Change and Development in the
Twentieth Century

Change and Development in the Twentieth Century

Thomas C. Patterson

Oxford • New York

First published in 1999 by
Berg
Editorial offices:
150 Cowley Road, Oxford, OX4 1JJ, UK
70 Washington Square South, New York, NY 10012, USA

Berg is the imprint of Oxford International Publishers Ltd.

Library of Congress Cataloging-in-Publication Data

A catalogue record for this book is available from the Library of Congress.

British Library Cataloguing-in-Publication Data

A catalogue record for this book is available from the British Library.

ISBN 1 85973 251 8 (Cloth)
1 85973 256 9 (Paper)

Typeset by JS Typesetting, Wellingborough, Northants.
Printed in the United Kingdom by Biddles Ltd, Guildford.

**This book is for Kathy Walker who asks
tough questions and demands good answers**

Contents

Preface

The first anthropology course I ever taught was Culture Change. That was in the fall semester of 1963 at the University of California, Berkeley. I had returned a few weeks earlier after thirteen months in Peru. While I had notes for the dissertation I was trying to finish, I had none for the course I was about to teach and only vague ideas about what I should include in it. Choosing an historical approach and talking about cultural evolution, acculturation, and innovations were endorsed by my new colleagues and former/current teachers; choosing to explore the impact of depopulation in colonial areas and the consequences of the Japanese Relocation Camps in California during the Second World War received less enthusiastic, more critical responses. 'You probably shouldn't talk about that,' one professor told me. A couple of others merely smiled at the choices. I was never quite sure what their smiles meant, but clearly they didn't mean the same thing, since one was sympathetic to the Left and the other was a Cold Warrior. I should have asked, but I didn't.

I have taught social and cultural change courses on a pretty regular basis since those days. However, the content has changed steadily over the years. It has changed in tandem with my understanding and appreciation of the dialectical development of Western social thought. That began when I was volunteered to teach thirty-five students each year in a required 'Western Intellectual Heritage' course that none of them wanted to take. Student approval ratings began to soar once they grasped the dialectical nature of what they were reading and discussing in class and its relevance to their everyday lives.

The idea for this book began to crystallize a couple of years ago. I was having dinner one evening with Kathy Walker, my friend and colleague at Temple University, who asked me what I had been thinking and reading about in recent weeks. Since I was trying to understand the dissolution of the socialist states – especially the USSR, which only a few years earlier had usually been portrayed as one of the world's two great 'superpowers' – I told her about Soviet agricultural statistics in the 1980s. She then described the hundred thousand or so men and women she had seen at a railway station a few years earlier in the Yangzi Valley. They had been displaced from land in the countryside and were swarming into the cities in search of wage work. It reminded me of Peru in the 1950s. After coffee, when the bill arrived, she was still asking me questions about the connections I saw between these events. While I didn't have too many answers at that moment, I knew that I had to incorporate this kind of material into the social change course. The course outline I prepared a month or so later became the outline for this book.

A couple of months later, Kathryn Earle of Berg Publishers, the best editor I have ever worked with, asked me what I was writing. I told her about a book manuscript on twentieth-century theories of change that was still on the launching pad. She expressed some interest. Since Berg had published my Inca book, which was selling well, we talked. I asked for a large advance and translation rights during the negotiations. Berg did not agree to the advance but promised to pay royalties on time; I got the translation and movie rights. I continued to write, now with Kathryn Earle's persistent encouragement and support.

Writing has not been a solitary venture for me for a number of years. I talk to friends about what I and they are working on; I read paragraphs to them and try out ideas over the phone; I give them drafts of chapters hoping, given their busy schedules, that they have time to read and criticize what I have written.

Kathy Walker has provided a steady stream of constructive comments, criticism, and questions. My friends and colleagues Christine Gailey, Karen Spalding, Ananth Aiyer, Jennifer Alvey, Karen Brodkin, Carla Freeman, John Gledhill, Peter Gran, Antonio Lauria, Richard Lee, Jeff Maskovsky, Don Nonini, Bob Paynter, John Stinson-Fernández, Ida Susser and Eric Wolf have as always been forthcoming with useful observations and remarks. I have also benefited from the clarity of thought of Tom Bottomore, whom I have never met but whose writing is a model of excellence. Gavin Smith, my anonymous reviewer, provided extensive, detailed comments on the manuscript. Wendy Ashmore provided instantaneous comments on the clarity and coherence of the revisions I made. David Phelps' copy-editing caught ambiguities and omissions. All of them have contributed in significant ways to the themes I will explore in the following pages, as have the students enrolled in my cultural and social change course since 1995, who helped me think and write clearly about these topics. I thank all of them for their help, inspiration and support.

Introduction

This book is about the ways social theorists have written about social change and development during the twentieth century. They have had to deal with the fact that the political-economic, social and cultural conditions in the current era of the internationalization of capitalism are more similar to those of the decades preceding the First World War than they are to the ones that existed from the 1920s through to the early 1970s.

Karl Marx, Émile Durkheim and Max Weber provided textured analyses of the kind of industrial capitalist society that was developing at the end of the nineteenth century during an era marked by the concentration and centralization of capital, imperialism and class conflict. Since they influenced most subsequent theorists of social change and development, their perspectives are still relevant today. In fact, their views have been continually reworked for the last hundred years to explain the changes associated with the development of world capitalist society. It is not erroneous to claim that virtually all the important statements made about social change and development during the twentieth century build directly or indirectly on their writings or on the debates they provoked. However, given the power relations that prevailed before the First World War and again today, social scientists and their audiences were more receptive for various reasons to the ideas of Durkheim, Weber and their successors than to Marxist perspectives.

Marx, Durkheim and Weber wrestled in different ways with modernism, which proclaimed that change was directional, that old forms of society were continually replaced by more modern ones, and that the only really significant differences were those differentiating modern from traditional societies or civilized from primitive ones. Modernists masked the extent of social and cultural differences in the world. In their view, traditional peoples would either follow the road to capitalism that the West had taken earlier, though perhaps at a slower pace, or they would be condemned to extinction. The engine driving progress was the West – its superior technology and the capacity of its elites. The rest of the world's population – the masses in the industrial capitalist countries themselves and the members of traditional societies elsewhere – lacked agency and either were destined to follow the West's lead or were doomed. Weber, for example, argued that all the world's religions except Protestantism actually impeded the growth of rational institutions and economic development.

Contemporary descriptions of the global world emerging today are stunningly similar to modernist accounts from the 1890s or early 1900s. For today's post-modern commentators, the motor of change is still located in the capitalist countries – especially in the markets they have created, in their technology and in the power of their leading classes. The core capitalist states organize the world economy and control the activities of the other states. The significant cultural and social differences today are those between the capitalist (civilized) West and the Other (an analytical category, like traditional or primitive society, that homogenizes diversity), whose members live in de-industrialized parts of the capitalist world or on its semi-periphery or periphery. The Other will eventually be enveloped by modern social relations as globalization proceeds along its current path. However, even the idea of society itself has come under attack from neo-liberal theorists and politicians like Margaret Thatcher who have proclaimed that society does not exist or that it is in reality merely an aggregate of individuals who buy and sell in the market in order to consume. The postmodernists, like their modernist predecessors and neo-liberal contemporaries, believe that most of the world's population lacks the ability to organize collectively or the power to initiate structural changes. At best, agency involves individual acts of resistance in which individuals mark themselves or their bodies in ways that establish an identity they might possibly share with others in a world that is increasingly shaped by consumerism and the Janus-faced desire simultaneously both to belong and to be different.

The distinctive features of the mid-twentieth century were shaped by the success of the Russian Revolution, decolonization and national liberation or revolutionary movements in various colonial countries. The successes of these collective under-takings were buttressed by alternative visions of what societies not dominated by capitalist or colonial social relations might be like; these visions imagined societies with more egalitarian social relations and circumstances in which individuals had opportunities to fulfill their needs and achieve the real potential of being human.

The period from the 1920s to the 1970s was a time of crisis and conflict, when people got together and acted collectively to initiate changes that were not always under conditions they chose. As a result, their actions had unintended consequences because of the uncertainties of processes over which they had little or no control. These struggles scarred the fabric of modernist–postmodernist discourse. They showed what revolutionaries and anthropologists had long known: that the actually existing political-economic, social and cultural differences mattered. These differences were infinitely more important than theoretical distinctions drawn between modern and traditional societies that oversimplified and distorted reality. The diversity of societies also showed that the history of humanity could no longer be viewed as a mere extension of what had happened in Europe and North America.

The events of the mid-twentieth century showed that the world was racked by contradictions, protest and civil unrest, which neither the Weberians, nor the

Durkheimian functionalists nor the social evolutionists, who had resurfaced, could adequately conceptualize and explain. As a result, it was the time when Marxist theorists most successfully challenged the hegemony of Durkheimian and Weberian explanations of change and development. Intense debates occurred between their proponents and the Marxists, as well as among the Marxists themselves. These discussions produced theoretical perspectives that were more diverse and more finely textured than those crafted later as the capitalist classes re-established the hegemony of their discourse in the 1980s and 1990s.

This did not mean that the Durkheimian and Weberian strands of social theory disappeared during the mid-twentieth century. Modernization theorists kept them alive and well. They combined the dichotomy between traditional and modern types of society with Weber's views about rationality, bureaucracy, and political parties. They argued that power resided in the upper levels of an organization, and agreed with Durkheim's claim that the state was the central nervous system of modern society – i.e. its prime mover and organ of moral discipline. Since power involved both the capacity to produce certain results and to command but never completely to control, subordinate members, agency was the possession of the political elite. The modernization theorists linked this conceptualization of the dominance of the political realm of society with Keynesian political-economic theory. The Keynesians criticized neoclassical claims that an unregulated market system had the capacity to exploit the full productive potential of a society; they argued instead that the state should intervene in the economy in order to stabilize demand, fluctuations in the financial sector and prices. For some, the state was autonomous. Its power was separate from class power, and it had the capacity to pursue its own interests or those of the society as a whole even when they came into conflict with the interests of the dominant class.

This Book and its Organization

The processes of social change set in motion by the development of capitalism had profound, long-lasting consequences and implications. They affected the views of late nineteenth-century theorists – like Marx, Durkheim and Weber – who sought to explain them, as well as those of later theorists, who have had to cope with both the changes that occurred and the views of their predecessors. As a result, our understanding of social change in the twentieth century has developed through a series of ongoing dialogs, both imagined and real, between theorists with different points of view.

Social theorists have usually viewed change either as a quantitative alteration in the form of society or as the replacement of one type of society by another. However, this statement is complicated by the fact that most – including Marx, Durkheim and Weber – have portrayed the *idea* of change in terms of synonyms and metaphors that convey subtle differences of meaning and evoke a wide range of images. For example, they have depicted change as growth, unfolding, emergence, metamorphosis, maturation, succession, progression, alteration, modification, refashioning, evolution, mutation, transformation, progress, development, advancement, enhancement, gain, improvement and modernization.

Chapter 1 explores briefly how some of the more important metaphors used to describe change emerged historically, and sketches how they have been used at different times during the last 2,500 years to address issues of change and development. Theorists of social change have produced a series of seemingly contradictory explanations both of what happens and of the processes involved. For example, some argue that social change lack directionality; others portray it as cyclical or as a teleological process that unleashes a potential inherent in society that develops progressively and steadily as it unfolds toward some final end-product like civilization. Some view social change as a slow, gradual, continuous process; for others, it is a sudden metamorphosis – the radical transformation of one social form into another. Some view change as the product of motors that are internal to society itself, while others see it as a consequence of forces or events that impinge on society from the outside to either modify or disrupt the normal course of development.

Chapter 2 examines theories formulated by Karl Marx, Émile Durkheim, and Max Weber around the turn of the century to account for the development of industrial capitalist society. Their theories are important, because they have had a continuing influence on virtually all subsequent writers who have dealt with issues of social change and development. Marx, Durkheim and Weber had critical relationships with the social and political-economic theories of society and change discussed above. Marx argued that the classical political economists ignored the historical specificity of capitalist social relations when they failed to distinguish different kinds of class structures and forms of exploitation. Durkheim was concerned with the conditions that promoted morality and the evolution of the moral individual in industrial society. In his view, the real foundations of society resided in the religious, moral, and legal institutions that regulated behavior rather than in the social relations shaped by the economy. Like Marx, Weber related forms of social organization and consciousness to economic processes. However, where Marx located the motor for the development of modern capitalist society in the sphere of production, Weber focused his attention on exchange relations in the market.

Chapter 3 explores how social theorists conceptualized the consequences of the interrelated developments of industrial capitalism and the national state between the 1880s and 1914. These fueled the appearance of a new form of imperialism based on economic expansion and territorial acquisition, as various capitalist national states scrambled for overseas markets and investment opportunities and vied with one another to gain territorial possessions and to extend their political power into regions, such as Africa or Asia, where the indigenous populations were too numerous to crush and too culturally different to be easily assimilated. As the imperial states consolidated their overseas empires, relations with the inhabitants of their new territories shifted from ministries of foreign relations to offices of colonial affairs and departments of the interior. The statuses of the formerly autonomous inhabitants of those possessions shifted to those of colonial subjects, indigenous or tribal peoples, or national or racial minorities. There was a resurgence of nationalism in Europe surrounding the efforts to achieve political unification in the Balkans, Germany and Italy, the struggles to free Poland from Russia and Hungary from Austria, and the nascent attempts of the newly constituted colonial subjects, especially in Asia, to free themselves from their imperial overlords. The resurgence of nationalism was further fueled by the tens of millions of people from Eastern and Central Europe who emigrated in search of work and eventually found it in racially and ethnically stratified labor markets. The lives of rural agricultural workers were transformed as capitalist production relations penetrated the countryside.

Chapter 4 investigates how social analysts conceptualized and explained the processes of change and development that were unleashed by the crises underpinning the two world wars, the Russian Revolution of 1917, and the Great Depression of the 1930s. Marxist critics argued that the economic crises of the late nineteenth and twentieth centuries were not accidental as liberal neoclassical economists seemed to suggest, but rather that they were a fundamental feature of capitalism itself. They further argued that the crises had political as well as economic dimensions. The First World War left unsettled conditions in its wake. A revolution had already raged in Mexico for seven years; workers and students there and in Spain, Argentina, India, Indonesia, Australia, Germany, and Hungary recognized their affinity with the participants in the Russian Revolution. The political map of the world was redrawn as territories changed hands and new countries appeared. Consequently, national states had to confront old issues – nationalist movements, capitalist penetration into the countryside, the ongoing transformation of rural life, increasingly tense relations with colonial subjects seeking to reassert their political autonomy, and the promotion of capitalist development at home and abroad. The Soviet Union also had to confront many of the same issues; in addition, its theorists had to discover how to cultivate non-capitalist development in the agricultural and industrial sectors of its economy.

Chapter 5 considers how social theorists grappled with the issues of change and development after the Second World War in a milieu shaped by the Cold War and national liberation movements. The capitalist countries precipitated the Cold War in 1946 to contain the expansion of socialism. It pitted them against the Soviet Union and the socialist states established in Eastern Europe. Nationalists seized opportunities provided by the weakness of the colonial powers after the war to proclaim their independence or to launch popular struggles for political autonomy. By 1960, 1.3 billion people – a third of the world's population – had gained independence, and the number of independent countries in Africa and Asia increased from a handful to more than fifty. Decolonization created a Third World that was neither capitalist nor socialist. It pitted the poor countries of the emerging Third World against the capitalist colonial powers and would create a major arena of Cold War struggle. From 1946 onwards, liberal analysts underpinned theories of capitalist economic growth and modernization by recycling social evolutionism and the ideas of progress and modernity. Third World and Marxist writers pointed out that the world economy was characterized by uneven development, and that the poor countries were not in fact becoming more similar to the capitalist ones. In addition, both theorists and activists investigated national and rural class structures in the colonies, their linkages, and their potential as agents of reform or revolutionary social change. Social scientists with an evolutionary perspective saw analogies between the contemporary conditions of the Third World countries and those that had prevailed in the West during the transition from feudalism to capitalism.

Chapter 6 assesses critically how theorists conceptualized and attempted to explain certain changes and developments they perceived to have occurred during the last quarter of the twentieth century. Some critics argued that the existing theories do not adequately explain the globalization of capitalism as a foundational principle that would shape the world uniformly but not in the same way everywhere. They further argued that the existing theories did not account for the dissolution of the socialist states during the final stages of the Cold War in the 1980s, the rise of new capitalist countries in East Asia, or the efforts of various Third World countries to attract capital rather than to delink from it so that they could steer independent political and economic courses. These events marked either the triumph of capitalism, the crystallization of a new phase of capitalist accumulation on a world scale, or the consolidation of a post-industrial, postmodern condition. Globalization was a process that has already brought about a more profound reorganization of social relations across the world than national states and transnational (multinational) corporations had initiated and achieved during earlier phases in the internationalization of capital. It weakened the grasp of national states on the economy. It changed how and where people gained their livelihoods. It penetrated deeply into the fabric of their everyday lives, changing for ever where and how they lived, what they consumed, and how they viewed themselves in relation to the images produced by an increasingly internationalized media.

1

Theories of Social Change and Development

There have been a few moments when the established explanations of social change and development no longer provided satisfactory accounts of what had just happened or what was taking place. One occurred with the consolidation of industrial capitalism in the late eighteenth century; another involved the rise of finance capitalism and imperialism a century later. Recognizing the novelty of these moments impelled theorists to develop new accounts of the changes that had been set in motion. The thesis of this book is that the processes of change and development set in motion during the latter half of the nineteenth century had profound, long-lasting consequences and implications. They not only affected the views of the late nineteenth-century theorists and critics – like Karl Marx, Émile Durkheim and Max Weber – who sought to explain them, but have also influenced the perspectives of their successors who have struggled to explain the subsequent changes that unfolded in the twentieth century.

Social theorists have typically formulated and refined their explanations of change in terms of concepts and ideas that were already part of the intellectual baggage they inherited from previous generations. While some analysts recycled earlier accounts, others refined them, and a few – notably Marx, Durkheim and Weber – came up with truly novel insights about the processes of change that were unleashed before 1900. Consequently, subsequent theorists have also had to confront the views of those three analysts about social change and development.

One thing is certain. Social theorists have never been innocent observers who stood outside the societies and changes they were trying to explain. They have always been participants in those societies and have always belonged to particular classes or groups within them. As a result, their analyses have been shaped in significant ways by their own experiences of everyday life, by their own empathy and by the understandings they have shared with the members of their own and other groups. It is often the case that theorists who give voice to the sentiments of different class fractions and who therefore have different relations to the structures of power use different pieces of the intellectual baggage they have inherited to conceptualize and explain the changes they perceive taking place in their own and contemporary societies.

In this chapter, I want to examine briefly the more influential theories that have been proposed to explain social change and development and to consider the circumstances in which they emerged. Nineteenth- and twentieth-century social theorists have built on the analogies and metaphors used by earlier analysts to describe processes of change to explain capitalist development and imperialism. These models still influence how we understand the processes being described.

Change as Growth

Greek social theorists who lived 2,500 years ago on the edges of the expanding Persian Empire in Asia Minor – i.e. in Ionia – characterized social change as growth. The analogy they drew between human society and a biological organism laid the foundations for a debate over the nature of human society and social change. They implied (1) that both society and the organism were composed of a fixed number of continually interacting parts, and (2) that both developed through a fixed progression of stages – birth, youth, maturity, and senility. Materialist and idealist interpretations of the growth analogy have been recurrently popular since the fifth century BC. Theorists of change employing the analogy have typically distinguished between what occurred regularly according to some law of natural growth and what happened by chance when some outside event or force impinged on the social organism. Furthermore, such conceptions of change also left the door open to idealist interpretations that argued that human society was created and controlled by a divine prime mover (Bock 1956:1–2).

Materialists, like Heraclitus (*c*.544–*c*.483 BC), believed that the world and human society were real and that they changed in response to internal or external pressures. The world was a *cosmos* – an organized whole whose structure and development, while not immediately apparent, could be discovered through rational inquiry. They based this belief on seasonal regularities they had already observed in meteorological and celestial phenomena. They also believed that there was no radical difference between nature and human society, and that the appearance of human beings merely represented the latest stage in the development of the cosmos.

Heraclitus explained the evolution of the cosmos in terms of the interactions of its constituent elements (Kahn 1960:188–99). He argued that the natural world and the *polis* (city-state) as a social form developed from a primordial starting-point when simpler conditions prevailed. Change was continuous as the constituent elements of the cosmos were driven apart because of the oppositional forces inherent in them, and the changes that occurred in the cosmos appeared in a certain order (Kahn 1979:16–23, 159–63). In other words, the cosmos and the city-state were self-creating, self-governing and self-contained.

Heraclitus' account of the evolution of the cosmos was thoroughly materialist. However, Anaximander (*c*.610–546 BC) and other idealist theorists in Ionia argued that the development and the dynamic equilibrium of the cosmos had been set in motion by a universal god power who stood outside the world itself (Kahn

1960:238–9). Thus, while Heraclitus and Anaximander agreed that the development of the cosmos and human society was analogous to the birth, growth and decay of a biological organism, they disagreed over whether the motor driving their development was internal or imposed from the outside.

The Ionian theorists laid the foundations for a debate over the nature of human society and social change, and questions concerning the development of human society continued to intrigue Greek writers in Classical Antiquity. In the fourth century BC, for example, Aristotle (384–322 BC), Alexander the Great's tutor and the great encyclopedist of classical Greek philosophy, described the development of society and the state in more detail:

Every state is a community of some kind, and every community is established with a view to some good; for everyone always acts in order to obtain that which they think is good. But, if all communities aim at some good, the state or political community, which is the highest of all, and which embraces all the rest, aims at good in a greater degree than any other, and at the highest good (*Politics* 1252^{a}1–6). . . .

He who thus considers things in their first growth and origin, whether a state or anything else, will obtain the clearest view of them. In the first place there must be a union of those who cannot exist without each other; namely, of male and female, that the race may continue (and this is a union which is formed, not of choice, but because, in common with other animals and with plants, mankind have a natural desire to leave behind them an image of themselves), and of a natural ruler and subject (*Politics* 1252^{a}24–31). . . .

Out of these two relationships [i.e., with wife and slave] the first thing to rise is the family (*Politics* 1252^{b}10). . . .

When several families are united, and the association aims at something more than the supply of daily needs, the first society to be formed is the village (*Politics* 1252^b 16–18). . . .

When several villages are united in a single complete community, large enough to be nearly or quite self-sufficing, the state comes into existence. . . . Hence it is evident that the state is a creation of nature, and that man is by nature a political animal (*Politics* 1252^{b}28–29, 1253^{a}2–3).

Further, the state is by nature clearly prior to the family and to the individual, since the whole is of necessity prior to the part (*Politics* 1253^{a}19–20; Aristotle 1984: 1986–8).

Thus, the individual and the family were merely the first manifestations of the state – the seed, the incompletely formed substance of the primordial human cosmos from which the state arose. The development of the state was analogous to the growth of an individual plant or animal. It unfolded in a fixed sequence of stages of coming-to-be and passing-away. When one state decayed or degenerated, it was replaced by another. In Aristotle's view, the processes that were necessary for the formation of states in general could be studied scientifically, whereas the historically specific events that affected the development of a particular state could not, since there could be no science of the accidental (Nisbet 1969:38–40).

Aristotle and his successors schooled in classical Greek and Roman philosophy exerted a profound influence over early and medieval writers concerned with human society and social change. St Augustine's (354–430) *City of God* was the most influential fusion of Greek views on growth and decay of society with the biblical account of humanity's relation to God. Augustine was not concerned with the history of the Roman world *per se*, but rather with the problems that the imperial state confronted, and, more importantly, with the possibilities that might be open to human beings in the future. However, in order to understand the problems and options available, he believed that it was necessary to know how the world had come to be the way it was. This meant examining Roman history in terms of the same theory of growth and decay employed by other writers of classical antiquity: 'There is a process of education, through the epochs of a people's history, as through the successive stages of a man's life, designed to raise them from the temporal and the visible to an apprehension of the eternal and the invisible' (*City of God*, Bk. X, Ch. 14; Augustine 1984:392). For Augustine, conflict between the baser and nobler sides of human nature was the motor that drove human history and promoted the growth and decay of society. It began when Cain murdered Abel; it was exhibited again at the founding of Rome when Romulus murdered his brother, Remus.

When Augustine fused the growth analogy with the biblical account, he was forced to argue, unlike his pagan predecessors, that there was only one cycle of human existence. It began with Adam and would culminate with an eternal, unchanging state of grace. This meant that human history could be divided into three great epochs: pre-Christian, post-Christian, and the future. While the pre-Christian epoch corresponded to nature and the post-Christian epoch was marked by the rule of law, the future would be an eternity marked by grace, a time of continuous unchanging morality, justice and service (Deane 1963:91–2).

Change as Cyclical Renewal

Augustine's reworking of the growth analogy dominated Western ideas about change and development until the Renaissance (Lerner and Mahdi 1963). During the fourteenth and fifteenth centuries, commerce was transformed in the Mediterranean world, and the distribution of wealth changed with it. Historical scholarship enjoyed a resurgence in both Mediterranean North Africa and Europe, as thinkers struggled to explain what had happened to the traditional social order. Civil servants, clerics, politicians, and merchants began to study ancient texts and monuments (Ibn Khaldun 1967; Rowe 1965; R. Weiss 1988).

As a result, the Augustinian world-view was quickly eroded in this context. Social commentators constructed new theories to account for a social order that seemed to be continually in flux. They combined elements of Judeo-Christian thought with the ideas of classical writers whose views were preserved in the copyists' archives of monasteries and medieval universities. They believed humanity could begin to regain the freedom it had lost during the Middle Ages by retrieving and developing the capacities possessed by the ancient Greeks and Romans. In the process, they began to see history as a series of cyclical ups and downs – recurrences caused by outside forces impinging on a relatively fixed human nature – which one of them, Niccolò Machiavelli (1469–1527), described in the following way:

> Usually provinces go most of the time, in the changes they make, from order to disorder and then pass again from disorder to order, for worldly things are not allowed by nature to stand still. As soon as they reach their ultimate perfection, having no further to rise, they must descend; and similarly, once they have descended and through their disorders arrived at the ultimate depth, since they cannot descend further, of necessity they must rise. Thus they are always descending from good to bad and rising from bad to good (*Florentine Histories*, Bk. 5 Ch. 1; Machiavelli 1988:185).

The idea that historical change was cyclical had been widespread among certain circles of Hellenistic society. What the social theorists of Renaissance Europe actually did was to portray the artisans and writers of Greece and Roman as models of excellence. In the process, they revived and recycled ideas and works that were extinguished after Rome was sacked in 410.

Change as Progress and Becoming Modern

Sixteenth-century social theorists formulated the idea of change as progress to explain a world that was, from their viewpoint, increasingly shaped by repression and civil wars at home, overseas expansion and conquest abroad. It was a world witnessing the earliest stages of capitalist development. Progress, in their view, implied a form of directional change or development that has been described as

> the idea that mankind has slowly, gradually and continually advanced from the original condition of deprivation, ignorance, and insecurity to constantly higher levels of civilization, and that such advancement will, with only occasional setbacks, continue through the present into the future (Nisbet 1980:10).

This uni-directional change contradicted historical theories of cyclical renewal or of decline from an earlier golden age. It also resurrected St Augustine's idea that life in the future was potentially more desirable than life in the present.

In *The Nature of the New World*, written in the late 1570s, José de Acosta (1540–1600), the King of Spain's Jesuit emissary to the Pope, constructed a typology of non-Christian societies based on the kinds of idolatries their members practiced and on the methods needed to bring about their conversion. Monarchies like China and Japan had writing and governments; their members could be converted through peaceful teaching. There were illiterate barbarians, like the Aztecs and the Incas in the Americas, that had governments and fixed places of residence but lacked the intelligence and reasoning ability of the ancient Greeks and Romans; their conversion required a strong Christian ruler who would enforce their adherence to Christianity. Finally, there were savages – like the inhabitants of the Amazon basin – who lacked laws, government and permanent settlements; their conversion could be accomplished only by force, and required the collaboration of soldiers and missionaries (Rowe 1964:16–18).

Acosta proceeded to outline how one social type changed into another. He argued that

> Famous authors maintain by plausible conjectures that for a very long time these barbarians had no kings nor any regularly constituted state organization but lived promiscuously in bands after the fashion of the Floridans, the Brazilians, the Chiriguaná and numerous other Indian nations, who have no regular kings but hastily improvise leaders as the fortune of war or peace requires and try out whatever behavior lust or anger suggest. With the passage of time, however, men outstanding for strength and diligence began to rule by tyranny, as Nimrod did in times past. Increasing gradually [in power], they constituted the state organization which our people found among the Peruvians and Mexicans, an organization which, though barbarous, was very different from the barbarism of the rest of the Indians. Reason itself, therefore, leads to the conclusion that this savage kind of men has proceeded principally from barbarous and fugitive men (Acosta in Rowe 1964:19).

In Acosta's view, the development from savagery to barbarism occurred only in the New World, presumably because there was nothing in the biblical account resembling the stage of primitive savagery.

While many sixteenth-century writers did not believe that Acosta's typology actually represented historical development or a genealogical sequence that unfolded over time, Louis Le Roy (*c*.1510–77) did. He was familiar with Plato's claim that the first human beings were naked forest dwellers and drew the obvious inference: the ancient inhabitants of Europe must have been as rude and as uncivil-ized as the contemporary forest- dwelling savages discovered by the Portuguese and Spaniards in Africa and the Americas. He wrote that they were

> . . . not civil by nature, nor governed by discipline, nor conjoined in habitations, neither do they sowe or plant; helpe themselves little or nothing with manury [manual] trades; exchange in their bargaining one thing for another, not knowing the use of money; but living without houses, townes, cities . . . dwelling in fields . . . (Le Roy, *Vicissitudes* in Hodgen 1964:199).

These forest-dwellers progressed from their primitive, original condition to a more advanced one by means of intellectual, moral and social progress. In this civilizing process, they passed through a series of stages:

> Now whereas men have taken nourishment, first of tame beasts, before either of graine or of fruits: there is no doubt but that pasturage, grasing, and shepheardie, were before husbandry and tillage. . . . The tillage and planting of the earth have bin both invented after pasturage, and unto both have bin added hunting, fowling, and fishing (Le Roy *Vicissitudes*, in Hodgen 1964:466–7).

Jean Bodin (1530–96), political theorist and adviser to the French king, also used the idea of progress to propose a theory of universal history. He argued that human history was divided into three periods, each more civilized than the last (Bodin 1945:291–302). Each period was dominated by the peoples of a particular region. The Oriental peoples – the Babylonians, Persians, and Egyptians – dominated the first two millennia because of their innovations in religion, philosophy, and mathematics, and their ability to unravel the secrets of nature. The Mediterranean peoples – the Greeks and Romans – reigned for the next two millennia because of their practical knowledge, gifted statesmanship, and politics. Finally, the Northern nations came to the fore because of their skill in warfare and their mechanical inventions. Shifts in history's center of gravity were the result of geographical and climatic conditions acting on peoples who had different instincts, desires, and capacities for self-preservation. In other words, Bodin laid the foundations for a theory of historical development that is still dominant in many parts of the world today: civilization began in the Holy Land, passed to Greece and Rome, and then reached its highest levels in the nations of Northern Europe (and, later, the United States).

Progress, for Le Roy and Bodin, meant that knowledge and the arts gradually increased through time as a result of observation and experience. The recent discoveries of places and things unknown to the peoples of classical antiquity challenged Renaissance claims alleging the superiority of Greek and Roman civilization; as a consequence, they also called into question the validity of cyclical theories of change. These challenges laid the foundations for the quarrel between the ancients and moderns – a debate concerned with whether modern society was superior to those of ancient times. It examined the question of whether modern peoples were more advanced because they were able to incorporate and elaborate the ideas and discoveries of their predecessors (Baron 1959). The question it failed to answer was how progress actually took place.

Two Crown intellectuals – Francis Bacon (1561–1626) and René Descartes (1596–1650) – provided an answer to this question in the early seventeenth century. They argued that reason was a uniquely human attribute differentiating people from animals and nature. If reason were applied systematically, they held, then custom and superstition could be eliminated, nature conquered and social institutions improved. Reason was an abstract skill that did not depend on particular bodies of knowledge. Rather it was an instrument that any human being – properly schooled in the scientific method – could apply. When properly applied, reason became the engine of progress.

In the *New Organon* (1620) Bacon saw reason as the application of a set of procedures, now called the scientific method, that resembled a judge and jury sifting through piles of evidence to establish the facts of the case. Descartes wrote about reason in a slightly different way. In *Discourse on [Scientific] Method* (1637), he noted that half-savages began to behave rationally when they made laws to regulate crimes and quarrels. It was at this point that they became civilized; in his view, the application of reason was a civilizing process. He then argued that civilized (or modern) societies were both rationally organized and superior to their less rational predecessors and contemporaries. Their members applied reason to nurture progress and change, unlike the savages and barbarians of static, backward societies.

The growth of reason was also a hallmark of modernity. It freed people from the restraints of tradition. Rationality untainted by human passions, ethics or historical considerations was a hallmark of the modern nations of Northern Europe; possessing it distinguished them from their predecessors and from their more primitive contemporaries. The growth of reason and the increased rationality of the European states had already underwritten overseas expansion and technological innovation – such as advances in printing, military ordnance and navigational instruments. It would facilitate the conquest of nature, which in turn would unleash rapid, beneficial and profitable changes and offer unlimited opportunities in the future.

Seventeenth-century commentators carried this view to its logical conclusion: Modern society, which was the result of rationality, was clearly superior to earlier forms. Consequently, modernity was a goal that should be pursued. In 1651, Thomas Hobbes (1588–1679) described what might happen if this goal were not encouraged:

> Whatsoever there is consequent to a time of Warre, where every man is Enemy to every man; the same is consequent to the time, wherein men lived without other security, than what their own strength, and their own invention shall furnish withall. In such a condition, there is no place for Industry; because the fruit thereof is uncertain: and consequently, no Culture of the Earth, no Navigation, nor use of the commodities that may be imported by Sea; no commodious Building; no Instruments of moving, and removing such things as require much force; no Knowledge of the face of the Earth; no account of Time; no Arts; no Letters; no Society; and which is worst of all, continuall feare, and danger of violent death; And the life of man, solitary, poore, nasty, brutish, and short. . . . It may peradventure be thought, there was never such a time, nor condition of warre as this;

and I believe it was never generally so over all the world: but there are many places where they live so now. For the savage people in many of places of *America*, except the government of small Families, the concord whereof dependeth on naturall lust, have no government at all; and live at this day in that brutish manner, as I said before (*Leviathan*, Pt. I, Ch. 13; Hobbes 1968:186–7).

Hobbes's perspective made it difficult to idealize earlier stages of society that lacked agriculture, commerce and security, and whose members acted instinctively rather than rationally (Meek 1976:17).

Change as Development

Strong reactions to Hobbes's arguments and methods surfaced in the early eighteenth century as industrial capitalism and bourgeois culture began to take root in north-western Europe. Giambattista Vico (1688–1744), the Neapolitan social critic, was among those who constructed alternatives to Hobbes's perspective on the progress of human society. Vico (1970) argued that it was impossible to talk about some general entity called society or humanity; he focused instead on what happened in particular societies and on how the various aspects of those societies were inter-connected. While he viewed society as an organism composed of interrelated parts and made use of the growth analogy, he based his arguments on relativist rather than universal claims.

In *The New Science*, Vico (1970:74, ¶374) argued that political institutions were not imposed by a social contract, that social institutions were not the product of some innate human nature that was for ever fixed in time, nor were they part of the state of nature: '. . . this world of nations has certainly been made by men, [and] it is within these modifications that its principles should have been sought'. In his view, the customs and laws of a particular society – its social institutions – were the product of a long historical development that resulted from the fact that human nature changed with the passage of time. Social institutions appeared in a fixed order: '. . . first the forests, after that the huts, then the villages, next the cities, and finally the academies' (Vico 1970:36, ¶239). Furthermore, social institutions determined both the form of the ideas or culture of people and the order in which these ideas appeared: 'the order of ideas must follow the order of institutions' (Vico 1970:36, ¶238). He also noted that, while there were parallel developments in different societies, human nature was not the same everywhere; it varied from one society or nation to another as a result of the interplay between conditions that fostered intellectual advancement and those that eroded it. In his view, the growth of reason was not the motor of social change or the historical development of society, as Descartes and others had argued earlier. The development of society and the mind were instead parts of the same historical process.

In the *Discourse on the Origin of Inequality*, Jean Jacques Rousseau (1712–78) accepted Hobbes's claim that it was possible to examine systematically the original condition of humanity and the development of society. It was essential to do this, from Rousseau's perspective, in order to strip away the later human-made accretions and to show what people were like before civilization was introduced. This would also reveal the errors and prejudices of both ancient and modern writers regarding the original nature of humankind and the origins of social and political inequality. It would also reveal that Hobbes's view of the primitive condition of humanity as one that was 'solitary, poore, nasty, brutish, and short' actually appeared later and was part of the rise of civilization (Rousseau 1973:72).

In Rousseau's view, human beings were free and economically independent in the state of nature. They had no language, little capacity for thought, and few needs, but they did possess a natural sentiment – compassion or pity – which was the source of their humanity and most important virtues: kindness, generosity, and mercy. These virtues were rarely found in the modern civilized world, because civilized people were separated or alienated from their own natural feelings; this alienation

> . . . engenders *amour-propre* [a form of self-love composed of vanity and the desire to be superior to others and admired by them], and reflection that confirms it: it is reason which turns man's mind back upon itself, and divides him from everything that could disturb and afflict him. It is philosophy that isolates him, and bids him to say, at the sight of the misfortunes of others: 'Perish if you will, I am secure.' Nothing but the general evils as threaten the whole community can disturb the tranquil sleep of the philosopher or tear him from his bed. . . . Uncivilized man has not this admirable talent; and for want of reason and wisdom, is always foolishly ready to obey the first promptings of humanity (Rousseau 1973:68).

Amour-propre underpinned the beginnings of inequality. Inequality, which was limited in the early stages of society, became intolerable after the advent of agriculture when people began to claim private property: this

> . . . gave new powers to the rich; which irretrievably destroyed natural liberty, eternally fixed the law of property and inequality, converted clever usurpation into unalterable right, and, for the advantage of a few individuals, subjected all mankind to perpetual labour, slavery, and wretchedness (Rousseau 1973:89).

Rousseau (1973:104) then proceeded to point out that the civilizing process had different effects on the members of the lower classes and the ruling elites, and argued that civilization had different implications for each of them.

The former breathes only peace and liberty; he desires only to live and be free from labour. . . . Civilized man, on the other hand, is always moving, sweating, toiling and racking his brains to find still more laborious occupations. . . . He pays court to men in power, whom he hates, and to the wealthy, whom he despises; he stops at nothing to have the honour of serving them; he is not ashamed to value himself, on his own meanness and their protection; and proud of his slavery, he speaks with disdain of those, who have not the honour of sharing it. . . . [T]he source of all these differences is . . . [that civilized] man only knows how to live in the opinion of others.

Rousseau was skeptical of assertions about the benefits of progress or the development of civilization at the very moment that industrial capitalism, that most possessive of market societies, was experiencing explosive growth in northwestern Europe. He denied that progress and civilization improved the human condition and drew attention to the values that were lost in the process. In contrast to Rousseau, Scottish intellectuals employed by the state – like Adam Smith (1723–90) – explained the changes taking place in their world in terms that separated economics from politics and morality (Meek 1976: 68–130). Smith and several of his contemporaries in Scotland constructed historical narratives to explain the rise of commercial society – that is, civilization.

In his *Lectures on Jurisprudence*, Smith argued that social progress was a natural, law-driven process tied to changes in the mode of subsistence production. The first societies were composed of small numbers of individuals who provisioned themselves by hunting and foraging. As their numbers increased, they domesticated animals and became herders. When their number increased even further, those occupying favorable environments turned to agriculture. This was followed by a significant advance in the division of labor, as artisans – like carpenters, weavers and tailors – ceased to produce their own food and settled in towns to pursue their crafts and to barter goods or exchange them with other members of the community and with those of other nations (A. Smith 1978:200–20).

Smith was principally interested in the material and technical advantages that result from raising the productivity of labor. He accounted for the development of a technical division of labor in which the various members of a society pursued different activities, each producing commodities that were ultimately bartered or exchanged for money in the market. In his words 'the division of labor arises from a propensity in human nature to exchange' (A. Smith 1976, Vol. 1:17). The effect of a division of labor – once it was introduced into a sphere of production – was to increase the productivity of labor. In other words, the division of labor resulted from the voluntary actions of individuals engaged in production and exchange, and economic development occurred because these rational actors found it in their own best interest to engage in activities that promoted widespread production for exchange, specialization and innovation.

Human society, for Smith, was organized like a modern factory. In *The Wealth of Nations*, Smith (A. Smith, 1976, Vol. 1:72–397) he distinguished three economic classes on the basis of their source of revenue. Capitalists derived their income from stock, landowners from rent and laborers from wages. The classes had their origins in the functional differentiation of stock, land and labor as factors of production in an emerging technical division of labor rather than in either innate human differences or historical circumstances. Any uneven distribution of wealth and property among the various classes resulted from the differential contribution of stock, land and labor to the growing economy – i.e. the increasing division of labor and the expanding market. Smith further believed that, despite the inequalities that develop in societies with an expanding division of labor, the relations between the classes normally remain harmonious.

However, Smith's discussion concerning the appearance of a social division of labor – i.e. the crystallization of a class structure in which the members of one group appropriated either the labor power or goods of one or more classes of direct producers – was problematic. Because he conflated the technical and social divisions of labor, he was unable to discern how class structures actually emerged and how the various classes came to occupy particular places in a system of social production and have varying degrees of control over the conditions of their production, their labor power, and the goods they produced. It also prevented him from examining seriously the antagonistic relations that develop between classes. In other words, Smith was not as clear as Rousseau about the disruptive effects of a social division of labor.

For Smith, there was a complex relationship between politics and economics. Political economy was concerned with supplying people with the subsistence or revenues they needed to sustain themselves and providing the state with the revenues it required for public works and other expenditures – defense, justice, and 'supporting the dignity of the sovereign' (A. Smith 1976, Vol. 1:449; Vol. 2:213–340). Thus, law and government were central concerns in both *The Wealth of Nations* and the *Lectures on Jurisprudence*. In the former, he argued that 'the natural progress of opulence' took different forms in each stage of the development of the division of labor as production for the home market was ultimately surpassed by production for foreign markets.

Smith implied that the hidden hand of the market – humankind's continual effort to achieve order through exchange – could be thwarted, and that it operated only under certain conditions: when exchange is possible and when it is free from state restrictions and control. Consequently, the role and form of the government – which was to maintain social order and to provide the stability required for extending the division of labor, accumulating capital, and protecting the diverse forms of property ownership that arose in complex commercial societies (like Greece, Rome, or eighteenth-century Europe) – must also change from one stage of development to the next. Since each stage in the development of the division of labor reflected the increasing liberalization of politics, Smith believed that a centralized form of government with separate judicial and executive branches was a necessary precondition for the continued growth of modern civilization.

By 1800, liberal commentators in France and Scotland used the word 'civilization' to describe a process and an achieved condition characterized by social order, refined manners and behavior and the accumulation of knowledge. Civilization represented the development of the human condition and intellect. In the 1820s, the French began to wonder whether progress toward civilization was a universal process, or whether civilization was the product of particular peoples at different times and places. In other words, they revived relativist concerns about the development of particular societies and the functional interconnections of their various social institutions. Framing the issue of development in this manner allowed more detailed comparisons between past and present civilizations – such as ancient Greece or Rome and modern France.

Henri Saint-Simon (1760–1825) coined the term *industrial society* to describe the particular configuration of functionally interrelated and interdependent social institutions that was emerging in northwestern Europe in the early nineteenth century. The breakdown of the *ancien régime* and the appearance of a new epoch of industrialism occurred because of economic pressures and technological developments. Industrial society developed when '. . . science, learning and art replaced religion, metaphysics and law as the dominant occupations in the spiritual sphere, and the industrialists (or producers and communes) replaced the military in the temporal sphere' (Ionescu 1976:31).

The appearance of industrial society, in Saint-Simon's (1976a) view, marked both the internationalization of society and the end of the nation state. As a result, he paid particular attention to the political organization of this new social form. Industrial society, unlike earlier forms of production, was built around the institutions of civil society rather than the centralized political structures of the state. The scientists, artisans and industrialists – not the politicians and the leisured classes – were actually responsible for the real prosperity of France; however, they were '. . . kept down by the princes and other rulers who are simply more or less incapable bureaucrats' (Saint-Simon 1952:74).

Like Rousseau and Smith, Saint-Simon (1976b, 1976c) was concerned with the class structure of modern society. Unlike them, however, he had a vision of what society could be in the future – one in which social relations were more egalitarian. His goal was to rejuvenate European civilization with a new kind of politics – one that was based on ability rather than social position or power. What the class-stratified societies of Europe needed, in his view, was a new moral center – one that paid more attention to the needs of the poor. The productive class – the scientists, artisans, and producers who actually created wealth – would constitute this moral center, and its members would oversee planning, organization, and production.

Change as Evolution

Nineteenth-century writers increasingly emphasized that progress was inevitable and that it occurred through successive stages of intellectual and social development. They called it 'evolution', in order to convey the idea of alteration or modification through time. The ideas immediately underlying social evolutionist thought did not have their origins in the work of Charles Darwin (1809–82) but rather in that of Adam Smith and his contemporaries in France and Scotland. In other words, the core ideas of evolutionism preceded Darwin's notion of descent with modification; however, the social evolutionists and Darwin did share a few intellectual ancestors, like Thomas Malthus (1766–1834) who formulated a supposedly natural law about human behavior: populations grow geometrically, while their food supplies increase arithmetically (Young 1985:23–55).

The social evolutionists claimed that the human and natural worlds were governed by the same kind of immutable laws. Progress occurred slowly but steadily on a global scale. While they generally saw human nature as uniform, they also believed that human progress was uneven in a double sense: civilized societies were advancing more rapidly than non-civilized ones, and the pace at which a particular society had developed varied during the different stages of its evolution. That is, the advanced, civilized sections of humanity were different from the backward, uncivilized ones. They concluded that civilized societies were evolving more rapidly than primitive ones. They used this claim to buttress assertions about the existence of social, cultural or racial hierarchies.

Since the evolutionists did not constitute a coherent school of thought, let us consider the works of Herbert Spencer (1820–1903) and Lewis Henry Morgan (1818–81), who had slightly different conceptions of the evolution of human society.

Herbert Spencer, English engineer and popular writer, believed that human society, nature, and the cosmos were subject to the same immutable law of progress or evolution. It involved a slow, continual movement '. . . from the simple to the complex, through a process of successive differentiations . . .,' by means of which homogeneous structures were steadily transformed into increasingly more heterogeneous systems with functionally interrelated components (Spencer 1857:267, 1876:614–16).

For Spencer (1972:18–21), the evolution of human society – i.e. the rise of civilization – was law-driven, and merely one aspect of the general tendency toward progress in the cosmos. In his view, human society had evolved slowly under contradictory circumstances. On the one hand, following Hobbes, each society attempted to achieve the highest degree of happiness, which brought them into conflict with other communities; however, this actually hindered the development of civilization. On the other, each society had a desire to diminish the misery of inferior creatures – laborers, children, and primitive communities – by ameliorating their conditions of existence; this actually promoted the evolution of the social state. As a result, civilization could emerge only when the sympathetic circumstances based on the amelioration of misery outweighed the earlier unsympathetic ones rooted in the war of man against man.

Spencer (1876:569–70) classified human societies in different ways.

> Primarily we may arrange them according to their degrees of composition, as simple, compound, doubly-compound, trebly compound; and secondarily, though in a less specific way, we may divide them into the predominantly militant and the predominantly industrial – those in which the organization for offence and defence is most largely developed, and those in which the sustaining organization is most largely developed.

With regards to their composition, simple societies were, in his view, those nomadic and settled communities – like the Inuit and the Pueblos – that either lacked formalized political organization altogether or exhibited only rudimentary forms of political control. By contrast, compound societies – such as the Comanches or the Fijians – had recognized political leaders, different social ranks and more developed divisions of labor. Doubly compound societies – the Samoans or the Incas – were permanently settled and had even more developed social, political and ecclesiastical hierarchies. Trebly compound societies – the civilized nations of ancient Mexico or the Roman Empire – had overarching political organizations that enveloped other political forms and also functioned as the centers of those aggregates.

Societies representing the various stages in this process of compounding and re-compounding appeared in a fixed evolutionary sequence. Small simple societies were clustered together into larger groupings, and these, in turn, were aggregated into even larger units. While population growth was the motor for social evolution during the early stages of the process, its importance as an engine of change diminished as society became more complex:

> The gradual diminution and ultimate disappearance of the original excess of fertility could take place only through the process of civilization; and, at the same time, the excess of fertility has itself rendered the process of civilization inevitable. From the beginning, pressure of population has been the proximate cause of progress. It produced the original diffusion of the race. It compelled men to abandon predatory habits and take up agriculture. It led to the clearing of the earth's surface. It forced men into the social state; made social organization inevitable; and has developed the social sentiments. It has stimulated to progressive improvements in production, and to increased skill and intelligence. It is daily pressing us into closer contact and more mutually-dependent

relationships. And after having caused, as it ultimately must, the due peopling of the globe, and the bringing of all its habitable parts into the highest state of culture – after having brought all processes for the satisfaction of human wants to the greatest perfection – after having, at the same time, developed the intellect into complete competency for its work, and the feelings into complete fitness for social life – after having done all this, we see that the pressure of population, as it gradually finishes its work, must gradually bring itself to an end (Spencer 1852:267).

Spencer (1876:576–96) believed that all societies – except for simple ones inhabiting remote, sparsely populated regions – came into conflict with neighboring groups. As a result, they developed institutions and practices for defending themselves and for attacking their enemies, on the one hand, and for providing for the sustenance and other needs of their members, on the other. The two forms of organization, the militant and the industrial, coexisted in every society. In some societies, like Japan, the militant organization was predominant and shaped various aspects of everyday life; in other societies, like the Pueblos or the towns of the Hanseatic League out of which the Dutch Republic rose, the industrial organization predominated and affected other parts of the social structure.

In social evolution, there was a trend from the militant to the industrial type as a result of the growing importance of altruism – i.e. individuals became steadily more interdependent because of increasing social differentiation. As a result, militant organizations were more prominent during the earlier stages of social evolution, and industrial organizations became more important as the evolutionary process unfolded. Spencer (1876:596) contrasted the militant and industrial types in the following way: while the individual existed for the benefit of the state in the militant type, the state existed for the benefit individual in the industrial type. He also hinted that there might be a third type of society, one where 'work is for life' – i.e. for enjoyment and self-expression.

Toward the end of his career, Spencer recorded his thoughts about various aspects of modern industrial society; these notes focused mainly on institutional structures rather than any potential for social change. For example, in describing the impact of the factory system and the new forms of industrial organization associated with it, he remarked that

> The wage-earning factory-hand does, indeed, exemplify entirely free labour, in so far that, making contracts at will and able to break them after short notice, he is free to engage with whomsoever he pleases and where he pleases. But this liberty amounts in practice to little more than the ability to exchange one slavery for another; since, fit only for his particular occupation, he has rarely an opportunity of doing anything more than decide in what mill he will pass the greater part of his dreary days (Spencer 1896:515–16).

Spencer's views were very influential in the United States and Europe, where they underwrote claims that the differences between individuals, societies, races, nations, and even corporations were rooted in human nature or even in nature itself. This is the ideology of Social Darwinism, which saw and interpreted the world through a lens called 'the survival of the fittest' (Jones 1980). Since the Social Darwinists believed that all things progressed naturally from lower to higher or more advanced forms, they constructed various kinds of hierarchies to portray the developmental relationships of those elements. The 'fittest' forms found at the top of their hierarchies were those deemed more perfect or to have progressed further up the evolutionary ladder. For example, Charles Darwin (1874:142), who also happened to be a Social Darwinist, remarked that '. . . a nation which produced during a lengthened period the greatest number of highly intellectual, energetic, brave, patriotic, and benevolent men, would generally prevail over less favored [i.e. less civilized] nations'.

Lewis Henry Morgan, a Rochester lawyer, was one of the founders of an evolutionary anthropology committed to the discovery of historical laws. In *Ancient Society*, Morgan (1963) portrayed the development of human society through a progression of stages from savagery through barbarism to civilization. This pro-gression was a generalization about historical reality. Human society had, in his view, developed in this manner and could not have developed otherwise. Progress, the movement from one stage to the next in the sequence, resulted from techno-logical innovations that transformed the modes of subsistence and the kinds of social institutions that were inextricably linked with them:

> Without enlarging the basis of subsistence, mankind could not have propagated them-selves into other areas not possessing the same kinds of food, and ultimately over the whole surface of the earth. . . . [W]ithout obtaining an absolute control over both its variety and amount, they could not have multiplied into populous nations. It is accord-ingly probable that the great epochs of human progress have been identified, more or less directly, with the enlargement of the sources of subsistence (Morgan 1963:19).

Morgan argued that the different stages, or ethnical periods, in the historical development of humanity were marked by the appearance of particular inventions. For example, the three stages of barbarism were defined respectively by the development of pottery, plant and animal domestication, and iron technology; the beginning of civilization was marked by '. . . the use of a phonetic alphabet and the production of literary records . . .' (Morgan 1963:11). Certain institutions – such as monogamous marriage or private property – appeared quite late in the process of social evolution, only after civilization had already been achieved. Furthermore, these institutions would continue to change in the future as society itself changed (Morgan 1963:499).

Morgan argued that the early forms of political organization were based on personal rather than political ties (Leacock 1963:IIi–IIxx). It was only after societies became territorially based, which began with the advent of simple agriculture, that the first steps toward political organization were taken: clans that restricted the number of possible marriage partners were followed by chiefs and tribal councils, tribal confederacies, then nations with divisions between a council of chiefs and assemblies of the peoples, and, finally, '. . . out of military necessities of the united tribes came the general military commander' (Morgan 1963:330).

There was a functional relation between the economy and the form of the political organization. The transformation from a social to political organization occurred when agriculture and herding became productive enough to allow people to live in cities and to acquire private property. Using Classical Greece as a case, Morgan argued that the civil powers gradually withdrawn from the kin-based units were re-invested in institutions – like military commanders or municipal magistrates – associated with the new territorially based constituencies. In his words, 'the city brought with it new demands in the art of government by creating a changed condition of society' (Morgan 1963:264).

Two other changes were also linked functionally to the shift from a social to a territorially based political organization and the development of property. One was the increasing importance of the monogamous, patrilineal family, and the other was the diminished status of women. 'The development of property in cattle and land . . . led to the desire on the part of men to transmit it to their own children. First patrilineality in the gens [clan], and second, monogamy, were the consequences' (Leacock 1963:IIxv). The centrality and dominance of men in the patriarchal family – the complete control they had over the household and their ability to isolate its members from the larger society – placed severe restrictions on the participation of women in decision-making (Leacock 1963:IIxvi, IIIi).

Morgan discussed the growth of private property in the final part of *Ancient Society*. On the one hand, he believed that social classes were disappearing in the United States. On the other, he suggested that 'It was left to the then distant period of civilization to develop into full vitality that "greed of gain" (*studium lucri*), which is now such a commanding force in the human mind' (Morgan 1963:537). While he thought progress was ultimately both inevitable and beneficial, Morgan also believed that the rise of civilization had, in fact, destroyed something valuable: the values of those past and present-day peoples who knew neither private property nor the profit motive. He wrote that

Since the advent of civilization, the outgrowth of property has been so immense, its forms so diversified, its uses so expanding and its management so intelligent in the interests of its owners, that it has become, on the part of the people, an unmanageable power. The human mind stands bewildered in the presence of its own creation. The time will come, nevertheless, when human intelligence will rise to the mastery over property, and define the relations of the state to the property it protects, as well as the obligations and the limits of the rights of its owners (Morgan 1963:561).

The rise of civilization, in Morgan's view, was the product of a series of fortuitous circumstances.

Its attainment at some time was certain; but that it should have been accomplished when it was, is still an extraordinary fact. . . . It may well serve to remind us that we owe our present condition, with its multiple means of safety and of happiness, to the struggles, the sufferings, the heroic exertions and the patient toil of our barbarous, and more remotely, of our savage ancestors. Their labors, their trials and their successes were a part of the plan of the Supreme Intelligence to develop a barbarian out of a savage, and a civilized man out of this barbarian (Morgan 1963:563).

If progress were a law of human history, then the current state of civilization based on private property could not be the final destiny of humanity, the end of history. Instead,

Democracy in government, brotherhood in society, equality in rights and privileges, and universal education, foreshadow the next higher plane of society to which experience, intelligence and knowledge are steadily tending. It will be a revival in a higher form of the liberty, equality and fraternity of the ancient gens [clan] (Morgan 1963:561–2).

Social evolutionism was one of the most important doctrines of nineteenth-century Victorian thought; it affected virtually all of the writers of the day who laid the foundations for the development of contemporary anthropological and sociological theory.[1] French sociologist Émile Durkheim was well acquainted with Spencer's writings, and both Karl Marx (1974a:6–30, 95–243) and Frederick Engels (1972) read Morgan's *Ancient Society* and made use of his ethnological data and analyses to sharpen their own materialist understanding of the distinction between primitive and civilized society. Engels acknowledged the importance of Morgan's investigations in *The Origin of the Family, Private Property and the State: In the Light of the Investigations of Lewis H. Morgan.*

---

1. The list of nineteenth-century writers who were either influenced by evolutionism and/or advocated an evolutionist perspective is long. It includes Edward B. Tylor (1832–1917), John F. McLennan (1827–81), John Lubbock (1834–1913), James Frazer (1854–1931), Adolph Bastian (1826–1905) and John Wesley Powell (1834–1902), all of whom contributed in significant ways to the formation of anthropological and sociological thought during the last half of the century – a period that was also marked by imperialist expansion and by the concentration and centralization of capital to underwrite the high costs associated with the large-scale production of steel and other commodities.

Social evolutionism also provided the theoretical underpinnings for several alternative theories of change in the late nineteenth century. One was diffusionism, which claimed that particular cultural traits or complexes of traits, like civilization, developed in one geographical region and subsequently spread or were carried to other parts of the world. The structure of the diffusionists' arguments was similar to those of the social evolutionists, who claimed that some parts of humanity (i.e. the West) developed more rapidly than those in other areas, and that their ideas and the products of their labors spread by some implicit mechanism or were taken by colonists to backward regions. Examples of diffusionist explanations of change included assertions that the aboriginal earthworks of the Ohio River Valley were built by Romans or Vikings rather than the ancestors of the indigenous inhabitants of the region, that civilization developed in Egypt or Greece and spread to other parts of the world, or that it was the duty of the imperialist states to civilize the indigenous peoples of their colonial empires. In the late twentieth century, individuals who claim that human history was influenced in profound ways by extraterrestrial visitors structure their argument in the same way as the diffusionists: ideas and materials move from advanced societies (i.e. civilizations) to less developed ones.

Another theory underpinned by social evolutionism was the 'trickle-down' argument articulated in 1890 by Gabriel Tarde (1843–1904), a French writer and critic. Tarde (1895:62, 396–7) claimed that in class-stratified societies the lower classes usually imitated the behavior of members of the more cultured and refined ruling classes. That is, innovations originated at the top of a social hierarchy and moved downwards. This argument buttressed the development of cultural institutions, like museums, in the late nineteenth century (DiMaggio 1982). It has also been recycled with considerable regularity, particularly by the members of elite classes who frown on various forms of popular culture.

Discussion

Modern theorists of social change and development – including Marx, Durkheim, and Weber – were both influenced by earlier theories of change and critical of them. Marx built on Heraclitus dialectical understanding of the cosmos and human society and appreciated the significance of theories that described change in terms of progress, evolution or directionality. However, Marx was ultimately much less interested in the evolutionary schemes of Lewis Henry Morgan or Herbert Spencer than he was in Charles Darwin's theory of natural selection, which, he believed, provided a way of looking at the dialectically constituted, historical contingency of the natural world of which human societies were one part (Marx 1985:232). Durkheim drew on the organic analogy and responded to Spencer's evolutionism. He arranged societies along an axis of simplicity and complexity, and treated simpler communities as representatives of the developmentally earlier stages of complex society. While Weber undoubtedly believed in the superiority of industrial capitalist society, evolutionism was never a significant feature of his social thought. Contemporary analysts, both modernization and Marxist theorists, have portrayed the penetration of capitalist social relations in Third World countries in terms of cyclical growth.

Marx, Durkheim, and Weber conceptualized society in different ways. Marx argued that it was the natural condition of human beings and that human beings were social animals whose real essence or nature was realized only in a social collectivity; human nature was constrained by the historically constituted traditions it encountered, and it was modified as new relations of production and needs developed. For Durkheim (1938:102), society was an emergent phenomenon that was borne by its individual members and that had an existence independent of them: in his words, 'When the individual has been eliminated, society alone remains.' In Weber's (1978:14) view, categories like 'society' referred only to the likelihood that individuals would act in certain ways under certain conditions: 'When reference is made in a sociological context to a state, a nation, a corporation, a family . . . or to similar collectivities, what is meant is . . . only a certain kind of development of actual or possible social actions of individual persons.' Durkheim and Weber also believed that human nature was malleable rather than fixed, as their contemporary Sigmund Freud seemed to claim.

Marx, Durkheim and Weber were also critical of the political-economic theories of society and change devised by Adam Smith and his successors. Marx, for example, argued that they ignored the specificity of capitalist relations of production, distribution, and exchange. Durkheim (1888:29) agreed: the economists distorted reality by removing it '. . . from all circumstances of time, place and country in order to conceive of the abstract type of man in general; but in that ideal type itself, they neglected all that did not relate to strictly individual life'. Weber rejected economistic conceptualizations of society, because they abstracted individual actors from the capitalist social relations that structured their lives and avoided or subordinated ethical and political questions to economic ones (Clarke 1982: 190, 204).

Durkheim and Weber had important relationships with two strands of thought that appeared in the 1870s and crystallized in the 1880s. One was Neo-Kantianism, the other marginal utility or neoclassical economics. The Neo-Kantians were dissatisfied by the alternatives afforded by idealism and materialism and sought to bridge the gap between liberalism and socialism with Kantian ethics (Willey 1978). While Durkheim was interested in themes explored by the Neo-Kantians, Weber accepted their claim that the natural and human sciences needed different methodologies and the distinction they drew between facts and values (Giddens 1987: 183–4).

Marginal utility theory was the other strand of social thought that exercised Durkheim and Weber. The marginal utility theorists rejected the classical political economy of Adam Smith and his successors in order to develop a theory of prices that would account for the rational allocation of scarce resources in the market. They claimed that:

> the economic institutions of capitalist society can be abstracted from their social and historical context and can be considered as the rationally developed technical instruments appropriate to the optimal allocation of scarce resources. . . .
>
> In its theory of price, marginalism explains the formation of prices as an expression of the individual rationality of economic agents, competitive exchange serving optimally to reconcile the conflicting interests of these individuals so as to reconcile individual and social rationality. On the basis of this analysis marginalism then proceeds to demonstrate that all capitalist economic institutions are, in the purest and most abstract form, the most perfect expressions of individual rationality . . . (Clarke 1982:156–7).

In Durkheim's eyes, economic exchanges that occurred in the market constituted the fundamental problem of modern society, because the social relations that were established between individuals in the marketplace were not effectively constrained by the moral ethics of a wider community. Weber rejected the marginal utility theorists' claim that economic rationality was natural. In his view, it was only one possible value-orientation in modern society; however, while economic rationality provided an important starting-point for the development of industrial capitalist society, it had the capacity to undermine other ideals, such as independence, self-sufficiency, community, or national security.

In the next chapter, we will examine in more detail how Marx, Durkheim and Weber extended some of the metaphors and models of change outlined above in their efforts to explain the rise of industrial capitalist society.

2

Modern Industrial Capitalist Society

Capitalism was a new word coined in the 1850s and 1860s. It described the triumph on a world scale of a new economy based on the industrial production of commodities, '. . . of the social order it represented, of the ideas and beliefs which seemed to legitimize and ratify it: . . . reason, science, progress and liberalism' (Hobsbawm 1979:xix). The boosters of this new social and economic order believed that growth rested on unrestrained competitive private enterprise and the absence of government interference. However, the reign of unrestrained competitive capitalism was short-lived. It was eroded by the rapid expansion of domestic consumer markets in the 1860s and 1870s, the growth of large-scale producers, new sources of power, and the rise of international rivalries between different national industrial economies. These led the various industrial states to intervene to protect their national economic interests. In the late nineteenth century, the distinction between developed and underdeveloped rapidly assumed its modern form, and spectra of political parties – working-class, national and oppositional – appeared in the core industrial countries (Hobsbawm 1979:337–43).

A number of social theorists analyzed the changes that were taking place. Three perspectives came to dominate discussions of social change and development by the early years of the twentieth century. They were shaped by the analyses and arguments of Karl Marx, Émile Durkheim, and Max Weber concerning the formation of modern industrial capitalist society. In fact, their intellectual legacies still influence contemporary writers who are concerned with these issues. Marx produced his analysis of capitalism between the mid-1840s and 1882. Durkheim and Weber began their work a generation later, in the mid-1880s, and wrote until the 1910s. Consequently, the three analysts captured two different moments in the development of capitalist society.

As a result, more than one commentator has remarked that both Durkheim and Weber were engaged in critical discussions with Marx's ghost. However, their reasons for analyzing the development of capitalism were different. Marx wanted to change the world. Durkheim preferred to adapt to it – to preserve individual freedom and to strengthen the nation-state in order to forge a new moral order that would overcome the centrifugal tendencies of social relations created by the market. Weber was concerned with the historical development of humanity, the diversity of its social relations, and the constraints imposed by bureaucracies and instrumental rationality on its further development in the future. However, the views of Durkheim and Weber cannot be understood merely in terms of their opposition to Marx, since they were just as critical of late nineteenth-century economic liberal and conservative commentators as Marx was.

The Radical View of Karl Marx

Karl Marx (1818–1883) was born in the Rhineland, an area of west Germany whose inhabitants were influenced during the 1820s and 1830s by the Enlightenment, by the French Revolution and by socialist thought. During this period, Marx became familiar at home with writings of Rousseau and Voltaire and with the socialist ideas of Saint-Simon. Later, at the University of Berlin, the moral ethics of the Saint-Simonians – especially their concern with the future of the 'poorest and most numerous class', the whole mass of exploited, propertyless industrial workers – influenced his critique of Georg W. F. Hegel's (1770–1831) *Philosophy of Right*, and led him to the socialist movement (Marcuse 1960:333–4; Marx 1982). While Marx believed that the socialist and communist doctrines contained a new understanding of the kinds of social relations that were developing, he would nevertheless maintain a lifelong critical stance toward such views, particularly when they failed to base their moral claims on a theoretically informed conception of reality (Bottomore 1988:4–5).

Marx (1964a:106–19) launched his critique of political economy in a study that came to be called *The Economic and Philosophic Manuscripts of 1844*. He developed two arguments that he would elaborate in subsequent works. First, he took Hegel's observation that the essence of humankind was created through labor, and moved it from the realm of pure thought to the language of political economy. By laboring to transform nature, humanity not only produces wealth but also develops the uniquely human qualities and forms of social life that distinguish it from animals. In his words, man '. . . contemplates himself in a world he has created' (Marx 1964a:114). Second, he extended Feuerbach's notion of alienation to describe the real conditions of industrial society. He argued that, while workers should be developing their human potential through labor, they were in fact unable to do so, because the economic structure of the society was divided into a class of property owners and a class of propertyless workers. Since the workers did not own the products of their labor, they were estranged from the commodities they produced. Moreover, since their labor power was also a commodity, they were alienated from their own human essence, and they were separated from meaningful relationships with other human beings because they competed for the jobs they needed to sustain themselves (Bottomore 1988:7–8).

Marx and Frederick Engels (1820–1895), his lifelong collaborator, turned their attention to the historical development of society in the late 1840s. Their first conceptualizaton of the process appeared in *The Germany Ideology*, written in 1846 (Marx and Engels 1970:48–60). They emphasized that the class structure of industrial society is an expression of exploitation, where the members of one class – in this instance, the owners who controlled the means and labor of production – appropriate the surplus product and labor of the direct producers. As a result of exploitation, the relations between the classes are inherently antagonistic and marked by conflict, which is expressed in the open and hidden fights that structure everyday life in all class-stratified societies. They employed variants of this conception of history for next fifty years, continually stressing the dialectical interplay between the actions of human beings and the social structures that shaped their activity. In 1848, they provided a concise summary of their view in *The Communist Manifesto*:

> The history of all hitherto existing society is the history of class struggle. Freeman and slave, patrician and plebeian, lord and serf, guildmaster and journeyman, in a word, oppressor and oppressed stood in constant opposition to one another, carried on an uninterrupted, now hidden, now open fight that each time ended, either in a revolutionary re-constitution of society at large, or in the common ruin of the contending classes (Marx and Engels 1974:67–8).

Marx and Engels pointed out that Rome, with its complex and changing social hierarchy, the Middle Ages with its feudal lords and serfs, and modern bourgeois society with its owners and workers represented production at different historical stages in the development of human society. Later, in his preface to *A Contribution to the Critique of Political Economy*, Marx (1970:21) characterized '. . . the Asiatic, ancient, feudal, and modern bourgeois modes of production' as 'progressive [successive] epochs in the economic development of society'. What distinguished societies manifesting different modes of production was:

> the specific economic form in which unpaid surplus labor [or goods] is pumped out of the direct producers. [It] determines the relationship of domination and servitude, as this grows directly out of production itself and reacts back on it as a determinant. On this is based the entire configuration of the economic community arising from the actual relations of production, and hence also its specific political form (Marx 1981:927).

By 1857, Marx (1973) began to focus his attention increasingly on the capitalist mode of production and Western capitalist society. He argued that both had a number of features that distinguished them from other social forms, the most important of which involved the generalized production of commodities that are exchanged for money in the market (Bottomore 1985:6, 1988:11). In his words, 'The wealth of societies in which the capitalist mode of production prevails appears as an "immense collection of commodities"; the individual commodity appears as its elementary form' (Marx 1977:125).

Consequently, Marx began his examination of the capitalist mode of production with an analysis of the commodity, which he described in the following way. In industrial capitalist societies, production is organized through exchange. The commodities produced by workers are the property of the capitalist who owns the means of production. In the market, the owner confronts individuals who possess other, different commodities. In the exchange process, '. . . a definite quantity of one product changes place with a definite quantity of another' (Foley 1991:101). Thus, any given commodity has a dual character. On the one hand, it has *use value* – that is, it satisfies a particular need of the individual who acquires it. On the other hand, for the owner of the commodity produced by workers, it has *value*, because it can be exchanged for definite, but quantitatively different, amounts of other commodities. The *exchange value* of the commodity becomes apparent when it confronts other commodities in the market. Money is the universal exchange value, which facilitates the exchange process, and '. . . exchange value comes to have an existence independent of any particular commodity as money' (Foley 1991:101).

In the production process, the industrialist capitalist uses a certain amount of money to purchase the raw materials, the tools, and the labor power required to produce a particular commodity. However, one of the commodities he purchases has a unique property. That is the labor power of the workers, whose wages the capitalist pays in return for their knowledge and activity as the producers of the particular commodity. By exerting their labor power, the workers produce a given product that has value, which the capitalist – as the owner of both the means of production and the goods produced – realizes when he sells the commodity in the market. In other words, it is the workers, and only the workers, who create value.

To obtain the value of commodities produced, the capitalist must sell them for more money than the amount he initially invested in materials, tools, and wages. The difference between his initial investment and the amount he receives after the sale is the *surplus value* produced by the workers. The workers, however, do not receive any of the surplus value, nor do they necessarily use the commodities they themselves produced. Instead, to satisfy particular needs, they use their wages to purchase commodities produced by other workers. The capitalist also uses money – including that derived from the surplus value created by his workers – to purchase the commodities he requires to satisfy both his personal needs and those of his firm.

Capitalists producing the same commodity compete with one another for customers in the market. The value of the particular commodity they produce depends on the average amount of labor that is socially necessary to produce it. However, if an individual capitalist can increase the productivity of his workers above the general level attained by the other firms, then he can undersell his competitors and increase his profits. In other words, the capitalist is squeezing more surplus value from his workers, or he is extracting it at a greater rate than his competitors. As the value of the commodity declines because of the capitalist's innovation, his competitors must either adopt the innovation or face the loss of sales or even bankruptcy.

As a result, each industrial capitalist continually strives to increase both the amount of surplus value created by his workers and the rate at which he extracts surplus value from them. Over the years, the capitalist has accomplished this in two ways. On the one hand, he has extended the length of the work day or week without increasing his workers' compensation; however, there are absolute limits on the length of the work period. Moreover, the productivity of the workers declines as they become exhausted, and they increasingly resist their employer's demands (Marx 1977:320–416). On the other hand, the capitalist has increased the workers' productivity, so that they produce more commodities in the same period of time. This is done by increasing the efficiency of the workers – e.g. by bringing together specialized workers, each of whom carries out a particular step in the production process – and by purchasing machines that perform the same tasks more rapidly and make the workers mere appendages of their tools. The former involves new forms of cooperation and an increase in the technical division of labor. The latter involves the mechanization of the production process, the displacement of skilled workers, the incorporation of unskilled workers – often women and children – into the labor force, and rising unemployment or the growth of a reserve army of labor (Marx 1977:429–639).

Since machines are means of producing surplus value and lowering the value of commodities, the competition among capitalists is a very important stimulus for incorporating machines into the production process and for continual efforts to improve their productivity – an activity that rests, of course, on steady progress in science and technology. In other words, there is a constant, systematic tendency in industrial capitalist society to transform production so that it becomes more efficient. Marx and Engels (1974:70) were well aware of the consequences and implications of this tendency when they wrote *The Communist Manifesto*:

> The bourgeoisie [i.e., the capitalists] cannot exist without continually revolutionizing the instruments of production, and thereby the relations of production, and with them the whole relations of society. Conservation of the old modes of production in unaltered form, was, on the contrary, the first condition of existence for all earlier industrial classes. Constant revolutionizing of production, uninterrupted disturbance of all social conditions, everlasting uncertainty and agitation distinguish the bourgeois epoch from all earlier ones.

The increased use of machines had another effect as well, particularly after about 1850, when capitalist production intensified and began to shift from consumer goods to capital goods – like steel and machines – that were used to manufacture other machines. In the first volume of *Capital*, published in 1867, Marx (1977:775–80) referred to the processes involved as the *concentration* and *centralization* of capital. They were just beginning to crystallize at the time, and involved the concentration of increasingly large masses of capital in the hands of an increasingly smaller number of capitalists.

Because the new instruments of production developed during the latter half of the nineteenth century were often very expensive, any capitalist who wished to use them to increase his profits had to invest significant amounts of capital in their purchase. Not all of them were able to so do, and the weaker firms were either absorbed or driven out of business because of competition with those that did employ the new machines. This fueled the formation of larger and larger firms that came to dominate the production of particular commodities. It also underwrote the appearance of monopolies, the constant introduction of increasingly more expensive machines into the production process, the concentration and investment of steadily larger amounts of capital, and greater output and profits for those firms that could make use of the scientific and technological innovations (Bottomore 1985:10–11).

Capitalist production is vulnerable to periodic crises because of the interdependence of different sectors of the economy. In *Capital* and the *Theories of Surplus-Value* (written in 1862–3), Marx (e.g. 1968:470–546, 1978:468–564) sketched an incomplete theory of the periodic crises of the capitalist economic system, based on the *tendency of profit rates to fall* (Shaikh 1991a, b). Since profit is the driving force of all capitalist activity, the individual capitalist producer must lower the unit cost of his commodity below the average value of the article in order to compete successfully in the market against other firms that produce the same item. He reduces the unit cost by mechanizing production and raising productivity. While his profits increase initially, his actions simultaneously lower the social value of the commodity and diminish the profit rates of his competitors. The tendency for profit rates to fall affects not only his weaker competitors but also the entire economic sector defined by the commodity they produce. Investment in the sector declines, leading to underconsumption, excess productive capacities, and wage squeezes. Besides eliminating the weaker capitalists, the falling profit rates stimulate investment in other sectors of the economy.

After analyzing the capitalist mode of production, Marx turned his attention to the historical conditions and processes that underwrote the development of industrial capitalist society. He believed that in the class-stratified societies of the pre-industrial world, which were based largely on agricultural production, the peasantries retained effective possession of land – the principal means of production. He argued that a proletariat could only be created if, and when, peasants were dispossessed of the land, separated from their means of production, and forced to work for wages in order to survive (Marx 1981:873–6). He called this *primitive accumulation*. State legislation called the Enclosure Acts underwrote this process in England.

Marx outlined two theories to account for the simultaneous dissolution of the tributary relations typical of feudal society and the consolidation of capitalist social relations in their place (Aston and Philpin 1985; Hilton 1976a; Katz 1989). In the 1840s, following Adam Smith, he argued that the rise of industrial capitalism was the fruit of merchant capitalists who spread commercial networks, promoted commodity production, and dissolved the natural economy that dominated the countryside by restructuring labor processes and organizing rural putting-out industries. They removed production from the guild-imposed limitations of the towns, and eventually transformed the class and power relations of the existing feudal order. Two decades later, he revised his assessment of the merchants, describing them instead as a conservative fraction of the ruling class bent on accumulating money-capital, spending it on conspicuous consumption, and preserving the conditions and social relations, both at home and abroad, that permitted them to maintain their lavish lifestyles (Marx 1981:379–455).

In his later appraisal, Marx (1981:453–4) described the formation of industrial capitalism in the following way:

> The transition to large-scale industry depends on the technical development of the small owner-operated establishment. . . . The transition can thus take three forms. First, the merchant becomes an industrialist directly; this is the case with crafts that are founded on trade . . . where the merchants import both raw materials and workers from abroad. . . . Second, the merchant makes small masters into his middlemen, or even buys directly from the independent producer . . . [leaving] him nominally independent and . . . his mode of production unchanged. Third, the industrialist becomes a merchant and produces directly on a large scale for the market.

There were conservative and revolutionary pathways of industrial capitalist development from the feudal mode of production. The conservative route occurred when the merchant took direct control of production – selling raw materials to the direct producers, buying their finished goods, and slowly changing them into wage laborers. This path preserved the old mode of production and worsened the conditions of the direct producers. The revolutionary way, which had the capacity to transform social relations, occurred when the producer became merchant and capitalist.

Marx and Engels were aware of the expansionist nature of industrial capitalism and its capacity to transform societies enmeshed in European colonial relations. They linked their critiques of colonial expansion and the capitalist societies of Western Europe. They described the connection in *The Communist Manifesto*:

The bourgeoisie, by the rapid improvement of all instruments of production, by the immensely facilitated means of communication, draws all, even the most barbarian, nations into civilization. The cheap prices of its commodities are the heavy artillery with which it batters down all Chinese walls, with which it forces the barbarians' intensely obstinate hatred of foreigners to capitulate. It compels all nations, on pain of extinction, to adopt the bourgeois mode of production; it compels them to introduce what it calls civilization into their midst, i.e., to become bourgeois themselves. In one word, it creates a world after its own image (Marx and Engels 1974:71).

As early as 1853, Marx (1983a:333) realized that some Asiatic societies were organized on the basis of different principles from their European counterparts. There was an absence of private property, since land, the major means of production, was held by autonomous village communities rather than by individuals or the state. These village communities were tied to overarching states by tributary relations. The political dynamic between them focused on the amount of surplus labor and goods that the state, or its personification in the ruler, was able to appropriate from the direct producers. In an article on the native states of India, which appeared in the *New York Daily Tribune* on 25 July 1853, Marx wrote that:

On certain State occasions, the tinsel-covered puppet issues forth to gladden the hearts of the loyal. On his days of reception strangers have to pay a fee . . .; while he, in his turn, presents them with turbans, diamonds, etc. On looking nearer at them, they find that the royal diamonds are like so many pieces of ordinary glass, grossly painted and imitating as roughly as possible the precious stones . . . (Marx quoted in Avineri 1969:126–7).

Marx developed his ideas about Asiatic societies in a series of newspaper articles written in the 1850s (Avineri 1969). In the *Grundrisse* he took a new step toward conceptualizing the diversity of societal forms and historical trajectories (Marx 1973:471–513). Here, he examined the development of the social division of labor – that is, the simultaneous dissolution of the institutions and practices of kin-organized communities and the appearance of social classes (Hobsbawm 1965:36–8). Depending on historical circumstances, class structures developed in three or four different ways: (1) communal property and labor were appropriated by the state or the ruler as the personification of the state; (2) communal property remained as a substrate in societies whose members appropriated goods and labor through piracy, cattle rustling and slave raiding; (3) independent craftsmen organized into guilds gained control over their means of production; and (4) a proletariat whose members were separated from the means of production and who were forced to sell their labor power emerged.

At the time, however, Marx was hampered by the paucity of both ethnological and historical information about kin-organized, communal societies. This situation changed once anthropology began to crystallize as a discipline in the 1860s. In the 1870s, he read systematically about the peasant village communes in the Russian countryside; and, in the years before his death, Marx (1974a) began to read critically what the major anthropological writers of the day had to say about kin-organized, primitive societies and archaic states (Krader 1974; Wada 1983).

Marx's interest in the Russian communes and primitive societies was deeply influenced by the events surrounding the formation and destruction of the Paris Commune in 1871, which he discussed in *The Civil War in France* (Sayer and Corrigan 1983; Shanin 1983). What impressed him about the Commune was its relation to the capitalist state and the potentialities it possessed as a political form by which the workers could emancipate themselves '. . . from the usurpations (slaveholding) of the monopolists of the means of production' (Marx 1974b:252). His studies of the village communes in Russia made him realize that the expropriation of the peasants – that is, separating them from their means of production – would not necessarily proceed in the same manner as it had in England, since there were different historical environments in Western Europe and Russia.

> In the Western case, then, *one form of private property* [founded on personal labor] *is transformed into another kind of private property* [capitalist private property, which rests on wage labor]. In the case of the Russian peasants, however, *their communal property* would have to be *transformed into private property* (Shanin 1983:124, emphasis in the original).

Thus, the anthropologically informed investigations of his later years reinforced his earlier view about the significance of the Paris Commune. In Russia, he could envision a society without private property and a class-based division of labor – characteristics of primitive communities – combined with the productive capacities of capitalism; however, given the historical conditions that prevailed in Russia, a survival and further development of the commune depended on a particular kind of revolution (Shanin 1983:111–7).

By 1882, Marx and Engels saw Russia as the revolutionary vanguard of Europe. They posed the following question:

> Can the Russian *obshchina* [village community], a form of primeval common ownership of land, even if greatly undermined, pass directly to the higher form of communist ownership? Or must it, conversely, first pass through the same process of dissolution as constitutes the historical development of the West?
>
> The only answer possible today is this: If the Russian Revolution becomes the signal for a proletarian revolution in the West, so that the two complement each other, the present Russian common ownership of land may serve as the starting point for communist development (Marx and Engels 1989:426).

In other words, socialist revolution might begin in Russia rather than in the industrial countries of Western Europe. This was important. Marx and Engels rejected the idea held by the advocates of progress and evolution that social change was unilinear and occurred through a fixed progression of stages; they reasserted the importance of class struggle and the social and historical circumstances in which it was taking place. They also implied that socialism might be the end-product of uneven development and different developmental trajectories.

The Liberal Functionalist View of Émile Durkheim

Émile Durkheim (1858–1917) spent his formative years in Alsace-Lorraine on the German border in the wake of the French defeat in the Franco-Prussian War, the destruction of the Paris Commune and the tumultuous years at the beginning of the Third Republic. He was influenced by Enlightenment writers, particularly Montesquieu and Rousseau, by the positivism of Saint-Simon and August Comte and their interpretations of the rise of modern industrial society, by the rationalism and moral ethics of the neo-Kantian philosopher Charles Renouvier and by the arguments of contemporaries like Herbert Spencer and Wilhelm Wundt (Lukes 1977:54–5).

Durkheim believed that the promise of the French Revolution was largely unrealized because of the civil unrest and wars that had disrupted everyday life in France since the 1790s; France '. . . did not know how to create organs which could give these ideas life, institutions in which they could be embodied' (Durkheim 1977:305). He positioned himself between the monarchists and conservatives, who rallied around the Catholic Church and called for the restoration of the *ancien régime*, and the socialists and Marxists, whom he distrusted because of their working-class politics and whom he portrayed as economic determinists who ignored the moral problems of capitalism. In the mid-1890s, he felt that the similarities he perceived between his ideas and those of the socialists had cost him university positions he desired in Paris (Alexander 1986; Llobera 1981; Mauss 1958:3).

Durkheim was concerned throughout his career with the moral basis of modern industrial society and with the conditions required to establish a new morality, one that would promote social stability or equilibrium – i.e. social order – in conflict-ridden, class-stratified France. Morality was generated by stable patterns of inter-action; but French society during the Third Republic was unstable and in crisis (Llobera 1994). This was further complicated by the fact that individualism lay at the core of the collective conscience of the modern industrial nation. He contrasted this with the circumstances that prevailed in primitive society, where the life experiences of each individual were virtually identical, and individuals had similar feelings and attitudes that were manifest in a web of shared beliefs, values, symbols and rules of everyday life that they held to with an intense, religious-like fervor. In modern industrial society, the collective conscience no longer centered on the primacy of the group over the individual, and few sentiments were held in common because of the complex division of labor and the resultant diversity of personal experience. Those that were shared emphasized the differences between individuals and their mutual interdependence. Whereas primitive society had universal moral codes, modern society had particular moral codes that applied only to the members of certain classes or segments of the wider society.

The breakdown of traditional forms of collective authority was an important cause of the moral disorder of modern industrial society. It was accompanied by the growing importance of a new social category, the individual, who was concerned with his own goals rather than those of the collectivity, and whose natural milieu was his occupational role. Modern industrial society had erected a cult dedicated to the personal dignity of the individual. The bonds created by this cult were not really social, since it promoted individuated personalities, individuated beliefs, individualism and lack of interest in all that lay beyond the self (Durkheim 1964:172, 190). Moreover, it was forged in the same context that witnessed the rise of the state and the appearance of new relations between individuals and the institutions and practices of the state. Given the current state of affairs in France, Durkheim argued that only the civil servants of a reformist state, like the Third Republic, acting in the general interest of society and remaining apart from its conflicts, were capable of providing the moral guidance that would ultimately lead to social stability, justice and the preservation of individual freedom (Birnbaum 1976).

Durkheim (1886:61–9) believed that morality, religion and law were the three important control mechanisms of society; they dictated the sentiments and ideas of a group and regulated the actions of its members. Morality allowed people to live together; it 'adapt[ed] individuals to one another, to assure thus the equilibrium and survival of the group' (Durkheim 1887:138). However, it was religion that really stood at the core of this triad; it was ultimately the historical source, the foundation, of the entire institutional apparatus of society. In his view:

> Religion contains in itself from the very beginning, even if in an indistinct state, all the elements which in dissociating themselves from it, articulating themselves, and combining with one another in a thousand ways, have given rise to the various manifestations of collective life. From myths and legends have issued forth science and poetry; from religious ornamentations and cult ceremonials have come the plastic arts; from ritual practice were born law and morals (Durkheim 1898:ii, quoted by Pickering 1984:74).

The solidarity of society was constituted by the moral exchange and symbolic communication that occurred between its members; however, the particular form the solidarity took was shaped by the degree to which social differentiation had occurred. In other words, the development of the division of labor modified morality, religion and law. Durkheim (1964:174–92; Wallwork 1984) provided an evolutionary account of increasing social differentiation and functionally related social phenomena in *The Social Division of Labor* (1894). He used ethnographic and historical information to explore the nature and origins of the crisis of modern industrial society and to argue later in *The Elementary Forms of Religious Life* (1965 [1912]) that 'the religious nature of man . . . [is] an essential and permanent aspect of humanity' (Durkheim 1965:13).

Durkheim construed social evolution as a broadly linear and directional trend. There was a progression from primitive, undifferentiated and segmented societies that were more or less homogeneous to modern, structurally complex, highly differentiated and organized ones. This development involved a change from mechanical to organic solidarity – that is, from linkages born out of shared experience that directly tied the individual to society to linkages that were born out of diverse experiences that tied individuals into market exchange and made them functionally interdependent.

Since 'social life . . . [was] an uninterrupted series of transformations', change was naturally slow, gradual, and continuous (Durkheim 1938:134). As a result, the equilibrium of society and its functionally interrelated parts was not dramatically disturbed during the process of social differentiation. The motor for social change was either internal to society itself or lay in its relations with neighboring societies (Durkheim 1938:117–21). The engine driving the development of social differentiation was the concentration of population in a confined area or city. This intensified the interactions between individuals, which, in turn, suppressed the gaps between different segments of the population and led to an increased moral density. Durkheim was more concerned with how the various institutions and collective meanings of society were affected by increasing social volume and frequency of social interaction than he was with the quantitative changes themselves.

Social cohesion (order) was maintained in primitive bands, the simplest and earliest of the social types, because their members cooperated and shared natural sentiments – such as honor, respect, or affection – that shaped their conduct and interpersonal relations (Durkheim 1978). Since all the members of the band shared the same values, felt the same collective sentiments, and participated in the same kinds of activities, they resembled one another. Consequently, individual differences and individualism scarcely existed in these communities. Moral solidarity was rooted in friendship and in the collective conscience, the beliefs and sentiments shared by all the members of the group (Wallwork 1972:42–3). In the primitive band, the meaning of morality was infused with and informed by religious beliefs and practices: 'Religion comprises all, extends to all. It contains in a confused mass, besides beliefs properly religious, morality, law, the principles of political organization, and even science, or at least what passes for it' (Durkheim 1964:135).

The mechanical solidarity characteristic of primitive bands broke down when they became parts of clan-based tribes and each acquired its own distinctive features – such as territory, specialized functions, political authority, and sacred ancestors – in the process. Further social differentiation occurred when the various tribes united to form a confederacy in which each group assumed a particular function within the larger entity – for example, the Levites became priests in the ancient Israelite confederacy. The formation of tribal confederacies not only led to the increasing separation of the gods from everyday life, but also laid the foundations for a rudimentary division of labor – functionally interdependent social units. Thus, '. . . classes and castes . . . arise from the multitude of occupational organizations being born amidst the pre-existing familial organization' (Durkheim 1964:182). Because of the diverse social conditions in which they found themselves, the members of each incipient class or caste developed its own morality (Durkheim 1887:123; Filloux 1993).

Structural complexity and functional interdependence further increased with the emergence of the ancient city-state, which was an aggregate of clans, tribes, and confederacies. The principal subdivisions of the city-state were territorial rather than kinship groupings. Social and political unity became vested in the state rather than in either family or tribal groups or in the religious cults they maintained. As a result, political leadership differentiated from the institutions associated with kinship and religion. The domestic religious cults, so typical of tribes and tribal confederacies, were subordinated to a state religion that was simultaneously more abstract and less pervasive in its control of everyday life; in order to incorporate the diverse population that resided in the city, the symbols of the state religion were also more general than those of the kin-based cults (Durkheim 1964:156–62, 181–6). While the state encouraged those religious traditions and practices it deemed essential for the maintenance of social order, the Roman state did not '. . . lend its authority to religion except insofar as the attacks directed against it also menaced statehood indirectly' (Durkheim 1964:160). Thus, a new form of social solidarity emerged with the rise of the city-state – one that acknowledged the emerging differentiation, specialization, and individuality of the city-dwellers. This organic solidarity built on the differences and functional interdependence of individuals rather than on some tribal collective conscience that was rapidly diminishing in importance. It emphasized loyalty to place over loyalty to kin.

Two major changes occurred in medieval society, the stage preceding the development of the modern industrial nation. The first involved the emergence of specialized institutions that were concerned with government, religion, education, and economics. The second involved inter-regional differentiation in the European economy, which produced an international division of labor (Durkheim 1964:288–91). In these circumstances, the Christian religion became even more abstract, composed of '. . . articles of faith which are very broad and very general, rather than of particular beliefs and determined practices' (Durkheim 1964:289). By allowing more individual reflection, voluntary action, and rational investigation, Christianity facilitated the secularization of the state and the economy (Durkheim 1964:163–4).

Modern industrial nations were thus freed from the territorial constraints of the city-state and medieval society. They had large-scale, functionally specific institutions concerned with government, education, manufacturing, and commerce that operated across the state. These institutions were interrelated and subordinated to the state, which established, through procedural and restitutive laws, the conditions of their cooperation (Durkheim 1964:212–29). Furthermore, the division of labor in modern industrial society promoted individuation, differentiated personalities, and the growth of a market economy; this ultimately pitted one against another when they sought to buy or sell the same item.

As the collective conscience of primitive society waned, the bases for morality and social cohesion were transformed. Social solidarity was increasingly based on occupational specialization, the interdependence of individuals and diverse groups, and the rights of individuals, sentiments that recognized the importance of diversity in a heterogeneous society and of loyalty to the nation (Wallwork 1972:43–4).

The state came to life as the mechanical solidarity of primitive society was eroded by the increasing division of labor. It was the central organ that coordinated the functions of the various parts of the social whole. By virtue of this central place, it was better able than individuals to grasp the significance of the whole and to provide the identity of interest required to achieve and maintain equilibrium (Alexander 1982:107–8). It became '. . . the essential cog in the machine, since it alone makes it function' (Durkheim 1964:113). As society advanced, the state became a source of social control by virtue of its regulation of the moral exchange and communication that occurred between diverse individuals and groups (Alexander 1982:222–3). Its representatives accomplished this by making administrative and restitutive laws that determined the normal functions of the different parts of the social whole and their interrelations with one another (Durkheim 1964:126–7).

The problem with modern industrial society, especially as it was emerging in France, was that the division of labor had, in fact, produced less solidarity rather than more. Durkheim viewed this as an abnormal development, a pathology, rather than an integral feature of advanced society. It occurred because the economy had become separated from the social whole. The capitalist had wedged himself '. . . between worker and society, [and] prevent[ed] labor from being properly appreciated and rewarded according to its social value' (Durkheim 1958:25). There was a lack of exchange and communication between the workers and the wider society that had devastating consequences. Instead of increasing cooperation, it created economic failures, class conflict, a breakdown in social regulation, and disequilibrium (Alexander 1982:153). Since the relations between capital and labor were unregulated, they existed in a state of anomie. The inequalities resulting from unequal exchanges in the market imposed a forced division of labor that reflected wealth and family position rather than a natural distribution based on the talents and abilities of individuals (Durkheim 1964:354–70).

Durkheim did not believe that the real problems of modern industrial society were economic ones, since capitalism had excluded economic life from the processes of communication by which the state regulated the rest of society. Economic relations were not part of the real foundations of modern society (Bottomore 1984:115–6). Modern society rested instead on a substrate composed of religious faiths; legal and moral regulations; political, literary, and occupational associations; and, curiously, financial systems (Durkheim 1938:3–4).

In *Suicide* (1897), Durkheim (1951) argued that Christianity was an independent causal factor underlying the uniqueness of the West. It was partly responsible for the separation of the individual from the structure of modern society. The pathologies of modern society, the disequilibrium resulting from the absence of regulation in economic life, could be remedied, he believed, by the reconstitution of secondary professional or occupational groups, like the Roman or medieval guilds, that stood between the family and the state. These groups had been destroyed by the rise of modern industrial society, which now operated on a national scale rather than for local or regional consumption. The loss of occupational groups in modern society diminished the regulation of the economy and the marketplace, the maintenance of an occupational morality backed by collective authority, and a collective milieu that was worthy of loyalty (Wallwork 1972:103).

A society composed of an infinite number of unorganized individuals, that a hypertrophied State is forced to oppress and contain, constitutes a veritable sociological monstrosity. For collective activity is always too complex to be able to be expressed through the single and unique organ of the State. Moreover, the State is too remote from individuals; its relations with them too external and intermittent to penetrate deeply into individual consciences and socialize them within. Where the State is the only environment in which men can lead communal lives, they inevitably lose contact, become detached, and thus society disintegrates. A nation can be maintained only if, between the State and the individual, there is intercalated a whole series of secondary groups near enough to the individuals to attract them strongly in their sphere of action and drag them, in this way, into the general torrent of social life (Durkheim 1964:28).

The occupational groups would serve this function. They would also counterbalance any tendencies of the state to exert its control over individuals, on the one hand, and the growth of anomic individualism, on the other. Employers and employees would belong to different corporate organizations, because their interests were antagonistic under the circumstances created by capitalism. Group life would be based on education and mutual aid, and the members of an organization would be related to one another by moral exchanges and communication. In other words, they would share ideas, sentiments, and practices, and the groups would regulate the actions of their members by virtue of the moral authority and force invested in them.

The formation of secondary groups was essential for providing linkage between the individual and the state. The question for Durkheim was how could they be instituted and maintained. His answer was that the state must participate in their formation. Thus, in *Professional Ethics and Civil Morals*, written in the late 1890s, he modified his earlier view that the state was the moral regulator and authority of society, and argued instead that:

> . . . the State is a special organ responsible for elaborating certain representations which are valid for the collectivity. These representations are distinguished from other collective representations by their higher degree of consciousness and reflection. . . . [T]he State does not execute anything. The Council of ministers or the sovereign do not themselves take action any more than Parliament: they give the orders for the action to be taken. They co-ordinate ideas and sentiments, from these they frame decisions and transmit these decisions to other agencies that carry them out: but this is the limit to their office. In this respect there is no difference between Parliament (or the deliberative assemblies of all kinds surrounding the sovereign or head of State) and the government in the exact meaning of the term, the power known as executive. The whole life of the State, in its true meaning, consists not in exterior action, in making changes, but in deliberation, that is, in representations. It is others, the administrative bodies of all kinds, who are in charge of carrying out the changes. . . . Strictly speaking, the State is the very organ of social thought. As things are, this thought is directed towards an aim that is practical, not speculative. The State, as a rule at least, does not think for the sake of thought or to build up doctrinal systems, but to guide collective conduct. None the less, its principal function is to think (Durkheim 1992:50–1).

The state was no longer merely the moral regulator of society as it had been in the ancient city or in medieval times. In modern society, it had become a representation of the collectivity and a moral community that forged rules and inspired loyalty. It had the capacity to create the conditions required for forging a new morality, one that involved secondary groups in the regulation of economic life and that dealt with the contradictions between the social norms of equality and the inequalities and injustices arising from the inheritance of property and talent (Durkheim 1992: 213, 220; Wallwork 1985).

During its early stages of development in the ancient city and medieval society, the state and the civic morality it promoted were intimately bound up with religion and religious beliefs.

The destiny of the State was closely bound up with the fate of the gods worshipped at its altars. If a State suffered reverses, then the prestige of its gods declined in the same measure – and vice versa. Public religion and civic morals were fused: they were but different aspects of the same reality. To bring glory to the City was the same as enhancing the glory of the gods of the City . . . (Durkheim 1992:55).

There were striking similarities between the moral community constituted by the early state and the one constituted by religion – that 'unified system of beliefs and practices relative to sacred things' (Durkheim 1965:62). Both the early state and religion were the collective representations of society, which emphasized its sacred quality. Society

. . . is worshipped by believers; the superiority of the gods over men is that of the group over its members. The early gods were the substantive objects which served as symbols to the collectivity and for this reason became the representation of it: as a result of this representation they shared in the sentiments of respect inspired by the society in the individuals composing it (Durkheim 1992:161).

Religion, which originated in the collective behavior of a society, was ultimately the source of virtually every institution in modern society – law, morality, contract, property, arts, and science – except economic activity. It helped people live together in a single moral community and adapt to the circumstances of their existence, and it was also a system of representations that explained the world in which they lived. It underpinned and strengthened society. However, religion was also a source of change, especially on those occasions when individuals came together in a context of collective delirium, and new collective representations emerged as a result of their participation and actions (Pickering 1984:385, 412–4; Wallwork 1985).

Durkheim's concern in *The Elementary Forms of Religious Life* was the problem of social order: What prevents society, especially a modern democratic one, from collapsing into a struggle pitting one individual against another? Whereas the early state was indifferent to the individual, who subordinated his interests to those of the collectivity, the individual broke away from the social mass in modern society and gradually acquired rights, property and respect, as the cult of the individual replaced the cult of the gods as an object of worship (Wallwork 1972:106–7). Durkheim (1992:69–74) argued that it was the duty of the modern state to promote, protect and define the emerging rights of the individual and, at the same time, to forge a civic morality that would engender and promote the loyalty of the increasingly autonomous person to the wider collectivity – i.e. the nation and humanity. These rights and the ethic on which they were based would ultimately be rooted in the realm of the sacred, since only the beliefs and practices associated with sacred things, 'set apart and forbidden', had the capacity to create social bonds. These bonds were more fundamental than the ones forged in the world of the profane or in the market.

The Left-Liberal Nationalist View of Max Weber

Max Weber (1864–1920) was raised in Berlin in the years following the unification of Germany in 1871 under the leadership of Prussian landowners. During this period, he witnessed the transformation of Berlin from a provincial administrative center to a cosmopolitan industrial metropolis, the crisis of the German agrarian economy, the rapid and uneven development of the world's most advanced industrial capitalist economy, the formation of the German overseas empire, and a significant expansion of both state and industrial bureaucracies. He was influenced by Enlightenment discussions of rationality and reason, by political theorists like John Stuart Mill who explored the 'crisis of liberalism', by the Neo-Kantian views of Heinrich Rickert, by the political economy of the German Historical School, by Friedrich Nietzsche's cultural critique of modern civilization, and by the published writings of Karl Marx and his successors – notably Eduard Bernstein, who was associated with the German Social Democratic Party and the Second International (Gerth and Mills 1946; Mommsen 1987).

Weber (1958a:17) viewed the rise of industrial capitalism as '. . . the most fateful force in modern life'. It was the pre-eminent feature of the history of Western society, and rationality was its problematic expression in the modern world (Löwith 1982:29, 48). He sought to characterize and explain the particular processes of rationalization and the forms of rationality that made Western society distinct from the rest of the world. He focused on how reason had infused the institutions and practices of economic life, law, bureaucratic administration, and religious ethics (Brubaker 1984:1–48). His comparative and historical studies of other civilizations made him acutely aware that the rationalization of Western capitalist society had severe consequences: '[It] involved the depersonalization of social relationships, the refinement of techniques of calculation, the enhancement of the social importance of specialized knowledge, and the extension of technically rational control over both natural and social processes' (Brubaker 1984:2). It meant that '. . . the ultimate and most sublime values have retreated from public life either into the transcendental realm of mystic life or into the brotherliness of direct and personal relations . . .' (Weber 1946a:155).

Weber's initial studies of capitalism in the early 1890s focused on two concerns. One was whether capitalism existed in ancient civilizations like Rome; the other was the capitalist transformation of Germany. In his comparative studies of ancient civilizations, Weber argued that capitalism in the ancient world was based on market exchange: 'capital always means wealth used to gain profit in commerce' (Weber 1976a:48). However, capitalist enterprises that employed free wage labor and resembled those of the present day were rare in ancient civilizations and involved seasonal or irregular activities such as harvests or state-sponsored construction projects. The profit orientation of merchants and moneylenders was grafted onto a largely natural economy. Capitalism flourished in periods when ancient states had recently acquired vast amounts of land through conquest and were in the process of redistributing spoils to their soldiers and allies. Furthermore, the institutions on which it was based were very fragile; for example, the decline of the Roman Empire – marked by the disappearance of the standing army, salaried bureaucrats, interlocal commerce, administrative law, and cities – also witnessed the collapse of capitalist institutions (Weber 1976b:409). Thus, the commercial and moneylending activities of antiquity had different consequences from those associated with the industrial capitalism that was shaping Western European society (Collins 1980).

Capitalism is the provisioning of needs by private, profit-seeking businesses. In his *General Economic History*, he wrote that

> Capitalism is present wherever the industrial provision for the needs of a human group is carried out by the method of enterprise, irrespective of what need is involved. . . .
>
> The most general presupposition for the existence of this present-day form of capitalism is that of rational capital accounting as the norm for all large industrial undertakings. . . . Such accounting involves, again, first, the appropriation of all physical means of production – -land, apparatus, machinery, tools, etc. – as disposable property of autonomous private industrial enterprises. . . . In the second place, it involves the freedom of the market, that is, the absence of irrational limitations on trading in the market. . . . Third, capitalistic accounting presupposes rational technology, that is one reduced to calculation to the largest possible degree, which implies mechanization. . . . The fourth characteristic is that of calculable law. . . . The fifth feature is free labour. Persons must be present who are not only legally in the position, but also are economically compelled, to sell their labour on the market without restriction. . . . The sixth and final condition is the commercialization of economic life. By this we mean the general use of commercial instruments to represent share rights in enterprise, and also in property ownership (Weber 1981:276–8).

In 1892, Weber (1989a) launched his survey of the transformation of the agrarian economy and the condition of agricultural workers in Prussia in order to study the development of modern German capitalism. He analyzed both the rural class structure and the developmental tendencies underlying its formation. In his view, the emergence of capitalism was marked by changes in the relation between domination and the economy, and by changes in the world-views of both the tenants and landowning aristocrats as they became enmeshed in capitalist production relations. Labor relations, formerly based on voluntary contracts between lord and tenant in the traditional estate economy, were replaced by legal contracts that turned tenants into rural proletarians who worked for wages and paid rents. In the process, the tenants lost their economic independence, as they were separated from the land and as their right to the resources of the estate was replaced by a monetary wage.

This transformation was underwritten by legal measures that established the preconditions for change by allowing merchants to purchase or rent agricultural estates, which they ran in an economically efficient manner to maximize their profitability. Since the Prussian aristocracy was adopting bourgeois consumption patterns, they had a steadily growing need for the cash in order to maintain themselves in the style to which they were becoming accustomed; as a result, there was also increasing pressure for them to rationalize production on their estates. Finally, the large capitalist enterprises began to import Polish laborers, who would work for lower wages than their German counterparts. Thus, Weber linked rural class struggle to the national question (Riesebrodt 1989).

Weber (1989b:198) continued his analysis of class and state formation in his inaugural address as Professor of Economics at Freiburg University in 1895, where he argued for the primacy of interests of the German national state in all discussions of economic and political policy: 'The economic policy of a German state, and the standard of value adopted by a German economic theorist, can therefore be nothing other than a German policy and a German standard.' He then linked his analysis of the rural class structure in Prussia with an argument that it was not in the national interest for an economically declining class to remain politically dominant. The old ruling class – the landed nobility of Prussia, whose members filled the state bureaucracy and had access to the German monarch – were in 'the throes of an economic death-struggle' because of the rapid development of capitalism. However, the bourgeoisie, located in the towns and cities, had not yet consolidated the political power they believed was due to them by virtue of their economic successes in recent years. While the German bourgeoisie was in fact the repository of the real power interests of the nation, it was politically immature, like the German working class, and opportunist (Weber 1989b:198–207).

The processes of class formation indicated that individuals and groups of individuals were engaged in a competitive struggle for advantage as each sought to promote its own ideas and material interests (Clarke 1982:192–6). Since Weber's (1978:302–6, 926–39) view of society was rooted in neoclassical economics, the behavior of social collectivities – such as classes, corporations and nations – ultimately had to be couched in terms that related to conditions shaping the behavior and social action of individuals.

The social groups emerging in Germany represented the superposition and intersection of two contradictory forms of social stratification. Class stratification was based entirely on economic exchange in the marketplace, as individuals bought and sold the property and skills they possessed. Individuals with the same class situation – i.e. belonging to same class – had roughly the same '. . . probability of procuring goods, gaining a position in life, and finding inner satisfactions . . .'

(Weber 1978:302). The emerging class structure in Germany crosscut a stratified series of estates – traditional status groups – whose members shared legal rights and obligations that were different from those of people in the other estates. For example, the landed aristocracy of Prussia had one set of rights and obligations with respect to their tenants, while the tenants had different expectations and responsibilities toward the landowners. In his view, the social classes and estates were forms that competed for political power.

Weber viewed the struggle for political power in Germany as one dimension of the conflict that was naturally inherent in capitalist society because of the market behavior of individuals, each of whom was trying to achieve a particular goal. The problem plaguing Germany in the 1890s was that the bureaucracy, which had become a social stratum unto itself, held power and controlled the political and economic policies of the state. In order to promote the expansion of German influence, it was necessary to create the conditions required for the emergence of a political leadership that would effectively challenge the domination of the bureau-cracy and recognize the primacy of the nation-state, which from Weber's perspective was '. . . the highest organisation of power in the world . . .' (Mommsen 1971:111). To do so meant forging conditions in which charismatic individuals from the property-holding bourgeoisie, the only group capable of providing leadership in a capitalist state, could emerge to challenge the rational-legal domination of the bureaucracy (Bottomore 1984:125–7).

Weber believed that social change was initiated by shifts in behavioral regulari-ties. However, since the actions of individuals were constrained by social and economic conditions that were largely beyond their control, '. . . the average person at any rate has little choice other than to adapt his or her life-conduct to the prevailing social and economic circumstances; conformity to given conditions and traditions is likely to be the individual's normal reaction' (Mommsen 1989:150). Nevertheless, individuals occasionally did break out of their established patterns of behavior. These shifts were initiated by the innovative deeds of charismatic personalities whose ideals challenged the existing value orientations and behavior patterns of the society. Because their ideals disrupted the existing structures of power and gave new meaning to life and the cosmos, they attracted adherents from different segments of the society, who realized that they shared both ideas and interests. These interests underpinned new forms of social actions. As Weber remarked, 'Not ideas, but material and ideal interests, directly govern men's conduct. Yet very frequently the "world images" that have been created by "ideas" have, like switchmen, determined the tracks along which action has been pushed by the dynamic of interest' (Weber 1946b:280). While social action driven by ideals was potentially revolutionary, social action motivated primarily by material interests was adaptive and tended to promote routinization. The two involved different forms of conduct.

Weber (1958b) began to develop this view of social change in *The Protestant Ethic and the Spirit of Capitalism* (1904–1905), where he claimed that the economic ethic of modern capitalism was based on a set of moral attitudes that emerged with the rise of ascetic Protestantism in the sixteenth and seventeenth centuries. These included Luther's notion of a calling that granted moral dignity to worldly activity, and Calvin's notion that the individual was a tool of divine will, his abhorrence of sensuous activity, which made religion impersonal and individualistic, and his belief in the powerlessness of individuals to effect their own salvation. Thus, worldly economic success was a sign of God's blessing, and 'worldly asceticism – the disposition to work intensely and methodically in a worldly calling – was . . . the practical-psychological consequence of the theoretical doctrines of the Reformation, and more particularly of Calvinism' (Brubaker 1984:25). This worldly asceticism was adopted by the followers of Luther, Calvin, and other charismatic individuals, who challenged tradition and undermined institutionalized routines of work with their new value orientations. Their charisma was a powerful force for historical change – a characteristic that Weber (1978:243–5, 1115, 1148–56) subsequently attributed to those intellectuals who sought to explain the world as a meaningful whole.

Weber (1958b:72) proceeded to note that modern capitalism seemed more like an adaptation rather than a revolutionary breakthrough, because the economic ethic had become so institutionalized in modern society that '. . . it no longer needs the support of any religious forces, and feels the attempts of religion to influence economic life, in so far as they can still be felt at all, to be as much an unjustified interference as its regulation by the State'.

Since Weber believed that industrial capitalism was a uniquely Western phenomenon that never developed elsewhere, he explored various dimensions of the historical circumstances in which it emerged. In 1915, he examined the relationship between the work ethics of various world religions and the conduct of the social strata that '. . . most strongly influenced the practical ethic of their respective religions' (Weber 1946b:268). He suggested that the various classes – for instance, warriors, peasants, merchants, artisans, and educated intellectuals – have pursued different religious tendencies. Of these, the intellectuals and the business classes were the most open to rationalism, in contrast to the peasants, who were receptive to magical explanations of nature, and the warriors, who pursued worldly interests remote from mysticism. City-dwelling artisans, merchants, and entrepreneurs in China, India, the Middle East, and Western Europe were the most ambiguous in this regard and, at the same time, the most receptive to a variety of religious sects – Taoism, Buddhism, Sufism, and Puritanism. Yet, what all of the civic classes had in common was a tendency toward a *practical* rationalism.

Their whole existence has been based upon technological or economic calculations and upon the mastery of nature and of man, however primitive the means at their disposal. The technique of living handed down among them may, of course, be frozen in traditionalism. . . . [But] there has always existed the possibility – even though in greatly varying measure – of letting *ethical* and rational regulation of life arise. This may occur by the linkage of such an ethic to the tendency of technological and economic rationalism (Weber 1946b:284).

He proceeded to argue that, whereas the religious prophets of Zoroastrianism and Islam, for example, directed their revelations of worldly action toward the peasant, noble and warrior classes, the Puritan prophets directed their message of worldly asceticism toward the civic strata of Western cities, whose members were already receptive to arguments about the rationalization of everyday life (Weber 1946b: 287–9).

Since modern industrial capitalism was based on the rational organization of formally free labor attuned to the market, Weber also began to explore how this labor force '. . . had gradually emerged as an entirely new form of social organization, . . . and where and under what conditions an autonomous urban bourgeoisie developed' (Mommsen 1989:149). In *The City* (1958c [1921]), he was concerned with the political and economic challenges to social stability that occurred during the development of Western cities, which emerged in the twelfth century. When the economic interests of their citizens clashed with those of local lords, they used political and military means to gain autonomy and to establish civic associations. Furthermore, '. . . when the economic interests of the burghers urged them toward institutionalized association this movement was not frustrated by the existence of magic or religious barriers' (Weber 1958c:114). The political equality of the associations was subsequently dissolved when affluent members monopolized municipal offices and excluded those who were unable to pay their share of the taxes. Nevertheless, the members who were excluded from office still viewed themselves and were viewed by the officials as citizens. 'Once the self-esteem of the outs . . . had risen to a point where they could no longer tolerate the idea of being excluded from power, the makings of a new revolution were at hand' (Weber 1958c:148). Like their predecessors, they organized citizens' unions to redress their grievances against the municipal authorities (Alexander 1983a:50–5).

In the *General Economic History* (1981 [1923]), Weber renewed his interest in the economic and political conditions that buttressed the rise of modern capitalism and the modern state. He argued that modern cities

. . . came under the power of competing national states in a condition of perpetual struggle for power in peace or war. This competitive struggle created the largest opportunities for modern Western capitalism. The separate states had to compete for mobile capital, which dictated to them the conditions under which it would assist them to power. Out of this alliance of the state with capital, dictated by necessity, arose the national citizen class, the bourgeoisie in the modern sense of the word. Hence it is the closed nation state which afforded capitalism its chance for development – and as long as the nation state does not give place to a world empire capitalism will also endure (Weber 1981:337).

Thus, the rational nation-state, which was the only one in which modern industrial capitalism could flourish, was exclusively Western. The bases of this modern state were rational law, which was made and applied by full-time jurists for a population with rights of citizenship, and a bureaucracy, which was staffed by full-time professional experts. Rational states were also national entities that had well-defined economic policies. Mercantilism, which appeared in England in the fourteenth century, was the first modern state economic policy; it brought the viewpoint of the capitalist entrepreneur into politics (Weber 1981:347–50). The rational state acted as if it were composed entirely of capitalist entrepreneurs who sought at every turn to maximize their gains at the expense of their opponents. The state became powerful by increasing the taxes derived from its citizens. Mercantilist economic policies had two features: they promoted class monopolies by granting import rights only to those with royal concessions, and they protected national industries.

However, mercantilism did not provide the foundations for the development of modern capitalism, since the creations of mercantilist policies disappeared. As a result, modern

... capitalistic development was not an outgrowth of national mercantilism; rather capitalism developed at first in England alongside the fiscal monopoly policy. The course of events was that a stratum of entrepreneurs which had developed in independence of the political administration secured the systematic support of Parliament in the 18th century, after the collapse of the fiscal monopoly policy of the Stuarts. Here for the last time irrational and rational capitalism faced each other in conflict, that is, capitalism in the field of fiscal and colonial privileges and public monopolies, and capitalism oriented in relation to market opportunities which were developed from within by business interests themselves on the basis of saleable services (Weber 1981:350).

Following the First World War, Weber reasserted a position he had held through-out his career: it was essential to strengthen the modern capitalist state. Doing so would preserve the integrity of the nation, which he defined largely in terms of literacy and a shared language and of its international struggle for existence with other nation states. Since participatory democracy was all but impossible, except in the smallest of societies, democracy was reduced to a mechanism for selecting leaders – preferably charismatic individuals who possessed a vision of the future; however, democracy so defined and the rights of citizens associated were threatened in the modern state. The danger came from two directions: the increasing domination of economic and political life by large-scale organizations – i.e. by industrial corporations and the state bureaucracy – and by the irrational pressures that mass movements, like the U-boat agitation in Germany during the First World War, could exert (Beetham 1985; Mommsen 1974, 1984).

Discussion

With regards to the rise of industrial capitalism, the arguments of Marx and Weber were closer to one another than either was to that of Durkheim. Both Marx and Weber considered the historic specificity of capitalist development. While Weber viewed the advent of industrial capitalism as a uniquely Western phenomenon, Marx saw its development as a process that was gradually ensnaring a steadily increasing portion of the world's population in its social relations, as colonies or countries on the periphery were caught up in market exchange relations. Marx based his conclusions largely on an analysis of what happened in Western Europe; however, he did not preclude the possibility that the capitalist mode of production might have developed autochthonously in other parts of the world because of the conditions and social relations that prevailed in those regions when they were incorporated into the emerging world market. Subsequent writers using Marx's analytical method have explored whether industrial capitalism developed autochthonously elsewhere – e.g. in Egypt and Japan (Gran 1979; Moulder 1977).

Since Durkheim viewed society as a biological organism composed of functionally interrelated parts that were transformed through time, he only partly addressed the historic specificity of the rise of modern industrial society. He portrayed its development as the steady unfolding of a potential that was inherent in society itself and that was unleashed by the concentration of population in cities and increased social differentiation. Cohesion and order were maintained in an increasingly complex society by exchange, communication and adherence to a broadly defined civic morality that was underpinned by religion and the state, that dictated the sentiments and ideas of the society and that regulated the action of its members. Social differentiation increased because of the concentration of people, which intensified the interactions between individuals. This increased communication, which diminished distinctions between different segments, led to the increased moral density of the community.

Durkheim's theoretical framework was adopted in the 1920s by the British structural-functionalist anthropologists – Bronislaw Malinowski and A. R. Radcliffe-Brown – who were concerned primarily with indigenous, kin-organized communities in the colonies. While Malinowski elaborated Durkheim's notion of *collective conscience* or culture, Radcliffe-Brown actively eschewed the idea of culture and focused instead on social relations. In the 1930s and 1940s, US anthropologist Robert Redfield adapted Durkheim's evolutionary progression of social types to describe what he called the folk–urban continuum – the relations that exist between a city and a series of rural communities that had differentially adopted cultural patterns and practices emanating from the urban center. In the 1950s and 1960s, Durkheim's views of society would underpin those of the modernization theorists who wanted to ensure that Third World states would pursue capitalist economic and social development strategies. They would also characterize modernization in terms of Weber's ideas about increased rationality, bureaucracy and the importance of charismatic leaders.

Besides providing explanations for the rise of industrial capitalism, Marx, Durkheim and Weber also furnished explicit or implicit theories about the formation of national identities and the transformation of the countryside; Marx and Weber also examined the economic and political conditions underpinning imperialism. Let us briefly consider their contributions to these topics, which will be explored further in subsequent chapters.

For Marx and Engels the development of the capitalist mode of production destroyed local cultural and linguistic differences and homogenized formerly disparate populations as the market formed; the emerging national languages and cultures laid the foundations for territorially based, absolutist states (Nimni 1991: 18). Moreover, they also recognized the existence of 'peoples without history' in Eastern Europe – i.e. Slavic groups with distinctive cultures and languages residing in territories dominated by the German bourgeoisie (Rosdolsky 1980).

Durkheim also developed an implicit theory of national identity. He described social solidarity in ethnic or national terms resulting from a community of beliefs and sentiments that were rooted in the shared historical experiences that occur when people participate in the same organizations. Nations appear when groups united by culture, language and shared sentiments overlap and merge with states. By distinguishing between nationality and the state, Durkheim was able, like Marx and Engels, to differentiate distinctive nationalities, like the Finns or the Poles, that lacked their own states from national states, like France or England, that were dominated by the members of a single nationality (Llobera 1994).

Weber believed that nations exist when people share a common objective factor – language, values, culture, religion, patterns of thought or political experience – and believe that it is a source of social cohesion and solidarity that finds its expression in an autonomous state. He also believed that, while the idea of nationhood was found in all layers of the class structure, it was not held equally by all strata of the society. He asserted that:

> Certain sections of the community had a particular interest in it: the army and civil service in extending their power and prestige; the cultural strata in preserving or developing the character of national culture; the propertied class in the profits that accrued from overseas trade and colonisation (Beetham 1985:144).

With regard to imperialism, Marx never used the term; however, he did sketch the outlines of a theory to account for the geographical expansion of capitalism and its impact on non-capitalist societies. In his view, competition forced industrial capitalists to devise new methods of production to increase productivity, to develop new markets for their goods and to locate the cheapest supplies of the raw materials, goods and labor power they must purchase. The industrial capitalists satisfied these needs initially by enmeshing pre-capitalist societies in their social relations. Capitalist expansion was facilitated by imperial states that protected overseas markets and prevented their colonial subjects from developing industries that would compete with those of the metropolitan country (Brewer 1990:25–57).

Weber pointed out that different social strata gained prestige and had vested interests in imperialism. They included the propertied classes that profited from overseas expansion and the cultural strata, the military and the civil service that benefited from the expansion of national culture into new territories (Mommsen 1982:19–30).

With regard to the transformation of rural social relations, Marx was among the first to point out that the development of industrial capitalism in England began with the Enclosure Acts, which drove peasants and tenants from the land, creating a class of landless individuals who were forced to sell their labor power in order to sustain themselves and their families. In his analysis of Prussian agriculture, Weber showed that the traditional social relations between landowners and tenants were dissolved and replaced with legal contracts that transformed the tenants into rural proletarians who worked for wages and paid rents. Marx and Weber showed that, in both England and Prussia, many of the propertyless individuals separated from agricultural land ultimately moved to factory cities in search of work.

Durkheim's theory about the transformation of social relations in the countryside was implicit in his discussion of the shift from small, homogeneous communities to large, internally differentiated ones in which the motors for change were located in the exchanges taking place in markets and urban centers and in the actions of states, which were also centered in the cities. The rural communities that persisted in the face of these changes became increasingly dependent on practices and ideas emanating from the urban areas. By the 1950s, the persistence of rural communities was seen as the major obstacle to modernization by theorists and civil servants concerned with forging capitalist social relations in Third World countries.

In the next chapter, we will examine in more detail how Marx's successors and the contemporaries of Weber and Durkheim dealt with imperialism, nationalism, the transformation of social relations in the countryside and the related issues of indigenous peoples and colonial subjects.

–3–

Imperialism, Nations, Peasants and Indigenous Subjects

The development of capitalism, nationalism and imperialism was increasingly interdependent and intertwined after the 1880s. During the first two-thirds of the nineteenth century, capitalism had developed *relatively* autonomously in different national states through a process involving the creation of domestic markets, the exploitation of wage workers and the penetration of capitalist social relations into the agricultural sectors of the national economies. The appearance of capital-intensive industries – like steel and railroads – and joint stock companies in the 1860s marked the concentration and centralization of capital and the beginning of the age of monopolies. Some monopolies dominated the economies of their home countries; they controlled all aspects of the production, distribution and sale of particular commodities, and all of them had the capacity to produce more than the domestic economy could consume. The various national economies of the world were slowly integrated as these corporations began to export the excess goods they produced. This process also ensured that the inequalities between the capitalist countries and the underdeveloped countries on the periphery would be reproduced.

The corporations and the capitalist nation-states in which they operated ushered in a new form of imperialism during the 1870s and 1880s. It was based on capitalist economic expansion rather than the extension of political sovereignty. They exported excess commodities and capital to areas that offered high rates of rates of return on investments. The new imperialism fostered unprecedented migration, as peoples from various regions, stripped of their means of production, were forced to emigrate in order to provide livelihoods for themselves and their families. The mass movements of people from various countries fostered the growth of nationalist movements not only in the capitalist countries themselves but also in colonies like India or French Indochina.

Imperialism, the resurgence of nationalism, industrialization, the transformation of rural life and the incorporation of indigenous peoples into national and/or imperial states occurred at the same time that the social sciences were becoming professions and distinct fields of inquiry. Consequently, it is necessary to read across the current disciplinary boundaries forged in this technical division of labor in order to gain a full appreciation of how the processes taking place were understood.

Imperialism: Conquest Abroad, Repression at Home

The early theories of imperialism were framed in political terms involving '. . . the personal sovereignty of a powerful ruler over numerous territories, whether in Europe or overseas' (Mommsen 1982:1). However, after 1902 the main theories of imperialism referred to the economic policies of nationalist and national states – England, France, Germany, the Netherlands and the United States – that acquired overseas colonies in pursuit of profits. They emphasized the linkages between economic interests and territorial acquisitions, and saw imperialism as an inevitable by-product of capitalism, one that marked a new stage in the conflict between capitalists and their opponents.

John A. Hobson's (1858–1940) *Imperialism* (1965 [1902]) was the most influential turn-of-the-century account. It provoked intense discussion among Marxist and liberal writers (Arrighi 1978; Brewer 1990; Howard and King 1989; Mommsen 1982). Hobson argued that the mainspring of a state's imperial policy was to find overseas markets for surplus goods and profitable investment opportunities in order to supplement the diminishing profits that could be expected and extracted from saturated home markets. Imperialist policies resulted from underconsumption and oversavings, and foreign investment provided an outlet for the surplus savings and unsold commodities product that resulted from underconsumption.

> As one nation after another enters the machine economy and adopts advanced industrial methods, it becomes more difficult for its manufacturers, merchants and financiers to dispose profitably of their economic resources, and they are tempted more and more to use their Governments in order to secure for their particular use some distant undeveloped country by annexation and protection. . . .
>
> Everywhere appear excessive powers of production, excessive capital in search of investment. It is admitted by all businessmen that the growth of the powers of production in their country exceeds the growth in consumption, that more goods can be produced than can be sold at a profit, and that more capital exists than can find remunerative investment.
>
> It is this economic condition that forms the taproot of Imperialism. If the consuming public in this country raised its standard of consumption to keep pace with every rise of productive powers, there could be no excess of goods or capital clamorous to use Imperialism in order to find markets: foreign trade would indeed exist, but there would be no difficulty in exchanging a small surplus of our manufactures for the food and raw material we annually absorbed, and all the savings that we made could find employment, if we chose, in home industries (Hobson 1965:80–1).

Hobson noted that the primary advocates and beneficiaries of imperialist policies were large industrial firms and banking houses. They used war, militarism and foreign policy to secure outlets for surplus goods and capital. As a result, the public finances of states committed to imperialist policies rose dramatically in the late nineteenth century; about two-thirds of the money raised from the general public, often through taxes on consumption, went for military expenditures and the payment of military debts. Such policies did not equally benefit all classes of the imperialist states, since the tax burden fell disproportionately on the lower classes, whose members did not share in the overseas profits (Hobson 1965:105–6). Hobson concluded that the great industrial firms and banking houses promoting imperialist policies would grow steadily more parasitic on society as a whole and, consequently, would require increased protection by the state, not only from their own lower classes but also from capitalists in rival states.

Rudolf Hilferding's (1877–1941) *Finance Capital*, which appeared in 1910, elaborated themes that were embryonic in the work of Hobson and Marx: the formation of modern corporations – i.e. joint stock companies – laid the foundations for development of monopolies and signaled the appearance of a new relationship between industrial firms and banks. Before modern corporations appeared in significant numbers in the last half of the nineteenth century, the size of an individual enterprise was limited by the personal wealth of its owner and his willingness to invest profits in the firm. However, the size of joint stock companies was limited only by the number of individuals who were willing to invest personal wealth in return for a share of the corporation. In Hilferding's (1981:107–29, 305–7) view, the formation of joint stock companies underwrote the concentration of capital needed to launch costly, gigantic enterprises – like modern steel mills. They also concentrated production, since the new large firms usually produced units more cheaply than their smaller, less efficiently organized competitors. As the competitors ceased to manufacture the same commodities, capital was centralized. Thus, the concentration and centralization of capital accelerated tendencies toward the formation of monopolies.

However, this was only part of the story for Hilferding. Banks – which concentrate the money form of capital – also underwrote the growth of monopolies, since they supplied credit to industrial firms and became increasingly concerned with the long-term prospects of their clients. In order to ensure profitable returns on their investments in particular firms, the banks suppressed competition and promoted cartels, trusts and mergers. As monopolies emerged, industrial and banking capital, which had previously been distinct, fused into *finance capital*. The linkages between them were cemented by interlocking directorates where high-level managers or owners of one firm sat on the other firms' boards of directors. The interests of the industrial firms and the banks became so intertwined in the process that they could not be disentangled (Hilferding 1981:170–82, 223–6).

The rise of finance capital had several consequences. First, the industrial firms and banks inextricably linked together were able to force the government to enact tariffs that simultaneously protected the goods they produced from foreign competition and gave them greater control over the domestic market. Second, the rise of finance capital witnessed the transfer of profits from competitive to monopoly firms – i.e. the cartelized firms enjoyed increasingly high rates of profit at the expense of their smaller competitors. Third, as the monopolies increasingly dominated protected markets, consumers had a steadily diminishing number of sources from whom to purchase goods. Fourth, as monopoly control over national markets increased, investment in both the monopoly firms and their smaller competitors slowed; this led to an accumulation of capital in search of a safe investment that would yield maximum returns. Fifth, as a result, uninvested capital was moved into undeveloped areas of the national economic territory with rich resources and cheap labor, or the national economic territory itself was enlarged.

Hilferding realized that imperialism transformed social relations at home and abroad. The class structure and role of the state within the national economic territory were modified, and the social relations of the precapitalist societies enveloped by imperialist states were devastated.

> The export of capital, especially since it has assumed the form of industrial and finance capital, has enormously accelerated the overthrow of all the old social relations, and the involvement of the world in capitalism. Capitalist development did not take place independently in each individual country, but instead capitalist relations of production and exploitation were imported along with capital from abroad, and indeed imported at the level already attained in the most advanced country (Hilferding 1981:322).

While Hobson and Hilferding considered imperialism to be a special form of capitalist society, Rosa Luxemburg (1870–1919) did not. Imperialism was militarism in her view. Militarism served to defend the national interests of one state from those of competing states and to consolidate the dominant position of industrial and financial capital *vis-à-vis* other classes and strata in the state. Imperialism was:

> . . . an instrument of class domination over the labouring population inside the country . . . . [It was] closely connected with colonialism, protectionism and power politics as a whole . . . a world armament race . . . colonial robbery and the policy of 'spheres of influence' all over the world . . . in home and foreign affairs the very essence of a capitalist policy of national aggression (quoted by Mommsen 1982:35 and Nettl 1966:524).

Luxemburg discussed the relationship between capitalism and imperialism in *The Accumulation of Capital* (1951 [1913]) (Lee 1971). Capitalism emerged like a volcanic island in a vast sea of precapitalist societies that provided the milieu in which the accumulation of capital could occur:

> Capitalism arises and develops historically amidst a non-capitalist society. In Western Europe it is found at first in a feudal environment from which it in fact sprang . . . and,

later, after having swallowed up the feudal system, it exists mainly in an environment of peasants and artisans. . . .

The existence and development of capitalism requires an environment of non-capitalist forms of production, but not every one of these forms will serve its ends. Capitalism needs non-capitalist social strata as a market for its surplus value, as a source of supply for its means of production and as a reservoir of labour power for its wage system (Luxemburg 1951:368).

These pre- or non-capitalist forms, or 'natural economies', as she called them, were of no use to capitalists, because they responded mainly to internal demands, produced no surplus and had little use for foreign goods. As a result, the capitalists had to transform or destroy all non-capitalist forms in order to gain possession of their resources, to acquire wage labor, to introduce commodities and to separate trade from agriculture.

Thus, the world economy at the turn of the century was divided into two spheres: a static precapitalist sector and a dynamic capitalist sector. The motor driving the constantly expanding capitalist sector was the capitalists' continual need to transform the forces and means of production to ensure the highest possible rates of profits. As a result, uneven economic development was essential for the expansion of capitalism:

From the very beginning the forms and laws of capitalist production aim to comprise the entire globe as a store of productive forces. Capital, impelled to appropriate productive forces for purposes of exploitation, ransacks the whole world, it procures its means of production from all corners of the earth, seizing them, if necessary by force, from all levels of civilization and from all forms of society (Luxemburg 1951:358).

Since the capitalist mode of production could not exist in isolation and had to co-exist with non-capitalist societies in order for the accumulation of capital and the reproduction of the capitalist system to take place, capitalism could never become a universal form of society (Luxemburg 1951:350, 365, 467). Consequently, as it repressed its own workers and engulfed non-capitalist societies through expansion, it also sowed the seeds of an economic crisis and its own destruction, since it was '. . . assimilating the very conditions which alone can ensure its own existence' (Luxemburg 1951:366).

The implication of Luxemburg's argument was that markets situated in areas with non-capitalist social relations rather than the exploitation of wage workers, as Marx had argued earlier, were essential for the realization of surplus value and constituted the condition necessary for accumulation of capital to occur (Tarbuck 1972:29–33). This was a practical question on the eve of the First World War: Should the workers in capitalist countries ally with the capitalist classes of those national states, or should they ally themselves with the peoples of non-capitalist countries (Luxemburg 1972)?

Nikolai I. Bukharin's (1888–1938) *Imperialism and the Accumulation of Capital* (1924) was the most thoughtful response to Luxemburg's theory of capitalist collapse (Bukharin 1972). He disagreed with her view that capitalism could not exist without non-capitalist societies. He further argued that her theories of imperialism and capitalist collapse were also inadequate, because they were defined largely in voluntaristic, political terms and ignored the transformative effects that monopolies had already had on capitalist social relations. However, he agreed that all national economies were parts of a single world market. They had become increasingly politicized and competitive, because their '. . . productive forces had developed beyond the point where they could be operated efficiently within the confines of any nation-state' (Howard and King 1989:246; Bukharin 1973:87–8, 168–9).

Bukharin (1973) reorganized and developed Hilferding's ideas in *Imperialism and the World Economy*, which was written before the Russian Revolution but not published until 1929. While Hilferding had focused on the concentration and centralization of capital in a single national state, Bukharin argued that two contradictory processes had already been occurring simultaneously on the eve of the First World War. On the one hand, the various national economies constituting the world economy were becoming increasingly interdependent through international trade; on the other, national blocs of capital were emerging in the context of this world economy as the interests of the monopolies and the capitalist states in whose territories they were located intertwined. Consequently, imperialism was a problem of the world economy.

> Just as every individual enterprise is part of the 'national' economy, so every one of these 'national economies' is included in the system of world economy. This is why the struggle between modern 'national economic bodies' must be regarded first of all as the struggle of various competing parts of world economy – just as we consider the struggle of individual enterprises to be one of the phenomena of socio-economic life (Bukharin 1973:17).

For Bukharin, international trade had established the relations of production on a world scale; however, differences in the level of economic development and the different natural conditions in various parts of the world laid the foundations for a growing international division of labor.

> Important as the natural differences in the conditions of production may be, they recede more and more into the background compared with differences that are the result of the uneven development of productive forces in the various countries. . . . The cleavage

between 'town' and 'country' as well as the 'development of this cleavage', formerly confined to one country alone, are now being reproduced on a tremendously enlarged basis. Viewed from this standpoint, entire countries appear today as 'towns', namely, the industrial countries, whereas entire agrarian territories appear to be 'country' (Bukharin 1973:20–1).

While Hilferding argued that the concentration and centralization of capital typically occurred within the confines of a given country because of the linkages between its monopolies and state apparatus, Bukharin argued that these processes occasionally splashed over those boundaries, and that the

> ... various spheres of the concentration and organisation process stimulate each other, creating a very strong tendency toward transforming the entire national economy *into one gigantic combined enterprise under the tutelage of the financial kings and the capitalist state, an enterprise which monopolises the national market.* . . . It follows that world capitalism, the world system of production, assumes in our times the following aspect: a few consolidated, organised economic bodies ('the great civilised powers') on the one hand, and a periphery of underdeveloped countries with a semi-agrarian system on the other (Bukharin 1973:73–4, emphasis in the original).

The uneven development of the world system focused attention on the relations between capitalists and the state that emerged in the wake of the formation of finance capital – i.e, the creation of monopolies and the protective economic policies of the state. Uneven development meant that tendencies toward the formation of monopolies in one national state did not signal the end of competition but rather the emergence and intensification of a new form of competition that took place in the international arena as the smaller, less developed states were enveloped by their larger, more developed neighbors. In Bukharin's (1973:119–20) view, 'Imperialist annexation is only a case of the general capitalist tendency towards centralisation of capital, a case of its centralisation at that maximum scale which corresponds to the competition of state capitalist trusts.' In other words, the state was an active agent both in the various advanced capitalisms rooted in different national states and in their imperialist overseas ventures.

Vladimir I. Lenin's (1870–1924) widely read *Imperialism, The Highest Stage of Capitalism: A Popular Outline*, written in 1916, was partly a wartime polemic attacking the theory of ultra-imperialism, which claimed that the capitalist powers would agree to exploit the world jointly rather than waging war over its division (Lenin 1964a, 1968; Brewer 1990:129). For Lenin, imperialism was the stage of development in which the dominance of monopolies and finance capital was already established; it had the following characteristics:

(1) the concentration of production and capital has developed to such a high stage that it has created monopolies which play a decisive role in economic life; (2) the merging of bank capital with industrial capital, and the creation, on the basis of this 'finance capital', of a financial oligarchy; (3) the export of capital as distinguished from the export of commodities acquires exceptional importance; (4) the formation of international capitalist associations which share the world among themselves, and (5) the territorial division of the whole world among the biggest capitalist powers is completed (Lenin 1964a:266).

In Lenin's view, monopolist associations headed by larger employers were the principal feature of imperialism (Lenin 1964a:193–4, 260). The export of capital to underdeveloped or undeveloped areas was an outlet for surplus capital and a means of checking the declining rates of profit in the various national states; capital export also intensified competition and conflict between the capitalist states in the world market. By exporting capital rather than commodities, the monopolies made superprofits, part of which they used to bribe the upper strata of their own working classes, through direct and indirect means, and to turn them into champions of nationalism and reformism. This was one reason why the European working classes supported the various national capitalist classes during the First World War. The export of capital also promoted the growth of a stratum of rentiers who received fixed incomes from stocks, bonds or property and thus lived by 'clipping coupons'; who were isolated from production themselves; and who lived by exploiting the labor of overseas countries and colonies.

Thus, for Lenin, monopoly capitalism was the essence of imperialism. Once a monopoly has gained control of a market, it

... engenders a tendency to stagnation and decay. Since monopoly prices are established, even temporarily, the motive cause of technical and, consequently, of all other progress disappears to a certain extent and, further, the *economic* possibility arises of deliberately retarding economic progress. ... [Nevertheless] monopoly under capitalism can never completely, and for a very long time, eliminate competition in the world market ... (Lenin 1964a:276, emphasis in the original).

Lenin believed that the tendency toward stagnation and decay undermined the capacity of monopoly capitalism to reproduce itself and threatened its continued existence; however, this tendency did not guarantee an inevitable breakdown, as Hobson and Luxemburg suggested.

Thus, between 1910 and 1920, Marxist analysts constructed alternative theories of imperialism that examined the formation of finance capital and monopolies, the convergence of capitalist and state interests, the encapsulation of underdeveloped countries into economic blocs that were part of a world economy, and the existence of precapitalist social relations in the colonial areas.

In 1919, the Austrian economist Joseph A. Schumpeter (1883–1950) formulated an alternative view in *The Sociology of Imperialisms*. It was a critique of the analyses of Hilferding and Luxemburg and, by extension, of those of other Marxist theorists mentioned above. Imperialism, in Schumpeter's (1951:7) view, was '. . . the object-less disposition on the part of a state to unlimited forcible expansion'. While there may be an economic explanation for this phenomenon, he argued that the Marxist theorists had reduced imperialism to economic class interests, which, given the '. . . customary modes of political thought and feeling can never be mere "reflexes" of, or counterparts to, the production of that age' (Schumpeter 1951:7).

Schumpeter's alternative was a restatement of liberal economic theory. He argued that imperialism did not represent the highest stage of capitalist development but was actually a transitional phenomenon resulting from the survival of residual political and social structures from the age of absolutist monarchies. While the monopoly capitalists had sought to control markets before 1914 through protective tariffs and policies, the monopolies themselves emerged only after the protective tariffs imposed by various national states were already in place. In other words, the industrialists and bankers found reasons to support these measures and were ultimately able to profit from the export of goods and capital in that milieu (Schumpeter 1951:83–5, 110–18). Imperialism

> . . . does not *coincide* with nationalism and militarism, though it *fuses* with them by supporting them as it is supported by them. It too is – not only historically, but also sociologically – a heritage of the autocratic state, of its structural elements, organizational forms, interest alignments, human attitudes, the outcome of precapitalist forces which the autocratic state has reorganized, in part by the methods of early capitalism. It would never have been evolved by the 'inner logic' of capitalism itself. This is true even of more export monopolism. . . . That it was able to develop to its present dimensions is owing to the momentum of a situation once created, which continued to engender ever new 'artificial' economic structures, that is, those which maintain themselves by political power alone. . . .
>
> The precapitalist elements in our social life may still have great vitality; special circumstances in national life may revive them from time to time; but in the end the climate of the modern world must destroy them. . . . Whatever opinion is held concerning the vitality of capitalism itself, whatever lifespan is predicted for it, it is bound to withstand the onslaughts of its enemies and its own irrationality much longer than essentially untenable export monopolism – untenable even from the capitalist point of view. Export monopolism may perish in revolution, or it may be peacefully relinquished; this may happen soon, or it may take some time and require desperate struggle; but one thing is certain – it *will* happen. This will immediately dispose of neither warlike instincts nor structural elements and organizational forms oriented toward war . . . (Schumpeter 1951:128–30, emphases in the original).

Schumpeter interpreted imperialism in the decades preceding the First World War as a departure from the normal path of capitalist development, the internal logic of which was rooted in a competitive, *laissez-faire*, free market economy. In his view, once the precapitalist survivals in modern society were replaced, imperialism would disappear.

The National Question: Nations, Nationalism and National Minorities

The concepts of the nation as a form of collective identity and of nationalism as an ideology and movement with both political and cultural dimensions crystallized in the wake of the American and French Revolutions in the late eighteenth century and those in Latin America during the first three decades of the nineteenth century (Hutchinson and Smith 1994:4–10). As was noted in Chapter 2, the relationship between the nation and nationalism, on the one hand, and the capitalist state, on the other, was debated from the mid-nineteenth century onwards in a world increasingly shaped by capitalist industrialization, imperialist expansion, massive population movements and struggles to establish sovereign nation-states in Central Europe.

From the 1840s onwards, the goals of unifying the German-speaking peoples of central Europe into a sovereign nation-state or, by extension, the members of other language groups into sovereign states built on the works of Johann G. Herder (1744–1803) and other German Romantic writers in the 1770s (Walicki 1982).[1]

---

1. While the German Romantics used the idea of nation – a culturally, linguistically, and geographically bounded group – to underpin a nationalist ideology calling for the political unification of separate states, nineteenth-century writers in France and the United States conflated this definition with conceptions of class and race in order to argue that social inequalities were rooted in nature. For example, in the mid-1850s, Count Joseph de Gobineau (1816–82) claimed that the French ruling class and lower classes belonged to different races, and that intermarriage between them had led not only to the decline of French civilization but also to horrible things like democracy, the French Revolution, and industrialization (Gobineau 1915). In the 1890s, the American anthropologist Daniel Brinton (1837–99) combined cultural, linguistic, and geographical criteria with physical traits to define four European races. The 'Aryacs', whom he viewed as the most advanced and civilized of the European races, were separated in his hierarchy of races from Africans, Asians, and American Indians as well as from the white races of Eastern and Southern Europe, who were then immigrating to the United States in large numbers. Brinton's scheme also provided the ideological foundations for a shared cross-class identity in the southern United States between the old planter elite and poor yeomen farmers, both of whom were identified as 'Aryacs' (Brinton 1890; Patterson and Spencer 1994).

While the French and the Americans used race to code social differences in their societies, the Germans saw it as an expression of the underlying unity of the German nation and state. However, this does not mean that German social theorists did not use the concept of race or believe in racial hierarchies. For example, in his Freiburg lecture of 1895, Max Weber (1989b) racialized national differences when he separated the Polish and German farmers of East Prussia on the basis of physical

Herder and his contemporaries had elaborated a theory of cultural nationalism. Nations develop because of the creative energies of a people who share the same language and patterns of thought in the course of everyday life. These shared beliefs and practices were found among the farmers, artisans, traders, and intellectuals of remote, relatively unstratified communities whose members retained close ties to the natural environments in which they lived; they were not shared by the aristocratic rulers or by the poor (Barnard 1965; Beiser 1992:189–244; Markus 1991).

The Prussian nationalist Georg W. F. Hegel (1770–1831) disagreed, and elaborated a theory of political nationalism in the *Philosophy of Right* (1821) and *Lectures on the Philosophy of World History: Introduction* (1830) (Hegel 1952:155–74; 1975:97–102). He

> . . . argued that the network of governmental and political institutions of the state – its constitution – is typically a product of history and expresses the culture of a particular nation – its values, religious beliefs, views about the world, traditions and customs. That culture (or 'spirit') of the nation permeates also other human relations (least of all, however, those which have come under the relative sway of civil society) and gives the whole unity, and cohesion. The values of the national community and the operation of its central government are linked together through mediating institutions (such as corporations, estates and the representative system), which ensure that the activities of the government broadly express the basic ideals and interests of groups within the community or its individual members. If such mediating links do not exist or cease to perform their proper function the nation or important sections become alienated from the government and the integrity or independence of the political community is jeopardized (Pelczynski 1984:266).

For Hegel (1964:153–64), the nation was a political entity shaped by the state, and cultural or linguistic unity were not sufficient to weld a group into a nation.

While Marx and Engels were critical of cultural conceptions of the nation and nationalism, neither initially developed a systematic theory of the nation or the national question (Löwy 1974:371). Like Hegel, they conceptualized the nation in political rather than cultural and linguistic terms, and the national question, in their view, was one of peoples struggling for political independence and self-determination (Pelczynski 1984:266). In 1849, Engels (1974:232, 237) adopted Hegel's distinction between 'historic peoples', like the Germans and the French, who had dynamic histories and would be a force in the future, and 'peoples without history', like the Slovaks or Moravians, who had been marginalized by historical

---

and psychical characteristics. He subsequently rejected this view in 1910, when he claimed that the concept of inherent racial differences was overused, that it was too frequently used to explain everything (Beetham 1985:122).

development in Europe (Rosdolsky 1980). In other words, Engels used 'peoples' as a synonym for Herder's terms 'nations'.

Marx and Engels shifted their views on national movements in the 1860s in the wake of Irish resistance to British repression. In 1869, Marx (1987) examined the relations between class and nation and pointed out that the nationalism of the English workers, which bound them to their rulers, was ultimately harmful to themselves:

> The English working class . . . will never be able to do anything decisive here in England before they separate their attitude towards Ireland quite definitely from that of the ruling classes, and not only make common cause with the Irish, but even take the initiative in dissolving the Union established in 1801. And this must be done not out of sympathy with the Irish, but as a demand based on the interests of the English proletariat. If not the English proletariat will for ever remain bound to the leading strings of the ruling classes, because they will be forced to make a common front with them against Ireland. . . .

Engels (1990a) subsequently examined the material factors that simultaneously gave rise to the national state at the end of the Middle Ages and laid the foundations for the development of the new nationalisms.

Nationalism became an increasingly pressing issue in the Austrian-Hungarian Empire toward the end of the nineteenth century, when more than a dozen different national movements, many of them involving nations without history, sought to assert their identities in a Social Democratic Party that proclaimed its internationalism. This forced Austrian Marxists, like Otto Bauer (1881–1938), to confront the national question head on (Bottomore 1978:30–6; Nimni 1991:119–84). Bauer (1979) reframed the concept of the nation, and thereby opened a new phase in the debate over the national question.

Bauer's theory described the historical process by which modern nations emerged. With the rise of social classes, the old unitary communal culture of the nation was dissolved and replaced, on the one hand, by the common culture of the ruling classes and, on the other, by the fragmented, highly localized and differentiated cultures of peasants, farmers and workers that resulted from the disintegration of the old nation (Bottomore and Goode 1978:108). Thus, there are two classes in every nation – the politically powerful ones that create and genuinely participate in the national culture, and the subordinated groups that are excluded from national life but whose labor and efforts sustain the culture of the national classes (Nimni 1991:167).

Class and state formation, in Bauer's view, not only involved *ethnocide*, the destruction of a way of life, but also constituted a milieu in which *ethnogenesis* occurs – i.e. people who occupied the same position in a stratified society began to recognize that they had a shared identity. This identity was rooted in their *national character*, which, according to Bauer, referred to the distinctive configuration of cultural traits and characteristics that resulted from how their common position in a tributary or capitalist society developed historically through time. Language was only a partial manifestation of a cultural community, merely one trait that was the product of the complex historical development of the community itself. The diversity of culture meant that even when people spoke the same language, like Croats and Serbians, they often remained separate nations (Bauer 1979:5–168; Nimni 1991:146–60).

Bauer also argued that, in capitalist societies, national education, which represents the common culture of the ruling classes, gradually overwhelms the particular national cultures of the subordinated workers and peasants – i.e. those of the people without history.

> The working class section of the *nations without history* in Austria was nationalist: the state which enslaved them was German; the court which protected the property owners and threw the dispossessed in jail was also German; each death sentence was written in German, and German was used to issue the orders to the [multinational] armies which were sent to crush each strike by the hungry and defenseless workers (Bauer 1979:296, emphasis in the original).

Capitalism did not produce a homogeneous national working class but rather '. . . a *nationally* conscious proletariat' (Munck 1986:40).

Bauer's suggestions regarding the national question echoed sentiments expressed by other social critics who had also wrestled with Neo-Kantian thought. A decade earlier, during the early 1900s, in the United States, where ideas of nation and race were conflated, the civil rights activist W. E. B. Du Bois (1868–1963) and the anthropologist Franz Boas (1858–1942) were already challenging essentialist notions of race and examining both the context and the historical processes by which races were constituted in that country (Du Bois 1898, 1903; Boas 1894, 1911a). By 1911, Boas (1911b) was already pointing out that race, language, and culture were distinct from one another and that their interconnections were the result of complex historical processes. Unfortunately, the Europeans who dominated the debate over the national question failed to recognize the significance of their contributions.

In Germany, Max Weber had a slightly different understanding of the inter-relationships of class, nation, and state. For Weber

> . . . the national state rests on deep and elemental psychological foundations within the broad economically subordinate strata of the nation as well, that it is by no means a mere 'superstructure', the organization of the economically dominant classes. It is just that in normal times this political instinct sinks below the level of consciousness for the masses. In that case the specific function of the economically and politically leading strata is to be the repositories of political understanding (Weber 1989b:202).

Thus, a nation exists when the objective conditions shared by a group of people distinguish them from other groups. These conditions produce feelings of solidarity that find their expression either in autonomous political institutions or a demand for them (Beetham 1985:122–3). Over time, Weber came to agree with Bauer that culture, rather than race, provided the scaffolding for national identity. Moreover, he also believed that the intensification of nationalism in his time was due to the economic conflicts of imperialism and to the spread of literacy and national literatures among the previously uneducated masses (Weber 1978 [1922]:395–8, 919–26).

Karl Kautsky (1854–1938), on the other hand, was highly critical of Bauer's theory of the nation. In 'The Modern Nationality' (1887) he argued that it was difficult to define nationality, because the significance of the nation was continually transformed, and varied from one set of circumstances to another. The nation, in his view, was best understood in relation to economic development and state structures.

> . . . the classical form of the modern state is the nation state. But classical forms exist in general only as a tendency. It is rare that they are developed in a perfectly typical fashion . . . To the extent that economic antagonisms deepen, each economic region tries to develop its own urban and rural industry, but can do this less and less without hurting the industry of its neighbors. The different Austrian regions tend to separate, and the 'reconciliation' of nations becomes more difficult (Kautsky 1887 quoted in Haupt, Löwy, and Weill 1974:114, 116).

In 'Nationality and Internationality', Kautsky (1908) proposed an alternative to Bauer's theory. The national state emerged because capitalists desired to locate markets that were free from the interference of old state structures, and new state bureaucracies became increasingly important in the process. However, bureaucracies did not function very well without an official language and linguistic unification, which, of course, were also promoted by the commercialization of the society. However, when economic and political forces were powerful enough to foster a truly national language, the state's efforts to enforce linguistic uniformity actually promoted diversity, as groups that suffered under these policies turned to national identities and languages that they opposed to those of the state. In Kautsky's view, Bauer did not truly appreciate the power of language in forging national sentiments that were opposed to those of the state (Harman 1992:21–3).

Rosa Luxemburg (1976:176–7) combined elements of Bauer's and Kautsky's arguments concerning the national question and challenged other claims, especially their views on the right of self-determination for nationalist movements. Using Italy and Germany as examples, she located the rise of national movements in the economic activities of the big bourgeoisie, who were driven to find domestic markets. However, this was not the case in her native Poland. There, nationalism was rooted in the nobility's view of its own social position; consequently, the bourgeoisie was an anti-nationalist factor, partly because it was foreign and partly because its industries engaged largely in the production of commodities that were exported to Russia. As a result, the Polish capitalist class leaned toward Russia and did not demand the creation of a unified national state. 'In Poland there arose an opposition between the national idea and the bourgeois development, which gave the former not only a utopian but also a reactionary character' (Luxemburg 1976:177).

Luxemburg (1976:128–31) also disagreed with Kautsky's view that the spread of capitalism and the consequent rise of socialism would gradually remove all national distinctions, because

> The development of *world powers*, a characteristic feature of our times growing in importance along with the progress of capitalism, from the very outset condemns all small nations to political impotence. Apart from a few of the most powerful nations, the leaders in capitalist development, which possess the spiritual and material resources necessary to maintain their political and economic independence, 'self-determination,' the independent existence of smaller and petty nations, is an illusion, and will become even more so. The return of all, or even the majority of the nations which are today oppressed, to independence would only be possible if the existence of small states in the era of capitalism had any chances or hopes for the future. Besides, the big-power economy and politics – a condition of survival for the capitalist states – turn the politically independent, formally equal, small European states into mutes on the European stage and more often into scapegoats. . . .
>
> The very development of international trade in the capitalist period brings with it the inevitable, though at times slow ruin of all the more primitive societies, destroys their historically existing means of 'self-determination,' and makes them dependent on the crushing wheel of capitalist development. . . . The destructive action of world trade is followed by outright partition or by the political dependence of colonial countries in various degrees and forms (Luxemburg 1976:129–30, emphasis in the original).

V. I. Lenin (1964b, c) was critical of Luxemburg's views on the national question and on the right of self-determination (H. Davis 1976). He based his arguments on Kautsky's analysis of the rise of nations:

> For the complete victory of commodity production [i.e. capitalism], the bourgeoisie must capture the home market, and there must be politically unified territories whose population speak a single language, with all obstacles to the development of that language and to its consolidation in literature eliminated. Therein is the economic foundation of national movements. . . .
>
> Therefore the tendency of every national movement is towards the formation of *national states*, under which these requirements of modern capitalism are best satisfied.

The most profound economic factors drive towards this goal, and, therefore, for the whole of Western Europe, nay for the entire civilised world, the national state is *typical* and normal for the capitalist period . . . (Lenin 1964b:396–7, emphasis in the original).

In Lenin's view, the spread of capitalist social relations across the globe unleashed new national movements and calls for the formation of new national states, particularly in Asia. This meant, contrary to Luxemburg's arguments, that the national state provided the best conditions for the development of capitalism. It did not mean that the exploitation and oppression of nations were absent or could be eliminated in these states. It implied that the '. . . "self-determination of nations" . . . *cannot*, from a historico-political point of view, have any other meaning than political self-determination, state independence, and the formation of a national state' (Lenin 1964b:400, emphasis in the original).

Lenin proceeded to argue that it was essential to distinguish between two phases of capitalist development, which differ from each other with regard to national movements. The first was marked by the collapse of feudalism and absolutism, when national movements were mass movements calling for the formation of the bourgeois-democratic state. The second phase occurred in fully developed capitalist states in which there were already marked antagonisms between the capitalist and working classes. In other words, one would expect to find different kinds of national movements in each phase. The political implication of this for Lenin was that Marxists should take the general historical and concrete state conditions into account when assessing the revolutionary potential of any national movement's claim to self-determination.

The bourgeois nationalism of *any* oppressed nation has a general democratic content. This is directed *against* oppression, and it is this content that we *unconditionally* support. At the same time we strictly distinguish it from the tendency toward national exclusiveness . . . (Lenin 1964b:412, emphasis in the original).

From this, he concluded that, in 1914, the Russian working class was faced with

. . . a two-sided task: to combat nationalism of every kind, above all, Great Russian nationalism; to recognise, not only fully equal rights for all nations in general, but also equality of rights as regards polity, i.e., the right of nations to self-determination, to secession. And at the same time, it is their task, in the interests of a successful struggle against all and every kind of nationalism among nations, to preserve the unity of the proletarian struggle and the proletarian organisations, amalgamating these organisations into a close-knit international association, despite bourgeois strivings for national exclusiveness (Lenin 1964b:453–4).

Two years later, he asserted that it was also the duty of working classes in oppressor nations to

> ... struggle against the enforced retention of oppressed nations within the bounds of the given state, which means that they must fight for the right to self-determination. The proletariat must demand freedom of political separation for the colonies and nations oppressed by 'their own' nation ... [And] the socialists of the oppressed nations must, in particular, defend and implement the full and unconditional unity ... of the workers of the oppressed nation and those of the oppressor nation (Lenin 1964d:147–8).

This statement was directed to the workers of the capitalist states of Western Europe and the United States and to those of the backward, less-industrialized countries of Eastern Europe, semi-colonies like China and Turkey, and colonial outposts in Asia and Africa, which had a combined population of more than one billion persons.

The national question generated heated debates, and the political issues raised by the participants mentioned above, as well as by other writers who will be discussed in subsequent chapters, remained unresolved, in spite of the fact that they resurfaced repeatedly throughout the twentieth century.

The Agrarian Question: Capitalist Development and Peasantries

Marx was among the first to study the relationship between the development of capitalism and rural agricultural populations. He pointed out that, in the mid-nineteenth century, French peasant households were isolated from one another and from events that were taking place in the towns and cities. While they had gained ownership of their property in the wake of the French Revolution, their social and spatial isolation meant that they effectively had no political influence either during the Second Empire or under the Provisional Government. In 1850, they had rebelled against the Provisional Government's efforts to tax the wine they produced and, as a result, supported Bonaparte's *coup d'état*. They allied themselves with the industrialists, merchants, moneylenders and army against the workers and the landed aristocracy. Their loyalty to Bonaparte rested on his support of the Papacy and of their right to own the plots of land they worked to gain livelihoods that grew steadily smaller and more precarious each year as they went further into debt and as they increasingly sent their impoverished sons into an imperialist army stationed in colonial outposts around the world (Marx 1963:123–130; 1964b:69–76).

Even though the French peasants lived under similar conditions and were opposed to other classes,

> ... the identity of their interests begets no community, no national bond and no political organization among them, they do not form a class. They are consequently incapable of

enforcing their class interest in their own name. . . . They cannot represent themselves . . . [and] their representative must at the same time appear as their mass, as an authority over them, as an unlimited government power that protects them against other classes and sends them rain and sunshine from above. The political influence of the small-holding peasants, therefore, finds its final expression in the executive power subordinating society itself (Marx 1963:124).

This left the French peasants vulnerable to the desires and predations of the urban-dwelling capitalist classes. In spite of this, Marx (1971:77–9) still considered the French peasantry a potentially militant political force, even though it was isolated and kept in the dark by the state. He believed its potential would be realized as its members were drawn increasingly into capitalist relations emanating from the urban areas. At that time, the peasant smallholders were already beginning to feel the effects of modern capitalist agriculture – mortgages and debt, dispossession from their plots, the consolidation of landholdings by capitalist farmers who produced goods for sale rather than use and the steady growth of a rural proletariat.

During the 1870s, Marx (1983b) gradually realized that capitalist development was also occurring in the Russian countryside, and that this threatened the peasant *mir* or corporate landholding village organizations. He thought that the actions of the tsarist regime combined with those of the urban-based capitalists might drive the Russian peasants toward political action, although it might take a different form from what happened in England or France (Duggett 1975:173–7; Shanin 1983).

In 'The Peasant Question in France and Germany' (1894), Engels (1990b) pointed out that peasantries were organized differently in different parts of Europe. As a result, the breakdown of their self-sufficient natural economies as capitalist production relations spread from the cities to the countryside might also proceed along different paths. Capitalism had already eliminated the peasantry as an effective political and economic force in England and Prussia. The rapid formation of a rural proletariat in East Elbe, which Max Weber (1989a) had described a few years earlier (see Chapter 2), was especially important in Engels's view, since Prussia was becoming a locus of a political-economic struggle in which the rural wage-workers of the area occupied the same class position as urban, industrial workers.

In *The Agrarian Question* (1899), Karl Kautsky (1988) examined the develop-ment of agriculture in capitalist societies. He sought to explain why the development of capitalist agriculture was proceeding at a different pace and taking a different form from that of industry, and how capitalist social relations co-existed and articulated with precapitalist relations in the countryside (Alavi and Shanin 1988; Banaji 1976a, 1990; Byres 1991, 1996:20–39; Hussain and Tribe 1981a). Kautsky's (1988:13) initial assumption was that

With the exception of a few colonies, the capitalist mode of production begins its development in *towns*, in *industry*, leaving agriculture largely undisturbed initially. But the development of industry in itself soon begins to affect the character of agricultural production (emphasis in the original).

In the process, self-sufficient peasant families, whose members produced food and handicrafts for their own use, were inextricably drawn into market relations as urban crafts developed and displaced peasant domestic industry. As a result, peasant life became increasingly difficult to maintain without money. The only way they could acquire the money they needed was to produce commodities for the market; however, these commodities were usually not the ones they preferred to produce, but rather those ones that were not manufactured by urban industry. In order to sustain themselves and to produce for the market, the peasants either needed more land, which was not readily available, or they had to minimize the number of dependents: their children became rural or town-dwelling proletarians or emigrated to other countries, such as the United States. Changes in the nature of agricultural production meant that those that remained on the farms worked harder for less and that wage-workers were often hired on a seasonal basis (Kautsky 1988:13–17).

Like many of his contemporaries, Kautsky (1988:95–132) believed that large production units were more efficient than small ones, and that the processes of accumulation and centralization operated differently in the countryside and the cities. It was difficult to create large farms, since arable land was a relatively fixed means of production that was not easily expanded, unless, as in the areas where feudalism predominated, public lands could be enclosed or peasants expelled from their lands. The patterns of inheritance that prevailed in areas where the majority of the farmers were peasant smallholders also made it difficult to establish large farms that would benefit from the scientific and technical advances associated with economies of scale. Even if agrarian capitalists bought up the plots or mortgages of bankrupt peasants, it was unlikely that the fields they purchased would be contiguous. As a result, it was impossible for them to convert smallholdings into more efficient larger units.

Kautsky (1988:169–97) further argued that the persistence of peasant production was an integral feature of capitalism. Large capitalists' farms and *latifundia* – i.e. conglomerates combining agricultural and industrial production in rural areas – relied on the surrounding peasant farms to provide the particular combinations of year-round and seasonal labor they required. This meant that the peasants employed by agrarian capitalists had less time and energy to devote to their own subsistence production. As a result, they and their families often worked harder for less con-sumption, and they were forced to accept a pattern of self-exploitation based on a combination of excessive labor, underconsumption, and underselling. At the same time that the large farms curtailed the production of labor power on the peasant farms, their mere presence simultaneously increased the demand for it. Kautsky interpreted this contradiction to mean that large capitalist farms could never predominate in a country.

Lenin (1960a, b, c) was also concerned with the form that capitalist development was taking in the countryside. In *The Development of Capitalism in Russia* (1899), he aimed to show how the home market was being formed by the development of capitalism in Russia. However, unlike Kautsky, Lenin argued that the initial development of capitalist industry took place in the peasant household. This laid the foundations for the development of factories, first in the countryside and then in the cities, and for the formation of an urban proletariat. From his perspective, the question of the development of capitalism in Russia involved both the extent of capitalist relations in the countryside and how the relationships between the agricultural and industrial sectors of the economy affected the formation of the working class (Lenin 1960a:37–69; Hussain and Tribe 1981b:37–50).

Unlike Kautsky, Lenin believed that capitalist relations would eventually dominate the agricultural economy as a whole. He argued that rich peasants and poor peasants constituted the dominant classes in the old village communities. However, after the Emancipation Act of 1861, which shattered the old feudal relations between peasants and the landed aristocracy, the wealthy peasants began to transform themselves into capitalist farmers at the expense of their poorer neighbors; they purchased or rented land and hired their neighbors as permanent or seasonal waged workers. The poor peasants, who often had not been provided with enough land to sustain their families, were forced into the labor market in order to acquire those commodities they could not or did not produce in sufficient quantities to remain self-sufficient. The development of a rural class structure led to the formation of two home markets in the countryside – one based on the sale of commodities, and the other based on the exchange of land and other means of production. While the rural proletariat and bourgeoisie both participated in the commodities market, only the rural bourgeoisie was involved in the market where the major means of production were exchanged (Lenin 1960a:70–190).

After examining the differentiation of the peasantry, Lenin (1960a:191–251) investigated how the formation of a waged labor system in the countryside eroded the corvée system and transformed the economy of the large landlords into a capitalist one. When the corvée system was eliminated in 1861, the large landowners were compelled to hire waged labor to work their farms. Wealthy peasants, who possessed draft animals and heavy equipment, were less frequently lured into this labor market than poor peasants who owned only simple tools. While the poor peasants became proletarians, their wealthier peasant neighbors had no need to do so.

Thus, there were two forms of capitalist development in the Russian countryside. One involved the internal differentiation of the natural economy of the peasantry and rural class formation as capitalists and proletarians appeared. The other involved the transformation of estate farming into capitalist agriculture. Lenin (1960a:252–330) argued that the former was revolutionary; the latter resulted in the kind of agrarian capitalism that appeared in East Prussia and was dominated by the Junkers. The former promoted unfettered capitalist development, and the peasant became a free farmer; the latter impoverished and enslaved the peasantry, supported the private ownership of large tracts of land, and maintained the political and economic power of the landlords – all of which impeded capitalist development.

Capitalist agriculture developed differently from industry in Russia. While industrial commodities were gradually being standardized, those produced by capitalist agriculture were becoming more diverse, as a result of regional specialization, the growth of dairy-farming, and the appearance of vegetable and fruit farming in suburban areas. From Lenin's (1960a:331–453) perspective, the capitalist economy of Russia was still dominated by rural production and markets that supplied both capital and consumer goods.

In 1907, Lenin pointed out that the transition to capitalism in the countryside could follow two very different routes – the Prussian path and the American path – both of which differed markedly from the agrarian transition that had occurred in England. In the Prussian path, capitalism was imposed from above by a feudal landlord class that had transformed itself into a capitalist class. This contrasted with the English case, where the landlords survived as a capitalist landlord class rather than as a class of capitalist farmers. The Prussian path stifled any development of the peasant economy and prevented the development of capitalist agriculture by segments of an increasingly differentiated peasantry (Byres 1991, 1996:27–9). The American path by contrast represented capitalism from below, as the peasant evolved into the capitalist farmer in circumstances shaped by the growth of an enormous home market (Lenin 1962:239). It involved 'the free economy of the free farmer working the land' (Lenin 1963:140). The uniqueness of the American path resulted from the availability of free land that was appropriated from the Indian tribes that had possessed and occupied it (Lenin 1964e:88; Byres 1991, 1996: 30–2).

Rosa Luxemburg (1951:368) also addressed the agrarian question in *The Accumulation of Capital*. She argued that capitalism developed in a social milieu that fostered 'simple commodity production in agriculture and trade' among peasants and artisans. Commodity production and exchange disrupted the natural economy of self-sufficient non-capitalist communities – a process that was further exacerbated as new forms of transport – canals, railroads, and new shipping routes – provided the infrastructure required to spread the commodity economy. Once industry was separated from agriculture, the next step in the process involved the simultaneous relocation of industry to urban areas and the eradication of rural industry (Luxemburg 1951:386, 395).

Luxemburg indicated that states played an important role in the destruction of peasant economies. For example, in the United States

> . . . the Congress of the Union under Monroe had decided to transplant the Red Indians from the East to the West of the Mississippi. The redskins put up a desperate resistance; but all who survived the slaughter of forty Red Indian campaigns were swept away like so much rubbish and driven like cattle to the West to be folded in reservations like so many sheep. The Red Indian had been forced to make room for the farmer – and now the farmer in his turn was driven beyond the Mississippi to make room for capital (Luxemburg 1951:402–3).

She proceeded to point out that the best agricultural lands in the West were retained by land speculating companies and venture capitalists who used scientific methods and the latest technology to farm them efficiently and profitably, and that 'the American farmer could not successfully compete with such capitalist enterprises' (Luxemburg 1951:405). Small farmers went into debt, and many lost their homes and lands. Those who emigrated to the wheatlands of Canada soon faced the same problem again, once Canada began to export wheat to the world market. In her view, the agrarian question was not a uniquely European issue, since she described similar cases in North America, Asia, and South Africa.

Unfortunately, the contributions of analysts of the agrarian question in other countries – such as Mexico or Peru, where it was typically linked with national question and called the Indian Question – were not more widely recognized at the time. In 1909, the Mexican anthropologist Andrés Molina Enríquez (1868–1940) argued that government policies that allowed the formation of latifundia in the countryside destroyed communities that held lands in common, prevented the formation of a rural middle class, and slowed industrial development in urban areas. That the latifundia produced crops for export and did not pay their workers a living wage inhibited the development of a home market (Molina Enríquez 1978). In the years immediately preceding the Mexican Revolution, he condemned the reconstitution of feudal relations in the countryside and argued for the repeal of the federal legislation that underpinned those political-economic relations (Shadle 1994).

In Peru, anthropologist Luis Valcárcel (1891–1981) was also concerned with the rise of capitalist export agriculture on the coast and its impact on rural production, landownership, and everyday life in other parts of the country. He was particularly concerned with the struggles over land that existed between indigenous communities, whose members held land collectively, and neighboring *haciendas* in highland areas, like Cuzco. Like his contemporaries in Mexico, Valcárcel (1914, 1981:130–72) was also critical of the rural class structures that were emerging in the wake of capitalist penetration into the countryside, and, consequently, he too was an advocate of land reform.

Indigenous Peoples, National Minorities and Colonial Subjects

During the last half of the nineteenth century, England, France, and Germany staked out colonial possessions in Africa and Asia. The United States was also forging empires as it annexed adjacent lands and overseas territories – like the American Southwest, Hawaii, or the Philippines – and incorporated their inhabitants into the national state as indigenous peoples or national minorities. Perceptions and representations of peoples on the margins of imperial states and their circumstances were shaped by different world-views. Social evolutionists believed they occupied lower rungs on the ladder leading from savagery to civilization. Social Darwinists portrayed them as inferior cultures or races, who occupied the positions they did by virtue of their inferiority. Diffusionists argued that settlers, companies, and agents of the metropolitan states would bring new ideas and practices to the periphery and promote social and cultural change among their inhabitants.

The issue of how to represent indigenous peoples to the public came to a head in a clash over how anthropological exhibits should be organized for the World's Columbian Exposition of 1893 in Chicago (Rydell 1984:38–71). The theoretical views of the anthropologists from the Smithsonian Institution's Bureau of American Ethnology – most notably Otis T. Mason (1838–1908) – were rooted in a social evolutionism that combined the ideas of Morgan and Spencer (Hinsley 1981:125–42). Mason (1894) believed that anthropologists should study Indians in terms of their relations to the different geographical regions in which they lived; consequently, the exhibits should be organized in terms of areas – like the American Southwest or the Plains. This would allow the anthropologists to portray the passage from savagery to civilization by arranging contemporary objects like house types found in the same region in a simple-to-complex continuum that purportedly represented change and development through time.

Anthropologist Franz Boas disagreed, and argued that the displays should portray the lives, activities, and objects of particular tribes, like the Kwakiutl or the Kiowa (Boas 1887a, b). In his view, each of the present-day tribal peoples was the end-product of complex, historically contingent processes. For Boas – and for James E. Mooney (1861–1921), one of the anthropologists at the Bureau of American Ethnology – the members of each tribe occupied a particular place in a set of power relations, and were bound together by their culture which shaped the historically transmitted ideas, behavior, and objects that gave them a sense of a shared history and identity (Mooney 1896). That is, there was a plurality of cultures, each of which was shaped by its particular history.[2]

---

2. Boas was the first anthropologist to formulate the idea that there was a plurality of cultures – that is, different groups of people had different cultures (Stocking 1982b:202–3). This idea, which crystallized in the late 1880s, was one of his more important contributions to anthropological thought.

Boas and Mooney, unlike Mason, were concerned not with individual specimens collected from a tribe but rather with the particularity of the whole that provided the context in which the individuality of the particular specimens could be understood (Stocking 1982a:155–6). In other words, they stressed the importance of understanding the processes and events that shaped the historical development of the different tribal societies in an area. They also emphasized how important it was to have first-hand knowledge of these tribal groups.

Besides arguing that different tribal peoples had their own cultures which reflected their unique historical experiences, Boas along with W. E. B. Du Bois and others challenged the Social Darwinist claims about the existence of racial hierarchies, which was a pervasive view in the United States at the time. The Social Darwinists asserted that the various races were distinguished from one another by various hereditary differences – head form, intelligence, or the propensity to engage in criminal activity – and used them to legitimate oppressive and exploitative social relations. The Anti-Immigration League also used these arguments to force the US Congress to stem the flow of immigrants from Eastern and Southern Europe and Asia.

Boas (1940b) was not particularly interested in the static racial classifications of the day, but rather in the processes by which human populations came to have particular features and in the historical and environmental conditions that shaped and constrained those processes. He used anthropometric data and statistical arguments to show that there was greater variability within racial groups than between them, and that the human form was exceedingly plastic because of its sensitivity to various historical and environmental factors. By doing so, he effect-

---

He developed this view in the context of his critique of social evolutionary thought – that is, that development always follows the same direction and passes through the same sequence of stages in spite of different external conditions. Boas (1940a:663) stressed the importance of historical contingency, not progression through a fixed sequence of stages, when he wrote that:

> . . . the development of ethnology is largely due to the general recognition of the principle of biological evolution. It is a common feature of all forms of evolutionary theory that every living being is considered as the result of an historical development. The fate of an individual does not influence him alone, but also all the succeeding generations. Therefore, in order to understand an organism [and a culture] it is not sufficient to study it as a stable form, but it must be compared with all its ascendants and descendants. This point of view introduced an historical perspective into the natural sciences and revolutionized their methods. The development of ethnology is largely due to the adoption of the evolutionary standpoint, because it impressed the conviction on us that no event in the life of a people passes without leaving its effect upon later generations. The myths told by our ancestors and in which they believed have left their impress upon the ways of thinking of their descendants who were subjected to the influence of a foreign civilization. Even the most brilliant genius is influenced by the spirit of the time in which he lives, by his environment, which is a product of events of the past.

ively called into question the validity of the claims of the Anti-Immigration League and the scientific publications that supported them.

Beginning in the mid-1880s, the anthropologist James E. Mooney from the Bureau of American Ethnology began a series of ethnographic studies in the United States (Colby 1977; Moses 1984). He was concerned primarily, but not exclusively, with peoples, mostly American Indian tribes, whose members had been displaced, murdered, sold into slavery and generally abused in myriad ways by the spread of civilization and by its agents, both civil and governmental. His first studies took him to the mountainous region of North Carolina, where he interviewed both poor white and Eastern Cherokee informants. In 1890, he traveled to the West, shortly after the US Army massacred more than 200 men, women, and children at the Pine Ridge reservation in South Dakota. The Army had mistakenly believed that dancing associated with the Ghost Dance religion signaled an imminent uprising among the Sioux. Over the next three years, Mooney (1896) would talk with numerous individuals – Paiute, Arapaho, Sioux, and Kiowa – who had first-hand knowledge of the movement.

The Ghost Dance was a religious movement adopted by various American Indian tribes in the West and the Great Plains, whose members were witnessing the dissolution of their own tribal cultures in the wake of the deliberate destruction of the great buffalo herds a decade or so earlier and the influx of settlers into their tribal homelands. Mooney (1896:657) wrote:

> And when the race lies crushed and groaning beneath an alien yoke, how natural is the dream of a redeemer, an Arthur, who shall return from exile or awake from some long sleep to drive out the usurper and win back for his people what they have lost. The hope becomes a faith and the faith becomes the creed of priests and prophets, until the hero is a god and the dream a religion, looking to some great miracle of nature for its culmination and accomplishment. The doctrines of the Hindu avatar, the Hebrew Messiah, the Christian God, and the Hesûnanin of the Indian Ghost dance are essentially the same, and have their origin in a hope and longing common to all humanity.

The Ghost Dance was a pan-tribal movement that linked together peoples who had formerly seen themselves as distinct. It was an entirely new religion that spread rapidly. Individuals from the various tribes that participated in the movement saw themselves as sharing a common fate and a destiny revealed in its rituals and prophecies. They dreamed that the old ways and the buffalo would be restored, that the Indian would be reunited with ancestors and old friends, and that the ways of the white man would be cast aside.

In Mooney's (1896:928) eyes, the Ghost Dance was '. . . the inspiration of a dream. Its ritual is the dance, the ecstasy, and the trance.' It was like other great religious developments described in the Bible or linked with the growth and diversification of Christianity. Mooney's comparison of the Ghost Dance with religious movements among civilized – i.e. Christian – sects evoked a cautionary remark from John W. Powell, the director of the Bureau, who feared a public backlash that would jeopardize the Bureau's annual appropriation from Congress. Powell's views were typical of the day: the Ghost Dance was a fantasy that belonged to the prescriptural stage of culture (Powell 1896:lx). Nevertheless, Powell permitted the publication of Mooney's work, and Mooney persisted in his comparisons of the Ghost Dance with other religious movements that erupted suddenly in circumstances of rapid social and cultural change, when people were forced to seek solace from the wretchedness of their lives in a heartless world.

One of these was the Peyote Religion, which appeared among various tribes around the turn of the century. In 1918, in testimony concerning the use of peyote by American Indian peoples, Mooney told members of the Committee on Indian Affairs of the US House of Representatives that

> You must understand that this is an intertribal religion. Every tribe that has not lost entirely its old cult has a tribal religion, centering around some sacred object or palladium but this peyote cult has come and superseded the others. In other words, the Indian under the influence of this peyote religion, has given up the idea that he and his tribe are for themselves alone, and is recognizing the fact of the brotherhood of the Indian race particularly and beyond that the brotherhood of mankind (Mooney quoted by Colby 1977:495).

While his sympathies for the participants in the Ghost Dance and other American Indian religions, as well as for Irish Home Rule, conflicted with the views of federal bureaucrats, Mooney's account of the Ghost Dance laid the foundations for subsequent analyses of other resistance movements based on religions of the oppressed, especially those that appeared when indigenous peoples were forced, by circumstances that were often beyond their control, to confront civilization and capitalism. Powell (1880:46) had already coined the term *acculturation* to describe the kinds of changes that occurred in this clash between indigenous and civilized peoples.

In an essay exploring the policies of imperial states toward colonial subjects, the English anthropologist William H. R. Rivers (1864–1923) remarked that

> Whenever one people assumes the management of another, three lines of action are possible. One is to wipe out the indigenous culture as completely as possible and govern the people in accordance with the ideas and institutions of their new rulers. The second is to preserve the indigenous culture in its entirety and to attempt to govern the people in accordance with the ideas which have come down to them from their fathers. This third and intermediate course is to uphold the indigenous culture except where it conflicts with the moral and social ideals of the governing people (Rivers 1917:303).

Since most states pursued the third course, at least when it was convenient for them to do so, anthropologists did have something to contribute to understanding the consequences of culture change in these circumstances. Besides correcting errors of fact, their knowledge might prevent colonial administrators from making mistakes.

Colonial officials often made mistakes, Rivers argued, because they did not understand the culture and practices of their subjects – for example, the role of chieftains. He pointed out that, after establishing control over a region, the administrator's first order of business was usually to find or to create intermediaries who would link the colonial state with the indigenous peoples it ruled. The official

> . . . will either treat as chief one of those whom the people regard in this light and impose on him functions to which he is wholly strange, for which perhaps he is quite unfitted. Or, and this is the more frequent case, he treats as a chief one whom the people do not regard, and never have regarded in this light, some man of superior address or intelligence who may combine these qualities with others which lead to the unscrupulous use of his new position to exploit his fellows for his own ends (Rivers 1917:315–16).

Fifteen years earlier, of course, Rivers (1906) had documented the contradictions that appear among peoples experiencing the effects of class and state formation in colonial settings in the Nilgiri Hills of southern India. He described the struggles and alliances between a Toda headman appointed by the colonial government to collect taxes from his neighbors and kin and the traditional lineage and clan headmen of the Todas (Vincent 1990:109–11). He showed how the social organization of traditional Toda society was simultaneously distorted, disassembled, and reconstituted as class interests were increasingly given precedence over those of kin and neighbor.

Discussion

While late eighteenth-century Romantic writers located the engine driving the development of national identities in the cultural realm, liberal analysts writing in the wake of the French and American revolutions located the motor in the political domain. Marxists pointed out that the formation of national identities was linked both politically and economically to the development of capitalism. In those countries where industrial capitalism had developed, capitalists and wage workers typically viewed themselves as sharing the same national identity – one that was opposed to those of capitalists and workers in other national states. Marx and Engels pointed this out in *The Communist Manifesto*, when they urged the workers of the world to unite in opposition to the capitalist class. The problem of forging linkages and solidarity between the working classes of different countries was the single major concern of the labor and socialist movements from the mid-nineteenth century onwards. The First World War was partly a result of their inability to do so.

As Hobson and others indicated, the new form of imperialism that emerged in the late nineteenth century was based on the export of excess commodities and of capital to areas that promised high rates of profit. Millions of people from countries with developing capitalist economies emigrated to find work. In the United States, for example, they found themselves enmeshed in labor markets stratified by ethnicity, with native-born US workers at the top, Eastern and Southern European immigrants in the middle, and Blacks either at the bottom of the class or outside it altogether. In the 1890s, liberal nationalists, like Max Weber, expressed concern about the effects of immigration at the same time as they upheld imperial expansion, since it benefited the German state and its citizens and had the ability to bring civilization to those overseas peoples that were becoming enmeshed in the social relations of the imperialist state.

Various analysts were aware that imperialism – the spread of capitalist social relations – fostered the creation of nationalist movements across the globe, most especially in Asia. Lenin, as you will recall, argued that the national movements that were emerging along the capitalist periphery were often mass movements calling for the formation of bourgeois-democratic states. In his view, the working classes of the capitalist states should support these movements for self-determination and the formation of bourgeois-democratic states at the same time that they combated nationalism in all its guises in their own countries. Like Marx, he was aware that this was not happening to any significant degree. Rosa Luxemburg posed the problem of imperialism in different terms, when she argued that it could exist only if there were non-capitalist societies that afforded opportunities for the sale of surplus goods. The accumulation of capital occurred because of markets in non-capitalist areas rather than the exploitation of wage workers. As a result the proletariats of the various capitalist countries benefited from the economic penetration and exploitation of the non-capitalist peoples residing on the periphery – a view that Bukharin rejected.

Anthropologists were particularly aware of the ways in which imperialism and capitalist penetration into rural and colonial areas promoted class and state formation at home and abroad. Social relations were overturned as yeoman farmers became proletarians, as rural folk emigrated to the cities, and as the new bourgeoisies attempted to emulate the opulent lifestyles of European royalty and aristocracy. In the undeveloped areas, traditional social relations were also overturned as the colonial states, the capitalist enterprises, and their agents forged new and varied kinds of relations with some segments of the colonial populations and not with others. The members of these segments became agents of the colonial state, representatives of the capitalist enterprises, or the operators of businesses that served or satisfied their needs. Away from the centers of power, individuals from particular regions were often recruited as agents of the colonial state to collect taxes or to oversee the activities of their less acculturated kin and neighbors. This promoted the formation of class structures as well as the dissolution of precapitalist communal and tributary relations centered in the rural areas.

Imperialism created conditions that fueled the growth of nationalist sentiments and promoted both ethnocide and ethnogenesis. Questions about national identity and character flourished in multinational states, like Austria, and in colonial areas, like the Indian subcontinent, where some groups were already beginning to forge national identities in opposition to that of the imperial state and to lay the foundations for nationalist movements that would eventually challenge both the policies and the legitimacy of the state. In other areas, like the Americas, the lifeways of indigenous peoples were destroyed, along with the resources they used and too often with the people themselves. At the same time in the United States, various Indian groups forged pan-tribal identities, around the Ghost Dance and peyote religions, that took cognizance of the common position they shared in the national structures of power.

In Chapter 4, we will examine how social theorists of the inter-war years explained the crises of capitalism, social reform and socialist revolution, rural class structures and alternative pathways of agrarian development, the national question and acculturation.

−4−

Capitalism in Crisis and the
Search for Social Order

Capitalist crises laid the foundations for the First World War (1914–18), which was the first truly world war, even though most of the battles were waged in Europe and the Middle East. Initially, it was a European war that pitted France, England and Russia against Germany and Austria-Hungary; however, other countries – like the United States and Japan – eventually joined the fray. The war, whose brutality scarred its survivors and non-combatants in different ways, had other consequences as well.

From the viewpoint of the victorious capitalist states, the consequences included the emergence in Russia of a revolutionary Bolshevik regime that had to be contained; a Germany that must remain weakened; and the appearance of new nation-states in areas controlled only a few years earlier by the Russian, Austro-Hungarian and Ottoman empires, whose continued existence would be sustained as long as they remained sufficiently anti-Bolshevik (Hobsbawm 1996:24–31, 65–70). In addition, the capitalist states still had to confront the transformation of the agrarian sectors of their economies, the rise of nationalism at home and abroad, and policies concerning the assimilation or further marginalization of indigenous and minority communities. The new socialist government of the Soviet Union also had to confront these and other issues, such as how to promote non-capitalist industrialization.

Uneven development was a theoretical problem that became increasingly important during the first half of the twentieth century. It had practical implications as well as temporal and spatial dimensions. One issue was how to conceptualize change and development in those colonial societies and countries on the periphery of the capitalist world, including the Soviet Union, where large segments of the population were not involved in any obvious way in capitalist production relations. These countries were often portrayed by social scientists as having dual economies: small dynamic capitalist enclaves engaged in export-oriented activities, like mining or agriculture, located amid or side-by-side with traditional or feudal production relations. A second issue was how to analyze the ways in which capitalism transformed the colonial societies it came to dominate.

The Crisis of Capitalism: Social Reform or Socialist Revolution

The capitalist countries experienced a series of economic crises between 1873 and the mid 1890s (Hobsbawm 1987:34–45). Marx (1978:153–6; 1981:607–25) had argued that the periodic, increasingly deep economic crises of the nineteenth century were not accidental. They were an integral feature of capitalism, caused by over-production and the growing disparity between expanding production and lagging demand in societies where the great majority of the population were too poor to purchase and use the goods produced. As a result, capitalists would be unable to realize profits from the sale of all the goods produced by their workers; in order to maintain the same level of profits they had achieved in the past, the capitalists had either to find new markets, to reduce the costs of production, to cut back on the number of commodities produced or to invest in economic sectors that yielded higher profit rates. In Marx's view, the economic crises caused by the anarchy of production signaled both the contradictions and the conditions required for social revolution.

In 1898, Eduard Bernstein (1850–1932), who represented a reformist tendency within the German Social Democratic Party, challenged Marx and Engels's theory about the breakdown of capitalism. Bernstein (E. Bernstein 1961:79–80, 164–5) argued instead that the development of cartels, the expansion of domestic and colonial markets, and new forms of credit and democracy gave capitalism a new, long lease on life. Since capitalism was alive and well, it would continue to develop under these conditions in the future. Hence, socialist parties should strive not for revolutionary changes in the relations of production but rather for legislative reforms that would gradually alter economic and political relations, and ultimately yield an equality of rights for all members of the society. Moreover, the party should abandon the idea that the state should take over production and distribution. Socialism, in his view, would rise slowly out of the daily struggles of workers and out of reform rather than revolution.

Representatives of the revolutionary tendency among the Social Democrats responded quickly to Bernstein's proposal. In Germany, Luxemburg argued that, by snipping the concept of an economic breakdown out of the historical develop-ment of capitalism as Marx and Engels saw it, Bernstein got 'a nice comfy notion of evolution' that overlooked the history of class struggle:

> Comrades who think they can lead society into socialism peacefully, without a cataclysm, have no historical basis in fact. By revolution we do not have to mean pitchforks and bloodshed. A revolution can also take place on a cultural level, and if ever there were any prospect of that, it would be in the proletarian revolution, since we are the last to take up violent means, the last to wish violent revolution on ourselves. But such matters do not depend on us, they depend on our opponents (Luxemburg 1971:48–9).

In her view, Bernstein did not wish to establish a new kind of society, but rather to modify or reform the surface of capitalist society. His goal was to subdue the exploitation and excesses of capitalism instead of suppressing capitalism itself (Luxemburg 1970a:78).

Lenin was also critical of Bernstein and his defenders in the Union of Russian Social Democrats Abroad. They not only deprived socialists of the opportunity to show workers that their interests were opposed to those of the capitalist class, but also demoralized socialist consciousness by vulgarizing Marxist thought

> ... by reducing the working-class movement and the class struggle to narrow trade-unionism, and to a 'realistic' struggle for petty, gradual reforms. This was synonymous with the bourgeois democracy's denial of socialism's right to independence and, consequently, of its right to existence; in practice it meant a striving to convert the nascent working-class movement into an appendage of the liberals (Lenin 1961:362–3).

Luxemburg and Lenin sought tactics and organizational forms that would promote socialist revolution. Luxemburg (1970b:198–9) focused on tactics – mass actions (strikes and demonstrations) – that involved the participation, cooperation and support of the widest possible group (Geras 1976:111–32). Lenin, who recognized that different conditions existed in Germany and Russia, was concerned, not with mass parties or parliamentary activity, but rather with developing a stable organization of full-time activists who were aware of the threat posed by the police and other agents of the state. They would educate, strengthen local committees in the cities and rural districts and increase participation in trade unions (Lenin 1961:464–509).

The Social Democratic parties were never monolithic in their viewpoint. There were intense debates within the various Social Democratic parties over the relative merits and liabilities of particular proposals. Some members sought to reform the worst excesses of capitalism, while others supported revolutionary tactics and organizational forms in order to dissolve capitalism and forge a socialist alternative.

Moreover, the Social Democrats were never the only political party in a country. During the 1905 Revolution in Russia, for example, the three discernible factions of Social Democrats – the revolutionary Bolsheviks, the reformist Mensheviks and an interfactional group that sought party reunification – vied for power with other groups – the populist Social Revolutionaries, the government and conservatives of varying stripes. Briefly, the Social Revolutionaries proposed to socialize agricultural land in order to prevent capitalist penetration into the countryside and rural class formation; while they advocated increased benefits and privileges for industrial workers, they refused to socialize factories, arguing instead that the land on which factories stood might be socialized by the towns in which they were located (Radkey 1958:25–46).

The government, under the guidance of Peter Stolypin, sought to promote capitalist development in Russia. Stolypin, who viewed the influence of the Social Revolutionaries in the countryside as the greatest threat to the tsar, pushed through legislation that led to the privatization and colonization of agricultural lands; however, his proposals for administrative reforms and expanding the rights of the ethno-religious 'merchant minorities' – i.e. the Jews and the Armenians – were thwarted by the conservative nobles and monarchists, who viewed these reforms as a threat to their authority and to that of the tsar (Shanin 1986:236–51).

While the Mensheviks argued that Russia was not sufficiently capitalist for a proletarian revolution, Lenin and Leon Trotsky (1879–1940) learned other lessons from the failed Revolution of 1905 (Hill 1971). The radicalism of the peasants, especially those in Georgia who had joined the Social Democratic Party in large numbers, led Lenin to propose alliances between the Bolsheviks and the agrarian Social Revolutionaries and the Peasant Union. He also believed that any proletarian party, like the Bolsheviks, whose aim was to gain state power had to seek representation in any provisional government that would be formed in the future; this meant becoming a public rather than a clandestine party. Finally, he recognized that the particular conditions and balance of forces that emerged in a region or country were important. Thus, the radicalism of the Russian peasantry, combined with that of the industrial working class, opened up revolutionary possibilities for the future. Non-Russian nationalism, such as that expressed by workers in Riga or by workers and peasants in Georgia, was a potent weapon that could be turned against the tsar. In other words, the alliance of radical workers and peasants together with struggles for national liberation created historically contingent conditions in which a post-revolutionary state could potentially come into being in Russia, a country located on the periphery of the capitalist world rather than at its center (Shanin 1985, 1986:279–305).

In 1906, Trotsky (1969a) was also struck by the peculiarities of Russian historical development. He was as convinced as Lenin that a socialist revolution was possible in Russia, which he viewed as an underdeveloped, semi-feudal, largely pre-industrial country on the margins of the capitalist world. The prerequisites for a socialist revolution had '. . . already been created by the economic development of the advanced capitalist countries' (Trotsky 1969a:100). However, since bourgeois democracy was poorly developed in Russia, the Russian workers supported by the peasants would be able gain power before the liberal bourgeoisie could assert their political skills in a revolutionary situation (Trotsky 1969a:63). Unlike the situation in the Western countries, where socialist revolution had not yet occurred, there would be an uninterrupted movement through the democratic and the socialist revolutions in Russia (Löwy 1981:30–69; Trotsky 1969b:158–77, 239–43).

Russia was ripe for revolution in 1917. The war was going badly for its army, and there were food shortages in the cities. The tsar's regime collapsed when

Russian women and workers confronted the government, demanding food, better wages and shorter hours. A short-lived provisional government was established in its place, and the Bolsheviks, who participated in it, used the slogan 'Bread, Peace, and Land' to organize in the cities and to gain support among the peasantry. When the provisional government collapsed in October, the Bolsheviks assumed power. Many viewed this disciplined, centralized party as the only one capable of holding the country together, and the peasants who were seizing farmland preferred them to the old nobility. As soon as the Bolsheviks assumed power, they sought to sign a peace treaty with the Germans and their allies, an act that enraged the Western capitalist states. Nevertheless, while the Bolsheviks got the peace they desired, they had to confront during the next two years a civil war led by the deposed nobility and monarchists, the secession of various regions, foreign invasion, hunger, economic collapse and criticism from both the Mensheviks and Karl Kautsky, who believed that they were attempting to take a short cut to communism by precipitating a social-ist revolution in an economically backward country (Hobsbawm 1996:60–6).

The Bolsheviks had to deal immediately with the issue of what to do with the machinery of the state after they assumed power. Lenin (1964f) outlined his views in *State and Revolution: The Marxist Theory of the State and the Tasks of the Proletariat in the Revolution*, which he wrote as the provisional government crumbled in the fall of 1917. He grounded his views on Marx's and Engels's analyses of the Revolutions of 1848–51 and the Paris Commune, as well as on the conditions that prevailed in Russia. He argued that the state is the product of the irreconcilability of class antagonisms in a class-stratified society; more specifically, it was the means by which the capitalist class retained and reproduced its absolute grasp on power – a hold that was, of course, constantly threatened by the struggle of subordinated classes. Lenin's alternative to the dictatorship of the bourgeoisie was the dictatorship of the proletariat, which occurred when the working class succeeded in seizing state power; the development and success of the class struggle that underpinned such a transition was historically contingent and could not be programmed in advance. In Lenin's words, 'the transition from capitalism to communism is certainly bound to yield a tremendous abundance and variety of political forms . . .' (Lenin 1964f:418; Balibar 1977:58–60).

The core features of the state, but not its only features, were its repressive apparatuses – the army, the police, and the legal machinery, as well as the bureau-cracy itself. The proletariat could not eliminate exploitation and create a society without classes and exploitation until the existing state machinery was dismantled, and a new state dedicated to these goals – i.e. socialism or the dictatorship of the proletariat – was erected in its place. As a result, the politics and economics of the transitional state were intensely discussed at the time (e.g. Bukharin 1971, 1982). In Lenin's (1965a:25) view, since the state was marked by contradictions and class struggle, the proletarian state had to defend the workers against their enemies, on the one hand, and the workers had to defend themselves from the state, on the other (Lock 1977:13–25).

The events in Russia were a harbinger of the strikes and anti-war demonstrations that swept in Central Europe in January 1918. The desertion of peasants from the Bulgarian army and a sailors' revolt in the Austro-Hungarian navy signaled the crumbling of the old empires on the eve of the armistice. New nation-states, whose citizens desired land and harbored suspicions of cities, strangers, and government – as well as the short-lived socialist republics in Bavaria and Hungary – rose in their place in 1918 and 1919. Lenin hoped that the events in the Soviet Union would serve as a beacon and provide support for revolutionary workers' movements in other countries, whose members were disciplined activists committed to casting off the yoke of capitalism. The Third or Communist International was formed in 1919 to work toward this goal (Hobsbawm 1996:66–75).

In 1918, the Bolsheviks argued that the government they established in the wake of the October Revolution best represented the interests of the majority of the population. In the absence of a coalition government that included the Social Revolutionaries or the Mensheviks, the workers and the peasants, who constituted the majority of Russia'a population, agreed. Needless to say, numerous forces – the civil war, the invasion, economic collapse, as well as the intolerable hardships experienced by the workers and peasants during the war and the state's response to them – impinged on the government during the next two years, and constrained or channeled the courses of action that were open to it. The most important result was the New Economic Policy (NEP), which was implemented in 1921 following the defeat of the right-wing opposition. The NEP relaxed the government's control over the economy and permitted private enterprise among the peasants, which changed the conditions of everyday life in the countryside as well as the circumstances under which the government operated.

The NEP provoked intense debate. Lenin (1965b:61) viewed it as a strategic retreat – a concession to both the peasants and the capitalists – since the '. . . direct transition from the old Russian economy to state production on communist lines' had not, in fact, occurred. Bukharin, who recognized that peasant agriculture was even more dominant than it had been before the Revolution, wanted to implement the NEP slowly so that the economy would be gradually transformed. Trotsky wanted to abandon the policy as soon as possible in order to launch a massive drive to industrialize the backward economy (Knei-Paz 1978:269–78). By 1926, the NEP had restored the production of the poorly developed industrial sector of the Soviet economy to its pre-war levels; however, it was also clear that the NEP would continue to produce very slow industrial development in a country where more than 90 per cent of the population was still employed in agriculture. The implication was that the Soviet economy would continue to depend on the Western capitalist countries for many industrial goods.

The NEP spawned a growing bureaucracy as former officials and administrators were drawn back into the service of the state and new recruits were attracted (Carr 1953:273). However, at the same time as the Bolsheviks eased their control over the Soviet economy, they also banned the participation of organized oppositional groups in the soviets, or workers' councils, as well as in the Communist Party itself. They feared that the urban bourgeoisie, who had re-emerged and flourished under the NEP, would ally themselves with the intelligentsia and peasantry to challenge the power of the proletarian state. While Lenin and Trotsky viewed the ban as a temporary measure that would be lifted when the social and economic conditions of the country had become more stable, others in the party, given the conditions provoked by the NEP, viewed it as a more permanent arrangement (Deutscher 1954:518).

The fact that socialist revolutions failed to materialize in Europe by 1920, combined with the Soviet Union's continued economic dependence on the West, led to important policy shifts after 1924 as Joseph Stalin (1879–1953) began to consolidate power and to assert authority over both the party and the state apparatus. He implemented the policy of 'Socialism in One Country', which signaled the emerging importance of foreign relations with capitalist countries. Soviet diplomats began to stress the security and prosperity of the Soviet state in their relations with the capitalist countries instead of world revolution, which entered the picture only to the extent that it furthered the realization of these aims. World revolution was, in fact, viewed as dependent on the security and prosperity of the Soviet state (Carr 1964:19–20).

In December 1927, Stalin re-initiated the drive to industrialize the Soviet economy under the control of the state (Erlich 1960). He called for investments in certain sectors of the economy, price controls on basic materials, and subsidies for the production of particular goods. In the process, the guided market economy of the NEP would be replaced both financially and physically by direct planning. Stalin and the state planners realized that there were contradictions between their industrial development plan and the existing structure of peasant agriculture. The only way to resolve them in Stalin's view was '. . . to turn the small and scattered peasant farms into large united farms based on cultivation of the land in common, to go over to collective cultivation of the land on the basis of a new higher technique. . . . There is no other way out' (quoted by Nove 1969:148).

Thus, the first Five-Year Plan, launched in the spring of 1929, involved the collectivization of agriculture in spite of peasant resistance, massive financial investment in industry, and food subsidies to sustain the industrial development, as well as the defeat of the Left Opposition, whose members challenged these policies and who had earlier contested the NEP reforms on which they were based (Lewin 1974:3–124). The human costs of Stalin's Five-Year plans were high, as the state attacked existing social structures and created chaotic conditions. This led to even more state intervention and to the rapid expansion and growing importance of its bureaucratic apparatus (Lewin 1968, 1985). In spite of the human costs and the inefficiencies that resulted from the consolidation and centralization of power and decision- making, the Soviet Union achieved high rates of industrial growth and succeeded in becoming an industrialized country during the 1930s, even as the specter of fascism was rising phoenix-like from the ashes of the First World War in Central Europe.

Rural Class Structures and Alternative Paths of Agrarian Development

During the inter-war years, social scientists were concerned with analyzing peasant economies, rural class structures, and the processes underlying their development. Debates over these issues were particularly intense in the Soviet Union, where more than 90 per cent of the country's population still earned its livelihood from agricultural pursuits during the transition to socialism. However, the issues captured the attention of political activists and scholars in other parts of the world as well – for example, China, Italy, Mexico, and Peru.

During the time of the NEP, the Bolsheviks' understanding of rural class structures was based on Lenin's characterization of the socio-economic structures that articulated with each other in different configurations in different parts of the Soviet Union. Lenin and his contemporaries relied on data collected before the Revolution by officials concerned with agricultural practices and inequalities in the countryside and on studies that were then being carried out by both Marxist and populist social scientists – notably L. N. Kritsman (1890–1937) and Alexander V. Chayanov (1888–1939), both of whom had a profound appreciation of what was happening to the Soviet peasantry. Both Kritsman and Chayanov were critical of Stalin's Five Year Plan and the impact it would have on peasant agriculture (T. Cox 1986; Littlejohn 1984:68; Solomon 1977).

Kritsman also made use of the categories that Lenin (1965c:331) discerned in the countryside during the transition: self-sufficient peasant farmers, small commodity producers, private capitalists who used wage labor and sought to maximize profits, state-capitalist enterprises guided by the proletarian state, and socialist economic enterprises planned by the state. Kritsman added that there were also feudal structures in parts of Central Asia. This meant that class stratification took different forms in different regions, and that these differences reflected in part whether production was primarily for commodities or for domestic consumption. This was especially true after the NEP reintroduced the market in 1921 and breathed life into the possibility of developing capitalist agriculture (T. Cox 1984:55–6).

Kritsman and his associates launched a series of regional studies in the Soviet Union in order to acquire the kinds of statistical data required to produce an accurate picture of the development of rural socio-economic structures (T. Cox 1984; Shanin 1980). The studies focused on peasant households as the basic units of analysis and explored the contradictory developmental tendencies found in them, especially the ones that engaged in small-scale commodity production. They distinguished between those households that produced for the market and those that produced for consumption. They showed that most of the small commodity producers could move in a number of different directions in a transitional society. They could form cooperatives that might later become socialist or capitalist; they could move directly to capitalist production; or they could become proletarianized.

Kritsman (1984:139–41) and his associates made an important observation: the ownership of working animals and farm equipment that were hired out, rather than land, was the basic form of capitalist agriculture in the countryside. Households with draft animals and equipment were able to appropriate surplus value from the peasant families that were forced to hire these means of production to prepare the fields they owned. The peasant hiring animals or equipment paid by working on the farm of the family that owned them; thus, surplus value was created by the peasant who hired the means of production rather than by the owners of the animals or equipment that they hired. In some areas, three-quarters of the peasant farms experienced this form of exploitation. However, there were other forms of capitalist agriculture as well, which were based on hiring rural wage workers. They observed that trade and usury were often interconnected in the countryside through the extension of credit, which reflected the economic instability of peasant households. They further noted that the impact of the Soviet state's taxation was similar to that of trading capital and usury; the burden fell disproportionately on poor peasants who were forced to sell their labor power.

Chayanov was also concerned with the fate of the Russian peasants, given the potential for capitalist development created by the NEP during the 1920s (Banaji 1976b; Littlejohn 1977; D. Thorner 1986). Unlike Kritsman, he viewed peasant economy and society as independent of those of wider economic and social structures. While he agreed with Kritsman that the peasant household was a basic economic unit, his analysis followed a different path and focused instead on the organization and nature of peasant production processes. Thus,

on the family labor farm, the family, equipped with means of production, uses its labor power to cultivate the soil and receives as the result of a year's work a certain amount of goods. . . . The size of the labor product was determined mainly by the size and composition of the working family, the number of its members capable of work, then by the productivity of the labor unit, and – this is especially important – by the degree of the labor effort – the degree of self-exploitation through which the working members effect a certain quantity of labor units in the course of the year (Chayanov 1986a: 5–6).

What distinguished the autonomous peasant household from capitalist entrepreneurs and/or waged workers was that its members determined the time and intensity of the work required to produce the goods they would consume. The balance between labor and consumption was established by the consumption needs of the family and the degree of effort or drudgery its working members were willing to expend during the year to produce the amount of goods they needed for consumption.

The labor–consumption balance was the main regulator of the farm's economic activity. It also reflected the demographic cycle of the peasant family. Both the quantity of goods produced and the number of working members were small immediately after the household was established; both grew as the family had children who would soon become workers; and both began to decline as the children left to establish their own households or as the farmstead was partitioned. This implied that the farm's economic activity was large because of its family size and composition, and any differentiation of the peasantry was caused by demographic rather than social factors (Littlejohn 1977:131).

Chayanov (1986b:90–4) conceptualized the organization of the peasant farm in terms of a combination of three traditional factors of production – land, labor, and capital. If there were a shortage in any one factor, then there would be a proportional decline in the other two from the optimal level of the combination. Unless there were some increase in labor intensity and productivity, this would lead either to a reduction in the size of the peasant family farm or to its workers supplementing their earnings with non-agricultural pursuits in order to maintain the labor–consumption balance in instances where family demands could not be satisfied by income derived from the farm itself. This implied, however, that there was a market. It further implied that the market affected the labor–consumption balance of the household, and that the farm's products would ultimately be divided into commodities for sale and goods for family consumption.

The peasant farm, in Chayanov's view, was an autonomous economic unit until it hired workers from the outside. At that moment, it became a capitalist enterprise. Thus, his understanding of the emergence of capitalist relations in the countryside contrasted with Kritsman's, which emphasized the importance of peasants who rented farm animals and equipment. For Chayanov, who presumed that earnings of a family farm were proportional to the labor effort expended by its members, any peasant household that employed workers was making an entirely new set of economic calculations. Because of the market, the peasant household no longer had to produce everything it consumed; items its members needed but no longer produced could be purchased in the market with the income gained by selling excess amounts of the goods they continued to produce. This meant that the peasant household could begin to specialize in the production and sale of certain goods – ones that required lower levels of labor effort than it would take to produce the goods they were purchasing in the market.

Chayanov (1986b:255–69) believed that capitalist farms were not widespread in the Soviet Union, and that the social differentiation of the peasantry was still in its early stages. Capitalist social relations initially penetrated the countryside when trade transformed the isolated peasant farm into a small commodity producer who was linked through the market to other farmsteads, to traders, and to artisans and factories whose workers transformed the raw materials into commodities that were consumed in the city – e.g. the transformation of hides into shoes or gelatin. In his view, a system of wholesale and retail cooperatives, organized vertically, would strengthen these linkages. The cooperatives would also protect the family farm from the menace of large capitalist farms and insure that the continued existence of the rural market did not promote rural proletarianization, oppressive forms of credit, and sweatshop systems of capitalist exploitation as it forced the reorganization of the family farm economy. In his view, cooperatives subordinated to state control provided the best path for the development of Soviet agriculture.

In *The New Economics* (1965 [1926]), Evgeny Preobrazhensky (1886–1937) pointed out the significance of Kritsman's and Chayanov's studies of social differentiation among the Soviet peasantry under the economic policies of the NEP. The fundamental economic problem of the Soviet Union was: How could the revolutionary state promote the growth of state-owned industry in a country where much of the capital was held by wealthy peasants who had acquired the means of capital accumulation only a few years earlier when the large productive estates had been seized and divided among them? Another way of saying this is that two contradictory forms of accumulation co-existed in the Soviet Union during the NEP: socialist accumulation in the state-owned, urban-based industrial sector, and capitalist accumulation, the law of value, in the rural agricultural sector (Preobrazhensky 1965:79–145).

From the state's perspective, the proletarian government had to acquire material resources from outside the economic system it controlled in order to finance desperately needed industrialization. In the absence of significant foreign investment, there were two ways to get the private owners to invest in the state-owned industrial sector: direct taxation of the private sector, and state control of the market exchanges between the state and private sectors. Preobrazhansky favored the latter because of the high probability that the peasants would attempt to evade paying taxes. In his view, control of the market exchanges meant increasing off-farm sales to the state in order to feed the towns and the state-controlled export sector, increasing the efficiency and productivity of Soviet industry and controlling the prices of goods sold to the peasants so that socialist accumulation could proceed (Dobb 1966:183–91; Nove 1965:xi–xvii).

In China, Mao Zedong (1893–1976) was also concerned with rural class structures and social change in the late 1920s and early 1930s. At the time, China's population included nearly 400 million peasants and an urban proletariat with no more than 2 million members. In his 1926 analysis of the class structure of Chinese society, Mao (1965a) distinguished seven classes that included both the urban and rural segments of the population. The *landlord* class and the *comprador* class – i.e. the Chinese managers of foreign commercial establishments – were linked with the international bourgeoisie. The national or *middle bourgeoisie* represented capitalist social relations in both town and country. The *petit bourgeoisie* included owner-peasants, master craftsmen, traders, school teachers and low-level government officials. The *semi-proletariat* included small craftsmen, shop assistants, small traders, semi-owner peasants who worked partly on their own land and partly on landed rented from others and poor peasants or tenants who had no land of their own; he further distinguished between poor peasants who owned tools and had access to funds and those that did not and were forced to sell their labor power. The members of the urban *proletariat* were employed in the textile, mining, railroad, maritime transport and shipbuilding industries. Finally, there was the large *lumpen-proletariat* composed of peasants who had lost their land and craftsmen who were unable to find work.

In two later surveys, Mao (1965b, 1990:148–58) focused exclusively on rural class structures and social relations. He discerned five classes in the countryside. The *landlords* he divided into three layers based on income and whether they worked or derived most of their income from land rent, and supplemented their primary income by moneylending or by extracting surplus value from workers hired to toil in their commercial or industrial activities. The *rich peasants* owned their own lands, and had good implements of production and access to capital – they sometimes hired workers and rented some of their land. The *middle peasants* owned some of the land they worked and rented the remainder; they derived their income from their own labor. The *poor peasants* usually rented the land they worked, and, unlike the middle peasants, were forced to sell their labor power. The *farm workers*, who typically had neither land nor implements, made their living by selling their labor power.

Mao (1965c) was interested in the dynamics of social change in rural areas. In 1927, he reported on the formation of peasant associations in Hunan Province during the preceding year. The peasant associations, which had 300–400 thousand members in 1926, swelled to more than 2 million members and had a mass following of more than 10 million a year later. The peasant organizations brought about fundamental changes in the power relations that existed in the countryside.

> The main targets of attack by the peasants are the local tyrants, the evil gentry and the lawless landlords, but in passing they also hit out against patriarchal ideas and institutions, against corrupt officials in the cities and against bad practices and customs in the rural areas. In force and momentum the attack is tempestuous; those who bow before it survive and those who resist perish. As a result, the privileges which the feudal landlords enjoyed

for thousands of years are being shattered to pieces. Every bit of the dignity and prestige built up by the landlords is being swept into dust. With the collapse of the power of the landlords, the peasant associations have now become the sole organs of authority and the popular slogan 'All power to the peasant associations' has become a reality (Mao 1965c:25).

Mao (1965c:44–6) observed that relations between peasant men and women varied from one class to another, and that the authority of husbands was always weakest among the poor peasants, where the women toiled alongside their husbands and had an important voice in family decisions. He explained how peasant women from different villages formed women's groups to protect themselves from harassment and violence at the hands of men; he further described how the women's groups challenged and weakened the three traditional systems of authority in the Hunan countryside – i.e. the patriarchal clan, the religious shrines and their fathers and husbands – and how they were struggling for more egalitarian gender relations.

Mao then surveyed the goals of the peasant movement. These included bans on gambling, opium-smoking, the distilling of spirits and the use of sedan-chairs; limiting the number of pigs and ducks that could be owned by a family, because they destroyed grain; curbing the aggressive behavior of certain tramps and vagabonds; eliminating banditry; abolishing levies imposed on peasants by the landlords and gentry that controlled the rural state apparatus; education; the formation of consumers' marketing and credit cooperatives; and the construction and repair of roads and embankments (Mao 1965c:49–56).

Mao, of course, was not the only social commentator to write about the agrarian question in China. In *Peasant Life in China* (1939), the anthropologist Fei Xiaotong (b. 1910) described the interrelations of the economic system and social structure of a rural community in the Yangtze Valley, about 500 miles northeast of the area Mao had written about six years earlier. Fei (1939:120, 192) argued that there were no real social differences among the villagers, even though a few of them owned land and some were wealthier than others; the wealth differentials that existed were due to differences in the amounts of rent paid the absentee landlords. Thus, the economic circumstances of the villagers, including the decline of the local silk industry, were a consequence of outsiders who charged exorbitant rents, practiced usury and collected onerous taxes – all of which upset the well-adapted social system of the village. The international capitalist economy and the Nationalist government also created problems for the villagers.

Given his structural-functionalist assumptions, Fei made little reference to the chaos that existed in the countryside at the time. In his view, while land reform would ease the economic problems of the village, the real solution ultimately rested on rebuilding rural industry. However, the real problems were that the Nationalist government was spending too much of its revenues trying to defeat the Communists, and did not really understand peasant villages or the problems they faced (Fei 1939:110–16, 282–5). The political subdivisions imposed by the state on the countryside were artificial and had no foundation in the traditional economy and society; and the schools it established paid no attention to the tempo of rural life and taught skills the peasants did not find useful (Arkush 1981:74–9).

National Integration

The agrarian question merged almost imperceptibly with the national question in countries like Italy, Peru, Indonesia, or Mexico: How were peasants, national minorities, or tribal peoples living in rural regions to be integrated into the national state? The 'Southern Question', the 'Indian Question', 'dual economies', and 'the folk–urban continuum' are only a few of the concepts that emerged around this issue.

Antonio Gramsci (1891–1937) wrote extensively about political-economic, social and cultural developments in Italy during and after the period of national unification. He was concerned with developing a revolutionary political strategy that would be applicable in a particular, advanced capitalist country (Italy); he was reacting to economistic arguments, imperialism, the defeat of revolutionary movements in the 1920s, the rise of fascism, the economic collapse of 1929 and the growth of the corporatist-interventionist state in the 1930s. He focused on the exercise of state power and the role that coercion, fraud- corruption and persuasion-consent played in maintaining and reproducing the existing class relations. He was concerned less with the coercive apparatuses of the state than with the roles different kinds of intellectuals played in securing the consent of the populace and in organiz-ing the hegemony of the dominant class, whose political power ultimately derived from the economic base but could not be reduced in any simply way to it (Jessop 1982:142–52).

Since the complex relationship between town and countryside was the motor driving Italian history, any examination had to consider the interconnections of the Northern urban force, the Southern rural force, the North–Central rural force and the rural forces of Sicily and Sardinia. The complexity of this relationship resulted from the fact that industrial capitalism was thinly and unevenly developed on the Italian peninsula; it was concentrated almost entirely in the cities of the Northern Piedmont, where the bourgeoisie and the factory workers were tied to the capitalist mode of production and shared a world-view, ultimately rooted in the economy, that united them against the tempo and mode of everyday life in the countryside. The rest of the peninsula was dominated by a semi-feudal agrarian bloc composed of peasants, landowners and traditional intellectuals whose activities cemented relations between the two rural classes (Gramsci 1967, 1971a:90–102, 1992:133).

The political unification of Italy in 1870 brought together under a single state apparatus regions with different histories, different economic foundations, and different cultural practices. In Gramsci's view, political unification did not create the conditions for further capitalist development and expansion into the South; it merely compounded the old social and regional divisions that already existed. From an economic standpoint, the North colonized the South and drained it of both capital and labor, which fueled further capitalist growth in the Piedmont. From a political standpoint, the Northern bourgeoisie was unable to rally other groups, to constitute itself as the dominant economic class or to establish clear programs of its own. Thus, its members had to share state power with the semi-feudal landowners, who always promoted their own economic interests.

Gramsci (1967:45–7, 1971b:14–5) observed that the Southern intellectuals constituted 60 percent of the state bureaucracy. This meant that Southern agrarian bloc as a whole was the intermediary and overseer for Northern capital and the large banks. In the South, the traditional intellectuals of the rural towns – the lawyers, notaries, priests and teachers – were the intermediaries between the peasant masses and the state. As a result, Gramsci was especially interested in the cultural characteristics of that group. They came mainly from a stratum of small and middle landowners who derived their income by renting land to peasants rather than by working it themselves, and their standard of living was higher than that of the average peasant. The members of this class also viewed peasants as little more than machines, to be despised and feared because of their penchant for violence. The Southern priests, unlike the clergy in the North, which had artisan or peasant roots, also came from this layer of small and middle landowning families, and shared the views of their class toward the peasants.

Gramsci pointed out that the peasants held contradictory views about the traditional intellectuals. On the one hand, they respected them, and many hoped that at least one son could become an intellectual, especially a priest, and thereby raise the social and economic position of their families through the connections they would acquire by interacting more closely with the landowning class. However, the peasants' admiration for the intellectuals was mixed with envy and anger. Since the priests were mainly from the landowning class, the peasants viewed them as bailiffs and usurers whose womanizing and money dealings inspired little confidence in either their discretion or their impartiality.

The role of the Southern intellectuals, including the priests, was to block any efforts by the peasants to organize mass movements and to prevent splits from developing in the agrarian bloc. In effect, the Southern intellectuals who held positions in the liberal democratic government before the rise of fascism in the mid-1920s muted the desires and needs voiced by the peasantry and shunted them to the margins of the political arena by portraying the characteristics and interests of the peasants as oppositional to those of the state. For example, while peasant culture was simple and fragmentary, the state's was complex and unitary (Cirese 1982).

In order to overcome the weaknesses of the political programs of the democratic liberals, Gramsci stressed the need for genuine worker–peasant alliances. By contrast, the programs of the democratic liberals perpetuated the traditional forms of corruption and extortion in the rural areas. In the name of creating unity, the democratic liberals had built a bloc of urban industrialists and workers in the Northern cities that reinforced the economy and hegemony of the North and reduced the rest of the peninsula to a colony. The South was disciplined by police repression, by the periodic massacres of peasants, and by political measures such as personal favors and jobs for Southern intellectuals, and by not enforcing ecclesiastical laws in the rural areas.

In *Seven Interpretive Essays on the Peruvian Reality* (1971 [1928]), José M. Mariátegui (1894–1930) used a similar lens to analyze the circumstances that prevailed in Peru – a country that was still dominated economically by a semi-feudal latifundia system that involved landholding and servitude for the peasantry. This impeded the development of an indigenous capitalism and underwrote the stagnation and grinding poverty of urban life on the coast and of rural Indian communities in the mountains. The owners of the latifundia, who grew sugar and cotton for export, served as intermediaries between the native population and foreign firms engaged in mining, commerce and transportation. As a result, industrial development on the coast in the early decades of the twentieth century was confined largely to sugar mills located in close proximity to clusters of sugar-producing latifundia. Two other economic forms co-existed with the latifundia. One was the indigenous communal economies found in the mountainous regions, and the other was the small, backward-looking bourgeois economy found in some coastal areas (Mariátegui 1971:16).

Mariátegui (1971:18, 30, 158–70) called the political form that corresponded to the realities of the Peruvian economy *gamonalism* or bossism. That is, the big bosses in various parts of the country, many of whom were large landowners, and their underlings in the state bureaucracy controlled education, law enforcement, and the administration of justice in the regions where they lived. The control they exerted over regional government ensured that the feudal estates were regularly exempted from the taxes and other regulations imposed by the central government on the indigenous communities and the cities, and that the rural folks linked to the estates could be disciplined. In short, the regional bosses who held power did not oppose the central government; they colluded with it to ensure that the existing structures of power were preserved and reproduced.

Consequently, the bosses had no reason to address either the Indian problem or the agrarian question, which were often merged and focused mainly on the indigenous communities in the mountains. For Mariátegui and his contemporaries, like

Luis Valcárcel (mentioned in the last chapter), the indigenous communities were not a residue of the ancient pre-Columbian society that survived mainly in the mountains after it had been eradicated on the coast. Instead, they were a communal form of production based on cooperation and association that defended the rural populations from the latifundists' demand for labor service. They preserved the rural population, protecting it from the threats of the bosses, on the one hand, and, on the other, from the individualism promoted by liberal reformers, who argued fervently that the problems the Indian communities confronted could be overcome through education, assimilation and private ownership of the land. The liberals, from Mariátegui's perspective, failed to grasp the political and economic forces that threatened the highland Indian communities in the decades following the War of the Pacific (1879–1883).

Since the Indian communities were composed of farmers, Mariátegui (1971:32) saw the agrarian question and the Indian question as intimately linked; they were

> . . . first and foremost the problem of eliminating feudalism in Peru. . . .
>
> There are two expressions of feudalism that survive: the latifundium and servitude. Inseparable and of the same substance, their analysis leads us to the conclusion that the servitude oppressing the indigenous race cannot be abolished unless the latifundium is abolished.
>
> When the agrarian problem is presented in these terms, it cannot be easily distorted. It appears in all its magnitude as a socio-economic, and therefore a political, problem, to be dealt with by men who move in this sphere of acts and ideas. And it is useless to try to convert it, for example, into a technical- agricultural problem for agronomists.

The integration of Indian communities into the nation-state was a political problem whose solution must also be political.

The economist Julius H. Boeke (1884–1953) developed an alternative understanding of the kind of situation that Mariátegui described as the persistence of feudal social relations. Boeke elaborated the idea of *dual economies* in his analysis of the Dutch colony of Indonesia. Societies with dual economies, he wrote, were different from and more complicated than those found in the West, because

> . . . we are dealing with groups that touch and influence one another, two social systems, one which answers to western economic premises, while the other does not.
>
> Now a clash between two social and economic systems is not found only in Indonesia. Wherever western culture has penetrated eastern lands without blotting out primitive or eastern culture, similar phenomena, similar complications are to be found (Boeke 1953:11).

One economic system was capitalist, the other precapitalist. In a society with dual economies, the towns whose Westernized residents participated in world markets contrasted with the rural villages with their traditional, self-sufficient agricultural economies.

The village was '. . . a religious community of food-crop cultivators, all or not belonging to the same clan, and ruled by a common tradition' (Boeke 1953:27). Its residents were in regular contact with one another, and their fields were located in close proximity to the village. However, the communal bonds that held the villagers together had been weakened by the capitalist policies promoted by the government and by private interests. Thus, the villagers struggled to adapt to the changing circumstances that impinged on their lives: to retain rights to their means of production, to meet the duties and obligations of membership in the community, and to ensure community solidarity. In some areas, the population of the rural villages had grown so that there were able-bodied young men who were, in fact, superfluous to the village economy. As capitalist labor markets penetrated into such areas, these men were employed as unskilled, casual workers who could be paid well below the wage required to sustain themselves, since their needs and those of their families were still actually being met by their kin and neighbors in the villages (Boeke 1953:33, 81, 138–41).

The growth of capitalist export agriculture created a steadily increasing demand for land. Agrarian capitalist firms gained access to land, because native landowners 'had developed a need for money' to pay debts or taxes or to purchase goods that were no longer produced locally in the villages. The villagers acquired the needed cash by renting and/or selling both arable fields as well as waste land they did not farm (Boeke 1953:130–6).

Boeke argued for government intervention or control of economic policy. He pointed out the obvious:

> . . . *that Indonesia today is further removed from self-sufficiency than it was a century ago*; and that its national small industries, its rural and communal self-provisioning with manufactured products, has for the most part been ruined in the course of modern development. . . . [T]he economic development of the country has increased its economic dependence – the dependence, that is, of the rural population, of those born and bred in the villages (Boeke 1953:227, emphasis in the original).

In a word, Indonesia had become more dependent on capital that came less and less from Asia. While the state should intervene in the economy and control of capitalist development, it should do so in ways that would benefit the whole of Indonesian society, including the rural villages. To accomplish this, the government had to adopt an economic policy that addressed equally the issues of both the capitalist and the traditional sectors of the society (Boeke 1953:226–9).

Boeke explored problem areas that the state would have to address. However, most of his recommendations were for policies that dealt with the capitalist economy – e.g. the control of production, wage and price controls, the regulation of imports and exports, or the promotion of certain national industries. He briefly addressed the circumstances that produced unemployment in the rural areas:

The rapid growth of the plants in the tropics; the small holdings; the deficient markets; the unprofitable transport; the inevitable intermediaries; all these are factors that cannot be altered and make the problem of rural unemployment unsolvable. One can only try to fill the spare time of the peasant with non-economic interests and occupations (village restoration) (Boeke 1953:318).

While the peasants and those villagers who engaged in casual work in the capitalist sector could be supported, at least in part, by their villages, the rural proletariat employed by the agrarian capitalist estates or the migrants to the cities had become separated from their natal communities. As a result, they had no fund of foodstuffs and resources to fall back on. According to Boeke's argument, people from the traditional villages would be supported by their natal communities only during the early stages of their incorporation into the capitalist economic sector; once they were separated from their natal communities, unemployment would become an increasingly serious problem.

The US anthropologist Robert Redfield (1897–1958) elaborated an alternative explanation of the process of national integration based on investigations that he and others carried out in southern Mexico in the wake of the Mexican Revolution. From the late 1920s onward, Redfield developed an argument that incorporated significant elements of Durkheim's theoretical framework – e.g. a society and its culture were functionally integrated wholes; culture functioned to maintain existing social relations and changed slowly through time because of social differentiation. Redfield believed that the assimilation and integration of the rural communities into the Mexican state were inevitable, and that the task of applied anthropologists and development workers was to ensure that the transition experienced by the folk communities found in the peasant villages was as painless as possible (Hewitt de Alcántara 1984:21–31).

In Redfield's view (1962a), the development of culture in the tribal communities and peasant villages of rural Mexico resulted from contact and communication with cities, which were the source of modern Western ideas and practices. The tribal communities of Quintana Roo, for example, were relatively immobile and isolated from urban society; consequently, their cultures were quite homogeneous, because communication was still based largely on face-to-face encounters between members of the communities. This contrasted with the peasant villages, where at least some members of the community – such as teachers, artisans or shopkeepers – wore shoes, read newspapers and visited Mexico City. In contrast, their peasant neighbors lived on the edge of town, gained their livelihood primarily or exclusively by farming and continued to participate in traditional practices and follow customary ways. The more cosmopolitan residents of the towns had undergone a twofold process of change. They were deculturated as they gave up or rejected certain traditional beliefs and practices; they were acculturated as they adopted ideas and practices emanating from the modern cities. One of the attitudes they adopted was that the peasants were despicable, mentally inferior and driven by tradition. In Redfield's view, the peasants were increasingly puzzled by the behavior of their more acculturated neighbors.

While Redfield (1962b, 1962c) recognized that the incorporation and integration of tribal peoples and peasant villages into the national state was an historical process, he focused his attention on its spatial dimensions. The remote tribal peoples were more isolated from urban influences than the peasant communities. He portrayed the process as an ideal type – a steady progression that involved the breakdown of traditional beliefs and practices and the adoption of modern urban practices, which he called the folk–urban continuum. The cultural homogeneity of primitive tribal groups crumbled as one moved to the peasant villages and from those spaces to the modern cities with their cosmopolitan, outward-looking inhabitants. What distinguished communities at different points along the folk–urban continuum was '. . . their degree of isolation from urban centers of modifying influence . . .' (Redfield 1962c:250).

Redfield (1962d) was also struck by the mobility of merchants from peasant villages in the Guatemalan highlands. As many as 30 per cent of the men from one community were traders who spent about 70 per cent of their time on the road, peddling cash crops or commodities or acting as middlemen who participated in daily or weekly markets in other communities. While the traveling merchants were not isolated from the other communities, their interactions with the inhabitants of those villages was limited to the market. They viewed themselves as strangers in those villages, and, at the same time, retained a strong sense of identity with their natal community even though they were rarely there: 'Each town center with its dependent countryside . . . is conscious of its own individuality. The people of a given community do not marry with outsiders, and they have their own government – subject only to the authority of the Guatemalan nation' (Redfield 1962d:203). Redfield interpreted the particular combination of commercial activity and primitive practices as a stable cultural configuration that probably emerged before the Spanish Conquest rather than as evidence of capitalist penetration into the countryside in the late nineteenth and early twentieth centuries. These investigations reinforced the view that, left to themselves, folk society and culture were relatively stable. Redfield (1950:178) lamented the fact that these cultures were changing because of increasingly frequent, more intense relations with outsiders.

What Redfield missed with his relatively static notions of folk culture and society was the impact that capitalist social relations had on the peoples of the Yucatán Peninsula. The inhabitants of many folk communities were, in fact, rural proletarians who had been engaged in wage labor on henequin plantations since the end of the nineteenth century, and the tribal peoples of Quintana Roo were actively resisting the incursions of the Mexican state in the twentieth century (Mintz 1953; Sullivan 1989).

Acculturation and Culture Contact

Anthropologists trained in the United States and England reconceptualized the processes of acculturation and culture contact during the inter-war years. Much of their financial support came directly or indirectly from the Rockefeller philanthropies, whose goal '. . . was to prevent the collapse of liberal democratic capitalism' (Fisher 1993:232, 1988; Stocking 1995:391–426). The view of the US anthropologists resulted from investigations among Native American tribes at a time when the policies of the federal government were shifting from ethnocide or assimilation into the dominant culture to the recreation of native cultures (Herskovits 1938; Linton 1940; Steward 1977a:335–6). The view of the British-trained anthropologists built on investigations among the indigenous peoples in the African colonies (Malinowski 1938, 1945).

The Americans focused their attention on *acculturation* – '. . . those phenomena which result when groups of individuals having different cultures come into continuous first-hand contact, with subsequent changes in the original cultural patterns of either or both groups' (Redfield, Linton and Herskovits 1936:149). The British were concerned with *culture contact* – i.e. with the institutional changes that appeared when the emissaries of Western culture came into contact and dynamic interaction with their colonial subjects in Africa, and that led to transformations in the African cultures, to modifications in the European cultures that better adapted them to the African environment, and to the creation of new cultures that combined European and African elements. Both the Americans and the British adopted the functionalist views of Émile Durkheim, which saw culture or society as a structured whole composed of interconnected parts, so that a change in one part not only had effects on the other parts but also on the totality as a whole. The important difference was that the Americans were concerned largely with tribal peoples in the United States whose members were being enveloped by the numerically larger capitalist culture, while the British were interested mainly in the numerically dominant indigenous groups in the African colonies.

In an influential memorandum prepared for the Social Science Research Council (SSRC), Robert Redfield, Ralph Linton and Melville J. Herskovits (1936) raised a series of questions that they believed should be considered in studies of acculturation: (1) what was the nature of the contact – e.g. was it friendly, between entire groups or between certain kinds of individuals; (2) what were the circumstances surrounding the contact and subsequent acculturative processes – e.g. were there inequalities between the groups or was force involved; (3) what processes of acculturation were involved – i.e. how were traits selected by the donor and recipient groups and how were they integrated into the patterns of the recipient culture; (4) what psychological mechanisms underpinned the acceptance, rejection, and integration of the new elements; and (5) what were the results of acculturation – i.e. were large numbers of new traits accepted, were original traits from both cultures combined to produce a new smoothly functioning whole, or was the acceptance of new traits resisted? Their recommendations built on anthropological studies that were concerned with the interplay of personality and culture, such as Ruth Benedict's (1961) *Patterns of Culture* – and with the appearance of idealist conceptualizations of culture that stressed the patterning of its elements and the unconscious, core value orientations that shaped and brought both consistency and a distinctive integration to those configurations (Sapir 1949a, b). They sustained the belief that the unconscious inner core of a culture was more resistant to change than its overt, external or peripheral features.

The authors of the SSRC memorandum were particularly concerned with the psychology of acculturation – i.e. with determining the covert, core value orientations of the recipient cultures as well as the psychological characteristics of individuals from those cultures who might accept or reject elements from the donor culture under the particular circumstances of contact. They wanted to determine why some societies adopted new elements and others did not, or why some individuals in a particular society adopted foreign traits while others rejected them. This perspective was applied to examine early occurrences of the Ghost Dance and religious revivals among the Indian tribes of the Western United States (Gayton 1932; Nash 1937). A few years later, the anthropologist Clyde Kluckhohn (1905–60) pointed out how important it was for administrators in the US Indian Service to understand the covert culture – the unconscious value orientations – of a society in situations where acculturation was taking place or where the adoption of new traits was being resisted (Kluckhohn 1943).

The British equivalent to the SSRC memorandum on acculturation was the African Institute's *Methods of Study of Culture Contact in Africa* (Mair 1938). In his introduction, the anthropologist Bronislaw Malinowski (1884–1942), the Director of the African Institute, commented on the power relations between the colonial metropolis and the colony and the profound shaping effects they had on culture contact and change in Africa:

> The whole concept of European culture as a cornucopia from which things are freely given is misleading. It does not take a specialist in anthropology to see that the European 'give' is always highly selective. We never give any native people under our control – and we never shall, for it would be sheer folly as long as we stand on the basis of our present Realpolitik – the following elements of our culture:
>
> 1. The instruments of physical power: fire-arms, bombing planes, poison gas, and all that makes effective defence or aggression possible.

2. We do not give out instruments of political mastery [i.e. sovereignty or voting rights] . . .
3. We do not share with them the substance of economic wealth and advantages. . . . Even when under indirect economic exploitation, as in West Africa or Uganda, we allow the native a share of the profits, the full control of economic organization remains in the hands of Western enterprise.
4. We do not admit them as equals to Church Assembly, school, or drawing room. . . . [F]ull political, social and even religious equality is nowhere granted (Malinowski 1938:xxii–xxiii).

Malinowski (1938:xxiv–xxv) believed that studies of culture change must take into account not only the impact of the 'higher' or Western culture and the substance of the native culture against which it was directed but also the unintended consequences of the autonomous changes that resulted from the interaction of the two cultures. The impact of the two cultures on each other was more than the mechanical mixture of elements from both; it disrupted the equilibrium of the tribal group, producing maladjustment, deterioration, confusion, strain, and conflict, on the one hand, and cooperation and even compromise, on the other. Setting aside his observations about power relations, he stressed the give-and-take nature of culture contact situations and stressed the mutual dependence of the colonial and tribal cultures, as the old cultural forms were dissolved and new cultural realities emerged in their place.

Malinowski and his associates, like Monica Hunter (1908–82), also stressed the places and institutional contexts in which culture contact occurred – churches, schools, markets, foreign-owned mines or the capitalist economic system. Since these contexts were usually regulated by legal codes that combined customary and British law and were supervised by European magistrates who may not have been familiar with the customary legal practices of the natives, the anthropologists were particularly concerned with how and in what ways the sanctions that regulated social behavior under traditional conditions were modified by contact. This led them to examine the roles played by the various agents involved in culture contact – teachers, students, administrators, district commissioners, as well as the native men, women and children who left their natal communities and went to the towns and mines to engage in wage labor (Hunter 1938:23–4, 1936).

Meyer Fortes (1906–83), another of Malinowski's students at the African Institute, saw the contact agents as integral parts of native communities that were being rapidly but unevenly transformed as a result of the infiltration of foreign practices. In his view, however, it was the communities where change was taking place, rather than the customs themselves, that should be the objects of investigation. He focused his attention on migrant workers who left their communities to gain a livelihood. He raised a series of questions about the migrant workers: What were the circumstances that led or forced them to leave their natal communities? What was their reaction to their milieu? How did the other members of their communities react to immigration? What influence did immigration ultimately have on the institutional life, practices, habits, and beliefs of the tribal community? Fortes (1938:72–91) compared the effects of migrant labor on tribal communities in the Northern Territories of the Gold Coast and in Bechuanaland. He noted that, while migrant workers were rapidly reabsorbed into their natal communities on the Gold Coast, this was not the case in South Africa, where the migrants flouted traditional authority, grew lazy and dissolute, and were perceived as a problem by the elders. The differences between the Gold Coast and Bechuanaland communities was due, in his view, to the fact that they reflected different stages of contact. The Gold Coast communities were only marginally involved with the outside. Those of Bechuanaland had been completely drawn into the capitalist economic system as sources of labor; as a result, the morality of the towns was transferred to the reserve as the income derived from the migrants' work eroded the '. . . traditional closed system of tribal economics' (Fortes 1938:88).

In *The Analysis of Social Change*, Godfrey B. Wilson (1908–44) and Monica Hunter Wilson summarized much of the research on social and cultural change carried out in Africa during the 1930s and early 1940s (Wilson and Wilson 1954). They argued that the economy of Northern Rhodesia was already an integral part of the world economy and that the tribal peoples in the area were no longer economically self-sufficient (Brown 1973). The area and its inhabitants had been pulled into the world economy by virtue of the mineral wealth coming from the mines at Broken Hill and in the Copperbelt. For several decades, the mines had attracted workers from the neighboring areas, incorporating them slowly but inexorably into the capitalist economy of the mining towns and beyond. At the same time, they broke down the natal communities of the workers by stripping them of the human resources they needed to ensure both their demographic and social reproduction and by eroding the foundations of the traditional systems of political authority in the villages. One of the concerns of the colonial state, given the transformations taking place, was whether the tribal communities would continue to reproduce the labor force for the mines and provide for the extended kin of those members who had been incorporated into the capitalist economy and society of the mining towns (Wilson and Wilson 1954:3–22).

The labor demands of the copper mines, combined with the policies of the colonial state, had created uneven and unequal development on a massive scale. The emerging society of Northern Rhodesia, especially in the mining towns, was characterized by opposition and maladjustment. One opposition was the race problem, which pitted the large, subject African population and the European colonists against one another and left the small Indian community poised uneasily between them. This opposition spilled over into the workplace, where there were conflicts between African workers and European employers over wages and between African and European industrial workers over the admission of Africans to skilled jobs. These conflicts underwrote the 1935 and 1940 strikes and riots in the Copperbelt, which led to the death of a score of African workers. There was further competition between African and European farmers for land and between African and European men for African women. There was also conflict between various tribal communities whose members struggled to retain control over their lives and colonial authorities who sought to constrain practices and activities they deemed illegal, immoral, or threatening the authority and well-being of the colonial state.

The Wilsons (1954:15–16) described the social relations and sentiments produced by this opposition in the following terms:

> Courtesy very markedly fails to govern the relations of the races in town, and less markedly in the country also. In Northern Rhodesia post offices and shops commonly provide separate entrances and a lower standard of courtesy for their African clients, who resent the differentiation, and sometimes push and clamour for attention. The increasing assumption by Africans of European dress and manners, though it symbolizes an increasing civilization, is accompanied by more rather than less discourtesy from many Europeans, who sense in it a bid for conventional equality.
>
> To describe the character of this situation as a prevalent discourtesy is inadequate; it is rather an opposition of courtesies. Africans resent being passed over, but a shopman who should attend to an African in his turn when a European was waiting would be felt by the latter to have insulted him. To slight Africans is, in the European group, itself a convention, whose breach leads to embarrassment. . . .
>
> This opposition of the races is complicated by the fact that there is opposition within the European group itself over 'Native policy'; and within the African group between conservatives who would maintain traditional ways, and radicals who seek to approximate to Europeans in all things. . . .

The anthropologist Felix M. Keesing (1902–61) wrote about the cultural dynamics unleashed by colonialism and capitalist penetration into the Pacific, where he discerned two types of contact situation (Keesing 1934). The earlier one involved the appearance of traders and missionaries and produced what he called a 'native–trader–missionary' culture that, in the absence of further penetration, tended to reach some sort of equilibrium. The later one produced more controlled and exploitative situations, such as the Cultural System of Java, in which the indigenous peoples were compelled to work or produce for the outsiders. Land was taken, and the indigenous peoples of the region toiled to produce profits for the outsiders. In this context, he observed that

> Native leaders saw their people faced by loss of autonomy and of territory and looked back with poignant memory to the good old days, resented the confidently domineering

ways of the newcomers who were thwarting their activities at some many points, could foresee no future other than the displacement and destruction of their race. Group after group, therefore, resorted to arms, even to extremes of ferocity, in the attempt to drive back the invasion (Keesing 1934:449).

While the native peoples of New Zealand, Fiji and the Solomon Islands rebelled, other groups numbed by prolonged struggles with the outsiders were eventually overcome by sheer numbers. In their new circumstances, many communities began to assert a conscious cultural conservatism, clinging tenaciously to particular customs as they struggled to resist the penetration of Western or Japanese – i.e. capitalist – practices into their everyday lives. This cultural nationalism arose from feelings of inequality that could be compensated only partially by self-exaltation (Keesing 1934:453).

In contrast to the cultural nationalists who sought to preserve the past, other groups formed or participated in nationalist movements that struggled for political autonomy. The colonial powers were not able to deal effectively with political nationalists in French Indochina, the Netherlands East Indies, New Zealand, Hawaii, American Samoa, or Fiji, and they would not be able to deal with them in the future:

> . . . unless the dominant peoples can unbend in a way they show no signs of doing until forced by practical circumstances, and unless cultural-pathological manifestations are met with more effective remedies than reasoned arguments, legal phraseology, and military demonstrations, the cultural nationalism of the smaller groups is due to froth over with greater or less violence before reaching the level of readjustment at which their numerical size and position in the human perspective now causes us to place them (Keesing 1934:558).

Thus, Keesing described conditions that ignited and fueled the growth of movements for decolonization and political independence before and after the Second World War.

Discussion

Social commentators writing during the inter-war years realized that they were witnessing unprecedented social changes occurring on a world scale, and that peoples with diverse cultures in all parts of the world were being brought into closer proximity with one another than ever before in human history. They attempted to explain the complex interconnections that existed between economic crises and the political crises they precipitated in both the capitalist societies and their colonial possessions. These crises were not derived from the business cycles that were already an integral feature of capitalist society; they were more general and threatened the breakdown and even the collapse of the operating principles undergirding capitalist national states (Held 1991; Shaikh 1991a). Such crises created the conditions for the transformation of those organizing principles in the Soviet Union after the Russian Revolution and for significant modifications in the capitalist countries themselves, especially during the 1930s, when one state after another followed John M. Keynes's (1936) advice to intervene in their national economies in order to restore social order, regulate activity, and promote growth.

The forces unleashed by capitalist expansion and penetration were apparent not only in the industrial cities, whose populations swelled as men, women and children came in search of work in their factories, but also in the rural and colonial homelands of the immigrants. By the 1890s, Weber, Lenin and others had already begun to describe and analyze, at least in a preliminary manner, the processes set in motion in East Elbe and Russia. They portrayed these processes in terms of rural class formation or social differentiation and the appearance of alternative paths of agrarian capitalist development. In the 1920s, the new Soviet state directed Chayanov, Kritsman and their associates to investigate the structure and organization of peasant agriculture and the changes that were occurring in it as a result of capitalist development in the rural areas. Fei and Mao undertook similar investigations in China, even though they reached quite different conclusions about the nature of rural society. This research would subsequently lay important foundations for the development of peasant studies after the Second World War.

Investigations of rural class formation and structures were, by definition, also studies of the linkages that existed between urban centers and their hinterlands and how the uneven development of capitalism in town and countryside fueled their reproduction. The question of how capitalist enclaves located cities articulated with the pre- or non-capitalist economies of rural areas became increasingly important and pressing. Gramsci and Boeke explored the economic and political underpinnings of uneven development in terms of the Southern Question in Italy and the formation of dual economies in Dutch Indonesia. Redfield discussed the cultural dimensions of the linkages in terms of a folk–urban continuum that emphasized differences in the intensity of communication between Westernized cities, peasant villages and remote tribal communities, and largely ignored the political-economic relations forged by capitalist enterprises in the Yucatán Peninsula.

Marxist theorists – notably Mao, Gramsci, and Mariátegui – believed that peasantries were capable of developing an understanding of the conditions that were impinging on their lives, and, given an historically contingent balance of force, of making their own history. Liberal commentators – Redfield, Boeke, and Fortes, for instance – believed that the lives of peasants and tribal peoples would ultimately be shaped in fundamental ways by relations, practices, habits, and ideas that originated in capitalist civilization and emanated from the Westernized culture of the cities, whose residents were already enmeshed in the social relations of the capitalist world economy.

Anthropologists were acutely aware of the consequences that capitalist penetration had for tribal peoples and peasantries, not only in Africa and the Pacific but also in the Americas. Keesing and the Wilsons pointed to the destructive consequences of culture contact; they used the notions of anomie and alienation to explain the revivals and creations of the cultural nationalists; and the arguments for autonomy were promulgated by political nationalists such as Mohandas Gandhi, Ho Chi Minh or Jomo Kenyatta. The acculturation theorists in the United States attempted to ascertain the psychological traits or core value orientations that led different individuals and groups to adopt or reject certain capitalist patterns of behavior, to assimilate to capitalist social relations or to resist them passively or violently, or to propose political nationalist alternatives.

In Chapter 5, we will examine how social theorists from capitalist countries writing after the Second World War explained imperialism as economic growth and modernization, and how their contemporaries from Latin America or colonial states who championed decolonization and political independence described imperialism in terms of dependency, underdevelopment or neo-colonialism. We will also consider the relationships between peasant communities, rural development and social revolution.

–5–

The Cold War, Decolonization and Third World Development

The capitalist countries were in disarray at the end of the Second World War. The United States was the only one whose industrial base had emerged unscathed from the war; the economies of the others – England, France, Germany, and Japan – were severely damaged, and would require nearly a decade to rebuild. In 1946, the capitalist countries precipitated the Cold War, pitting themselves against the Soviet Union in order to halt the advance of socialism. The Cold War was an uneven balance of power that was maintained by enormous expenditures on weapons by both sides (M. Walker 1993). As the historian Eric Hobsbawm (b. 1917) observed, 'Entire generations grew up under the shadow of global nuclear battles which, it was widely believed, could break out at any moment and devastate humanity. . . . It did not happen, but for some forty years it looked a daily possibility' (Hobsbawm 1996:226).

Decolonization was the other feature that dominated the post-war era. Throughout the world, the colonial subjects of the United States, England, France and the Netherlands seized the opportunities provided by the weakness of the imperial states to proclaim political independence or to launch popular movements, both armed and otherwise, to gain autonomy. By 1960, nearly 1.3 billion people – more than a third of the world's population at the time – had gained their independence as a result of the national liberation movements that succeeded, and the number of independent countries in Asia and Africa had increased from a mere handful to more than fifty (Hobsbawm 1996:208–22).

Decolonization created a Third World composed of the newly independent but poor countries in Asia, Africa, Latin America, and the Pacific (Pletsch 1981). They were neither capitalist like the Western states of the First World nor socialist like the Soviet Union and the Eastern European countries composing the Second World. What countries as diverse as India and Mexico shared was poverty relative to the First World and ambivalence with regard to their former colonial masters. In 1955, they adopted a policy of non-alignment, in which they would pursue economic and political development that was neither capitalist nor socialist. In practice, both the United States and its allies and the Soviet Union made loans to promote development and allegiance in the Third World countries. One effect was that all the wars waged during the succeeding half century were in fact fought in the Third World (Hobsbawm 1996:344–71).

The Cold War and decolonization had a profound impact on the ways scholars conceptualized theories of change and development in a world where capitalism was alive, socialism provided an alternative, and the issues raised by imperialism, nationalism, and peasants remained unresolved. By the late 1940s, advocates of capitalist economic growth and modernization were already underpinning their theories with social evolutionism and ideas of progress and modernity. This provoked a series of richly textured responses from Third World and Marxist critics, who typically rejected transhistorical arguments. They analyzed uneven development and unequal exchange between the capitalist world and its periphery, as well as the similarities they saw between these circumstances and ones that existed during the transition from feudalism to capitalism in the West. In a milieu shaped by the struggles for political independence, social scientists also investigated the participation of national minorities, peasants, and tribal peoples in the national liberation movements and their integration into the newly independent states.

Economic Growth and Modernization

Social commentators supportive of capitalist development and the continued domination of the capitalist First World couched their analyses of economic growth and modernization in structural- functionalist terms. They recycled the growth analogy, arguing that all aspects of a society or culture were interconnected and that change was directional and proceeded gradually through a fixed succession of stages. They relied heavily on Durkheim's views and on new interpretations of their significance (Bock 1963; Parsons 1961a; A. D. Smith 1973).

Change, according to the anthropologist Julian H. Steward (1902–1972), was inevitable. Every culture, he argued, has a core, '. . . a basic economy which produces a configuration that [functionally] interrelates a large number of elements . . .' closely related to subsistence activities and economic arrangements (Steward and Seltzer 1938:7). This core, which involved historically determined technologies and productive arrangements that developed through a progression of increasingly complex stages, had potent shaping effects on the less fixed, secondary aspects of social organization (Steward 1955a, 1977b).

Steward (1949) was initially interested in the cross-cultural, cause-and-effect regularities that shaped the development of early civilizations in semi-arid areas, like Mesopotamia or Peru.[1] By 1950, he conceptualized world history in terms of

---

1. Steward's was not the only evolutionary theory of economic growth that flourished after the Second World War (Leacock 1982; Patterson 1987). The Australian archaeologist V. Gordon Childe (1892–1957) and the US anthropologist Leslie White (1900–75) had already elaborated evolutionary

a succession of stages that unfolded gradually as hunting and foraging bands developed village agriculture and then state-based political organizations; the succession culminated in contemporary Euro-American societies characterized by free enterprise and competition between business institutions.

> At first there were small communities of incipient farmers. Later the communities cooperated in the construction of irrigation works and the populations became larger and more settled. Villages amalgamated into states under theocratic rulers. . . . Finally culture ceased to develop, and the states of each area entered into competition with one another. . . . One or another state succeeded in dominating the others, that is, in building an empire, but such empires ran their course and collapsed after some . . . years only to be succeeded by another empire not very different from the first (Steward 1950: 103–4).
>
> For the historian this era of cyclical conquests is filled with great men, wars and battle strategy, shifting power centers, and other social events. For the culture historian the changes are much less significant than those of the previous eras when the basic civilizations developed in the Near East, or those of the subsequent Iron Age when the cultural patterns changed again and the centers of civilization shifted to new areas [i.e. Europe] (Steward 1950:104).
>
> . . . The industrial revolution brought profound cultural change to Western Europe and caused competition for colonies and for areas of exploitation. Japan entered the competition as soon as she acquired the general pattern. The realignments of power caused by Germany's losses in the first world war and by Italy's and Japan's in the second are of a social order. What new cultural patterns will result from these remains to be seen (Steward 1950:104–5).
>
> The general assumption today seems to be that we are in danger of basic cultural changes caused by the spread of communism. Russia acquired drastically new cultural patterns as a result of her revolution. Whether communism has the same meaning in other nations has still to be determined (Steward 1950:105).

Steward recognized one limitation of this conception of world history. It was too general, and certain areas, like colonial possessions, did not fit neatly into it. Thus, in the late 1940s, he initiated a project in Puerto Rico to study the impact of US capitalism on a largely rural, agrarian colony that depended on an export crop and imported '. . . nearly all of its manufactured goods and about half of its food'

---

theories of social development before or during the war. Building on Marx, Childe (1942) explained change in terms of social, political, and economic institutions and the role they played in underwriting technological innovations (Trigger 1989:250–63). White (1943) argued that culture was the extrasomatic ways and means humanity employed in the struggle for survival; it was the way in which its members captured and harnessed energy. Agriculture and stockraising, which greatly increased the amount of energy that could be harnessed, provided the impetus for further development and progress in all aspects of culture, including the development of property relations and the rise of private property (Carneiro 1981; Peace 1993).

(Steward 1950:129). The cultural heterogeneity of Puerto Rican society was due to the differential penetration of '. . . the processes by which production, social patterns, and related modes of life are selectively borrowed from the outside and adapted to local needs . . .' (Steward 1950:133–4).

He saw the social structure of the island as composed of two interdependent features: (1) a series of distinctive, localized sociocultural subgroups crosscut by class, ethnic, and other social categories that were arranged hierarchically throughout the island; and (2) extra-insular institutions – i.e. economic relationships and the legal and government system – that regulated the society and had be understood apart from the behavior of the individuals connected with them. In his view, 'the most important factors in Puerto Rico's cultural change . . . appeared to penetrate the Island along the axes of these basic institutions' (Steward 1950:145). The folk cultures of the island were not disappearing as this more complex stage of development was being reached; they were being modified instead, and becoming specialized, dependent parts of a new configuration – a multi- faceted national culture (Steward 1955b:51–3).

The weakness of Steward's theory of economic growth and world history became increasingly apparent after 1953, as the issues of decolonization and development loomed larger in the new nations of the Third World and as the reconstruction of the capitalist economies of Western Europe and Japan neared completion (Huntington 1976 [1971]; Preston 1982:58).[2] He did not address the crucial question resulting from organized opposition to capitalist development in Third World countries: how to identify and support the classes or groups in those countries that would promote capitalist economic development.

This was a political question that modernization theorists, unlike Steward and others who focused mainly on economic growth, attempted to address (Sztompa 1993:129–36).[3] For example, Walt W. Rostow (b. 1916), economic historian and presidential advisor in the early 1960s, provided an alternative explanation of world

2. Anthropologists focused their criticism on three aspects of cultural evolutionist theory. First, they questioned the functionalist assumptions related to the integrity of the economic core and the presumed association of given technologies with particular forms of social and political organization. Second, they demanded greater specificity in the relation between the economic and the political spheres of particular culture types. Third, they challenged Steward's separation of the study of cultural process from history, and advocated, instead, studies that synthesized and explained the historical specificity of the succession of cultural and social forms in particular areas.

3. There were numerous critiques of modernization and the distinction drawn between traditional and modern societies (e.g. H. Bernstein 1972; Frank 1972a; Tipps 1973). For example, the economist Albert Hirschman (1958) was critical of their emphasis on balanced development; he argued instead that, since individuals with decision-making and entrepreneurial skills were in short supply in most of the new nations, they should be concentrated in one or a few sectors rather than spreading them across the entire economy.

history in *The Stages of Economic Growth: A Non-Communist Manifesto* (Rostow 1971a), which sought to explain why a dynamic social type oriented to economic progress appeared in the West and why the transition from traditional to modern society was impeded elsewhere. Rostow claimed that all societies, at least in terms of their economic dimensions, belonged to one of five universal types. He outlined the conditions and processes that promoted the transition from traditional society to the era of high mass-consumption that appeared in the capitalist countries during the 1950s.

Traditional society was a diverse catch-all category composed of groups that employed primitive technologies and devoted a high proportion of their resources to agriculture. These hierarchically organized societies had regional political structures dominated by landlords. They could not improve per capita output, because '. . . the potentialities which flow from modern science and technology were either not available or not regularly and systematically applied' (Rostow 1971a:4). The preconditions for economic take-off, which had first developed in England around 1700, occurred when the insights of modern science were harnessed to increase agricultural and industrial production in a context shaped by overseas expansion. As the idea of progress became a more pervasive aspect of everyday life, resistance to the idea of continuous growth was overcome and the institutions of traditional society were ultimately dissolved (Rostow 1971a:4–7; 1971b:26–97). While the era of take-off was achieved in England and its colonies because of this technological motor, political regimes favorable to modernization were needed elsewhere.

During economic take-off, societies significantly increased investment to 10 per cent or more of their national income in order to enlarge agricultural and industrial production, to promote a new but relatively narrow complex of industry and technology, to expand urban-industrial employment, and to support the emerg-ence of a new class of entrepreneurs. After a decade or two, the social and political structures of these societies were transformed in ways that would sustain steady economic growth (Rostow 1971a:17–36; 1971b:98–183). The drive to maturity over the next fifty or sixty years was characterized by the spread of modern technology throughout the entire economy, by regular increases in output that outstripped population growth, and by continuous changes in the make-up of the economy as new industries appeared, import-substitution occurred, and new exports were created. At this stage:

> The society makes such terms as it will with the requirements of modern efficient production, balancing off the new against the older values and institutions, or revising the latter in such ways as to support rather than retard the growth process (Rostow 1971a:9).

Mature societies had the technological and entrepreneurial skills to produce virtually anything they wanted. This underpinned the age of high mass-consumption that appeared in the capitalist countries during the 1950s, when the leading economic sectors shifted toward the production of durable consumer goods. Real per capita income increased, and the structure of the labor force changed as a larger proportion of the total population worked in urban settings in office or skilled factory jobs. Thus, the Western societies were also able to allocate additional resources to social welfare and security. While the Soviet Union was technically ready for this stage, its leaders, in Rostow's view, had not yet faced the difficult political and social problems of adjustment that would occur if it were launched (Rostow 1971a:10–11, 73–92).

The modernization theorists built on Weber's views about the role of rationality, bureaucracy and political parties in social transformation.[4] Modernization, in their view, was a disruptive process that ultimately dissolved the social, economic and psychological commitments of traditional societies. The members of backward societies were exposed through the media, literacy, and urbanization to various aspects of modern capitalist culture – industrialization, rationalization, the affirmation of science and the scientific method (reason), individualism, bureaucracies, political parties and democratization. As modernization penetrated more deeply into the fabric of everyday life, the societies adopted modern behaviors and ideas that provided opportunities for new forms of mobilization (Deutsch 1961). For example, David McClelland (1961) and Everett Hagen (1962) appropriated Weber's 'Protestant Ethic thesis' and argued that successful entrepreneurs in modernizing societies believed in self-reliance and high standards of performance. This resulted from the declining importance of fathers, who reputedly were away from the home more of the time, and the expanding role of mothers, who reputedly spent more of their time in the home, in modernizing societies.

Modernization was a complex phenomenon. In economic terms, it meant developing technologies based on Western conceptions of scientific knowledge, replacing human and animal power with machines, moving from subsistence to commercial agriculture, establishing markets, creating urban-based industries, and consolidating an ever-larger proportion of an increasingly skilled and differentiated labor force in the cities. In political terms, it meant the shift from tribal forms of authority to suffrage, political parties, elected representatives, and democratization. In educational terms, it meant eliminating illiteracy and emphasizing knowledge, skills, and competency. In human terms, it meant diminishing the importance of the various kin and neighborhood institutions that provided a safety net for the

---

4. More precisely, the modernization theorists built on Talcott Parsons's interpretations of Max Weber's views. Parsons emphasized the systematic elements in Weber's work and portrayed him as a theorist of social action, rationality and sociological methodology (Hennis 1988:7–8).

members of the community and granting a greater role to the nuclear family (Eisenstadt 1973:21–2; Smelser 1961).

Modernization also implied that the social and political- economic systems of the capitalist West and the Soviet Union would ultimately converge, because the logic of industrialism promotes uniformity.[5] This occurs, according to the proponents of *convergence theory*, because

> As industrialism advances and becomes increasingly a world-wide phenomenon . . . the range of viable institutional structures and of viable systems of value and belief is necessarily reduced. All societies, whatever path by which they entered the industrial world, will tend to approximate, even if asymptotically, [the ideal type of] the pure industrial form (Goldthorpe 1971:263).

Modernization posed problems that Third World nations had to confront (Shils 1960a, b, 1963). They had to establish effective governments, which meant (1) organizing and maintaining a rational political apparatus that was viewed as legitimate by the masses; (2) staffing it with indigenous personnel schooled in or receptive to modern Western culture; (3) integrating the mass of the population, steeped in traditional culture, into the new national society; (4) developing new economic institutions and techniques to move the nation from traditional subsistence farming to commercial agriculture or industry; and (5) persuading the traditional masses to accept these innovations. Consequently, it was necessary to determine how various institutions, practices, and beliefs '. . . function in the articulation of the society, in attaching or detaching or fixing each sector [of the population] in its relationship to the central institutional and value systems of the society' (Shils 1963:23–4).

Modernization, in anthropologist Clifford Geertz's (b. 1927) view, was a broad process of social, political, cultural, and economic change that was shaped at some fundamental level by the values of the cultural system (Geertz 1956, 1963a). He rejected materialist conceptions of history that were concerned with growth and gave primary importance to the economic base. This included not only Marxist analyses but also the economic determinist arguments of Steward and other social evolutionists in the 1950s and 1960s. By relocating the motor of development from the economic base to the cultural realm, he adopted the views of Durkheim and Talcott Parsons (1902–79), his mentor (Geertz 1971:376, 1973a, b). This perspective also shaped acculturation studies after the early 1950s (Barnett, Broom, Siegel, Vogt, and Watson 1954).

Modernization theorists also made extensive use of Parsons's views about society and change, as well as his interpretations of the significance of Max Weber's work,

5. Dependency theory – as well as the theories of combined and uneven development and the articulation of modes of production – and the resurgence of peasant studies were critical responses in the capitalist West to convergence theory (Blomström and Hettne 1984; Löwy 1981; Taylor 1979).

in order to explain precisely how the processes they discerned actually took place and how they were reproduced. Parsons distinguished the changes that continually occur *within* society – e.g. when a new conjugal family was formed or when the personalities of children were shaped – from structural changes *of* society. He saw change in terms of shifts in the culturally determined motivations by which individuals or groups optimized gratification. Individuals and groups with vested interests blocked or attempted to prevent changes in motivation and need gratification in order to maintain the existing cultural system.[6] When competing kinds of motivation and need gratification appeared, strains appeared in the interactions defining the social system, in the values of the cultural system, and in the ways the personalities of individuals allowed them to cope with the new situation. For the changes to be reproduced rather than to remain isolated instances of deviance, the consequences of the new motivations had to become an integral part of the belief and value component of the newly reorganized cultural system (Parsons 1951:480–503; Savage 1981).

What fascinated Parsons (1961b:37, 1961c) was a category of change intermediate between those changes within society where the patterns of the institutionalized culture remained constant and those changes where the structure of the action system was transformed. He called this *structural differentiation*. It was initiated when a force originating from any number of sources – economic, political, or cultural – disrupted the existing boundary relationships between a society and its environment. Differentiation produced strains that shifted value commitments away from specific role performances; these in turn produced social conflicts, as vested interests affected by the strains simultaneously attempted to combat them and to reassert their legitimacy and control over any breakaway units. If they failed, further differentiation occurred, and

> The institutions associated with the different dimensions of society – with the functional demands of adaptation, goal attainment, integration, and pattern maintenance – become separated from one another. In the process, each develops the capacity to mobilize the resources of the other systems and to assert an independent, though partial regulation of them (Alexander 1983b:128).

The newly differentiated structures continued to develop, like a biological organism, until the equilibrium of the system was re-established, and the patterns of social solidarity were transformed as the system was reorganized.

---

6. In critical commentaries on *The Social System*, Lewis Coser (1956) and Ralf Dahrendorf (1957) argued that Parsons's theory of social change placed too much emphasis on integration or reformation and did not deal satisfactorily with social conflict. The dichotomy they drew between consensus and conflict perspectives also influenced the way anthropologists have looked at the issue of state formation (e.g., Fried 1967; Service 1975).

During the mid-1960s, Parsons attempted to account for certain universals he saw in the process of modernization. One involved the 'break out' from the primitive stage of societal evolution caused by the appearance of social stratification and the cultural legitimation of differentiated societal functions, especially the political function, that were independent of kinship. Their appearance led to the formation of intermediate societies – the ancient Mesopotamian empires, China, the Islamic empires, or Rome – that were neither primitive nor modern. Once literacy was institutionalized in those intermediate societies, two additional changes occurred – the development of administrative bureaucracies, especially in government, and money and markets (Parsons 1967, 1971).

Parsons (1966:24–7) was also concerned with how and why these intermediate societies were different from modern ones. From his perspective, the breakthrough they failed to achieve was the development of a generalized legal system – the kind that was instituted by English common law. While the antecedents for this breakthrough were found in the legal order established in ancient Greece and ancient Israel, neither was able to institutionalize its inventions under the prevailing circumstances. However, the legacy of these 'seed bed' societies was capitalized on more than a thousand years later by the English, who successfully made the breakthrough to modernity.

Modernization and economic growth theorists had set forth arguments to account for the changes that had taken place in the post-war world. Many agreed with Steward and Rostow, who argued that changes in the economic base had profound shaping effects on political, social, and cultural realms of society. Others agreed with Geertz or Parsons, who followed Durkheim's claim that the determinants of change were ultimately located in the cultural system. Unfortunately, proponents of the two positions never confronted this discrepancy. Implicit in the views of both the economic and cultural determinists was the idea of convergence. Societies that pursued modernization would increasingly resemble one another because of limitations imposed by the logic of industrialization.

Dependency and Underdevelopment

Deteriorating economic conditions in Latin America during the 1950s and 1960s provoked scholars in the region to scrutinize the theories of economic growth and modernization emanating from the capitalist countries – especially the United States. These theories implied that convergence would occur as growth or modernization proceeded; however, as Raúl Prebisch (1901–86), Director of the United Nations' Economic Commission for Latin America (ECLA) noted, the world economy remained differentiated and convergence was not taking place:

> In Latin America, reality is undermining the out-dated schema of the international division of labour, which achieved great importance in the nineteenth century and, as a theoretical concept, continued to exert considerable influence until very recently. Under that schema, the specific task that fell to Latin America, as part of the periphery of the world economic system, was that of producing food and raw materials for the great industrial centres. There was no place within it for the industrialization of those countries (Prebisch 1950:1).

The world economy was structured in terms of a dominant center and a dependent periphery that were linked together by exchange relations that were not equally beneficial to both. The patterns of economic development that had occurred in Latin America in particular and in the Third World in general depended on decisions made in the industrial capitalist countries – the United States, Western Europe, and Japan.

Prebisch, a former director of the Central Bank of Argentina, was acutely aware of that country's failed efforts at internal development and industrialization in the 1920s, where, contrary to the predictions of the economic growth and modernization theorists, putting financial resources into the economic base or into the hands of 'modernizing' entrepreneurs had not led to economic development, modernization, or convergence with the industrial capitalist countries. In fact, the social and economic structures of Argentina were less similar to those of the Western countries in 1950 than they had been fifty years earlier (Blomström and Hettne 1984:38–44; Girvan 1973; Preston 1982:145–7). Prebisch and his associates at ECLA viewed the fact that the history of Latin America contradicted the predictions of the economic growth and modernization theorists as a devastating critique of the development models emanating from the First World countries – most notably the United States.

The governments of Argentina, Brazil, and Mexico had attempted to lessen their vulnerability to world markets after the crash of 1929 through political alliances and state policies that controlled foreign investment and commerce. In spite of these and other efforts during the 1930s and 1940s, they found that their economies were even more dependent in the 1960s than they had been four decades earlier. However, the agents of dependency had changed; the new agents were not the extractive mining and capitalist export agricultural companies of earlier times but First World multinational (transnational) corporations, which integrated diverse activities in a single firm and operated in a number of different countries.

The power of the multinational corporations was their control over commercial technology. In order to gain access to their technology, local industrialists had to enter into joint ventures with them. This set in motion processes that simultaneously denationalized industry in the Latin American countries, opened up their internal markets to foreign commodities, and altered the balance of forces within the ruling classes. This economic restructuring had devastating consequences. Local capital was used to finance the joint ventures; the amount of locally generated capital exported from Latin America in the form of profits, royalties, and commissions to the dominant economies increased significantly; and, consequently, less local capital was available for investment in the various national economies (O'Brien 1975:16–19; Sunkel 1969).

Social scientists at ECLA called this perspective *dependency theory*. Its most distinctive feature was that the developed and underdeveloped countries of the world occupied different positions in an international system of production and distribution, which was held together by unequal exchange. The Brazilian economist Celso Furtado (b. 1920) described the process and condition of underdevelopment in terms of the theory of dual economies. When capitalist structures and practices like production for export were introduced into a country with a largely subsistence economy, only a small number of local workers were incorporated into the capitalist enterprise, and the archaic economic structures were not changed dramatically. For this to occur, many more individuals had to be employed in the capitalist sector and have income that could be spent on consumption or invested. However, the income generated by the capitalist sector in a dependent country was only partially linked to that country, since the larger portion of it was exported and invested to promote a dynamic capitalist sector in the metropolitan state. As a result, hybrid economies that linked a capitalist core to archaic structures on the periphery were forged repeatedly as the frontiers of Western capitalism were steadily extended during the nineteenth and nineteenth centuries. What emerged in the dependent countries were three-sector economies composed of a remnant subsistence economy, a capitalist export economy, and a small capitalist manufacturing economy concerned with domestic consumption. The only dynamic elements in the dependent countries were external demand and the wages generated in the export sector; however, as wage incomes grew, there might be an internal multiplier effect resulting in increased investment and employment in the domestic capitalist manufacturing sector (Furtado 1964:129–40).

Fernando H. Cardoso (b. 1931), currently the President of Brazil, and Enzo Faletto pointed out that certain important features of the capitalist system – notably the technological and financial sectors – were the almost exclusive possessions of the developed states. Since they were crucial for further development, the dependency of the underdeveloped countries, as well as the domination of the developed ones, was reinforced as the Third World states attempted to expand their economies. In their view, the dependent countries were like borrowers approaching a bank president for a loan (Cardoso and Faletto 1979:xxi–xxii).

In *The Political Economy of Growth* (1957), the economist Paul Baran (1910–64) observed that many underdeveloped Latin American states had small, highly productive industrial sectors combined with large, relatively unproductive agricultural sectors. While the potential for growth and employment lay in the industrial sector, the small size of the domestic market and the small amount of surplus available for investment and capital formation constrained expansion. Baran (1957: 170–248) noted that various forms of surplus extraction coexisted in the economically backward countries: landlords extracted land-rents from the peasants; moneylenders charged interest on credit; merchants made profit on trade; and the capitalists, mostly foreign, extracted surplus value from industrial workers. He proceeded to argue that none of these classes had any real interest in promoting industrialization. The traditional classes of the agricultural sector – the landlords, moneylenders, and merchants – opposed industrialization, because it threatened their access to surplus. The capitalists, both foreign and national, also opposed further industrialization, because it would promote competition that would ultimately challenge their monopoly control over domestic markets and threaten the high profit rates that they were already extracting from them (Martinussen 1997:85–8).

The Chicago-trained economist André Gunder Frank (b. 1929) did much to popularize dependency theory in the United States through his critiques of mainstream development and modernization theory (Booth 1975; Frank 1967, 1969, 1972a). Since the economic underdevelopment of Brazil and Chile in particular and Latin America in general was a consequence of an exploitative relationship that extended from the capitalist metropoles of Western Europe and North America to the most remote reaches of their economically backward satellites on the periphery,

> The now developed countries were never *under*developed, though they may have been *un*developed. It is also widely believed that the contemporary underdevelopment of a country can be understood as the product or reflection solely of its own economic, political, social, and cultural characteristics or structure. Yet historical research demonstrates that contemporary underdevelopment is in large part the historical product of past and continuing economic and other relations between the satellite underdeveloped and the now developed metropolitan countries. Furthermore, these relations are an essential part of the structure and development of the capitalist system on a world scale as a whole.
>
> . . . [T]he expansion of the capitalist system over the past centuries effectively and entirely penetrated even the apparently most isolated sectors of the underdeveloped world. Therefore the economic, political, social, and cultural institutions and relations we now observe there are the products of the historical development of the capitalist system no less than are the seemingly more modern or capitalist features of the national metropoles of these underdeveloped countries (Frank 1969:4–5, emphasis in the original).

The Latin American countries had been part of a world capitalist system since the early days of the colonial period. Consequently, it made no sense to describe their economic structures as feudal, semi-feudal, or archaic, because they had been forged by the same historical processes of capitalist development and underdevelopment that affected the West.

The underdevelopment of the Latin American countries was reproduced by the contradictions inherent in capitalism. Only a small portion of the economic surplus generated by their economic development was actually saved and invested in the underdeveloped country; the remaining larger portion was either appropriated by another part of the world capitalist system or was wasted on the consumption of luxury goods.

> . . . [T]his exploitative relation . . . in chain-like fashion extends the capitalist link between the capitalist world and national metropolises to the regional centers (part of whose surplus they appropriate), and from these to local centers, and so on to the large landowners or merchants who expropriate surplus from small peasants and tenants, and sometimes even from these latter to landless laborers exploited by them in return (Frank 1967:7–8).

Capitalist development and expansion were facets of the same historical process. It simultaneously produced economic development in the metropolitan countries and structural underdevelopment in those on the periphery. It also polarized the metropole and the satellite countries as well as different regions within the countries on the periphery. Polarization occurred because

> . . . for the generation of structural underdevelopment, more important still than the drain of economic surplus from the satellite after its incorporation into the world capitalist system, is the impregnation of the satellite's domestic economy with the same capitalist structures and its fundamental contradictions (Frank 1967:10).

This meant that the conditions required to maintain underdevelopment were manifested in the class structures of the underdeveloped countries (Frank 1972b:1–12). It also implied that the '. . . satellites experience their greatest economic development and especially their most classically capitalist industrial development when the ties to the metropole are weakest' (Frank 1969:9–10).

Frank and the dependency theorists believed that the underdevelopment of Third World countries was a consequence of unequal exchange with the developed capitalist countries of the West. They challenged the idea that international trade was equally beneficial to all the participants (Emmanuel 1972). The Third World produced raw materials that fitted the production and consumption requirements of the capitalist countries; the surplus they created and transferred to the West far exceeded the value of the finished goods they were forced to import. Moreover, capital flowed from the Third World to the West because of wage differentials; the lower wages paid to workers in the Third World permitted the extraction of higher rates of surplus value, which was then siphoned off by the West. This challenged modernization and dual economy theorists, who claimed

> ... that Latin America was a region of 'dual societies' divided between dynamic zones integrated into modern capitalism and backward zones languishing in feudal isolation. Capitalism, understood as profit-driven production of commodities for large-scale markets on unequal terms that benefited capitalists and metropoles, was the quintessential colonial legacy in precisely the impoverished regions considered 'feudal' and 'isolated' in the twentieth century (Stern 1993:28).

The Transition from Feudalism to Capitalism

Questions concerning the transition from feudalism to capitalism were debated in the post-war years. The debate was significant for several reasons. The participants discussed changes in agrarian structures and practices, the origins of towns, the development of handicrafts, the role of trade and the importance of prime movers in the development of capitalism in Western Europe. More important was the fact that these were the same issues being discussed by the economic growth, modernization and dependency theorists who were attempting to conceptualize social transformation in the societies of Latin America, Africa and Asia, which they often described as 'feudal' or 'feudal-like'.

The British economist Maurice H. Dobb (1900–1976) launched the debate. He rejected claims that economic transformation was best understood in terms of transhistorical economic or social evolutionary laws. Taking Marx's lead, he argued instead that economic development – the growth of labor productivity – had to be understood in terms of the possibilities and constraints offered by the historically contingent sets of production relations that were characteristics of a given era and mode of production (Dobb 1947).

Dobb's *Studies in the Development of Capitalism*, which appeared in 1946, was concerned with the transition from feudalism to capitalism. This question was, of course, the focus of economic growth, modernization, and dependency theorists, on the one hand, and those who were concerned with the agrarian question, on the other. Dobb brought into focus the structural similarities that existed in the West during the early stages of capitalist development and those that still prevailed in most of the world. He fixed attention on the processes involved in the dissolution of the feudal mode of production and the consolidation of capitalist social relations in rural areas and in undeveloped or underdeveloped countries.

The US economist Paul M. Sweezy (b. 1910) described the timeliness and importance of Dobb's book in the following way: 'We live in the period of transition from capitalism to socialism; and this fact lends particular interest to studies of earlier transitions from one social system to another' (Sweezy 1976:33). Transition was an important question at the time. Between 1945 and 1952, roughly a third of the world's population became governed by states that claimed to be socialist, and another third of the world's people had either proclaimed their political independence from the imperialist states or were in the process of doing so. Many of the countries – as various social analysts realized – had economic and social structures that were not quite capitalist and/or whose development had either been blocked or deformed by the spread of capitalism. They too were either undergoing or would experience shortly some sort of economic transformation.

Dobb built his analysis around Marx's concept of a mode of production. Feudalism was characterized by a particular form of surplus extraction – feudal lords used extra-economic forms of compulsion to extort surplus goods or labor from their serfs, and their ability to exact tribute was limited because the peasants retained possession of the major means of production. Dobb was critical of how historians had typically explained the rise of capitalism. The dominant explanation was the thesis proposed by the Belgian historian Henry Pirenne, which asserted that trade and merchant capital, both originating outside Western Europe, eroded feudal class relations and thereby paved the way for the development of a new capitalist class.[7] In his view, trade and merchant capital had little to do with the transformation. He argued instead that the new capitalist class – generated by the internal contradictions of feudal society itself and composed of free petty producers, peasants, and artisans – appeared alongside and existed in the interstices of the feudal social order before 1500. It subsequently gave rise to a class of industrial and agricultural capitalists that finally established its hegemony in England during the anti-feudal, bourgeois revolution of 1640 (Brenner 1978; Dobb 1947:38–42).

Sweezy responded to this argument. Unlike Dobb, who viewed feudalism as a mode of production, Sweezy (1976:34–5) saw it as an economic system based on production for use

---

7. The Belgian historian Henri Pirenne (1862–1935) elaborated a thesis about the historical development of Western Europe that was virtually unchallenged during the inter-war period (Havighurst 1958; Pirenne 1914, 1939, 1952). Briefly, Pirenne's thesis was that the unity of the world was ultimately broken by the spread of Islam in the seventh and eighth centuries, which disrupted the existing patterns of Mediterranean trade and left Europe isolated. Merchants from Italy and the Low Countries re-established commercial ties toward the end of the tenth century, which led to the formation of towns that incorporated artisans and peasants fleeing from the countryside; the towns relied increasingly on manufacturing and export for their revenues, especially after the thirteenth century; at the same time, they also became increasingly more specialized – for example, those in Flanders produced fine cloth, while banking monopolies appeared in the towns of northern Italy. Furthermore, each shift witnessed the rise and hegemony of a new capitalist class. Pirenne defined capitalism in terms of profit-making – that is, buying cheap and selling dear.

... in which serfdom is the predominant relation of production, and in which production is organised in and around the manorial estate of the lord. ... [In such systems], there is ... none of the pressure which exists under capitalism for continual improvements in the methods of production.

This did not mean that feudalism was stable, since both warfare and population increase among the serfs introduced instability into a society that was fundamentally resistant to change in both the methods and relations of production. Sweezy (1976:36–7) argued that Dobb had not sufficiently taken into account the inherently conservative nature of feudalism. If he had, then he would have revised his argument that over-exploitation and class struggle were the main causes of the breakdown of that economic system, and he would have sought '... to uncover the process by which trade engendered a *system* of production for the market, and then to trace the impact of that system on the pre-existent feudal system of production for use' (Sweezy 1976:41). What was needed, from Sweezy's perspective, was a theory that specified how long-distance trade might be a creative force that could bring into existence an exchange economy alongside the feudal system of production for use. In other words, he retained the Pirenne thesis and gave primacy of determination to exchange over production relations.

Dobb (1976a, b) acknowledged that there had indeed been a revival of trade in Western Europe after 1100, and that it had had important economic consequences – for example, an increasing demand for money rents payments rather than payments of produce or of labor time, as well as the growth of domestic markets and the artisanal production of weapons and luxury goods in the market towns. However, external trade and craft production were largely directed toward demands of the feudal lords, who also had the most to gain if the existing social relations were preserved. In other words, '... the economic effects of trade and of merchant capital were themselves shaped by feudal class relations' (Brenner 1978:123).

Dobb questioned whether the new desires of the landlords would lead them to increase output by rationalizing production on their estates or by replacing serf labor with wage workers. This perspective forced him to look for another, internal motor that dissolved feudal social relations and laid the foundations for the consolidation of capitalist relations. He located it in the crisis of feudalism generated by the lords' increased demand for money and/or surplus product and the peasants' control of the forces of production, combined, after the Black Death, with the abundance of untenanted land and the scarcity of peasant labor in the second half of the fourteenth century. Peasants moved onto the untenanted lands or fled to the towns to avoid the exactions of the feudal lords. In other words, internal conflicts accelerated the process of social differentiation among the class of small producers in Western European feudal society.

Once the small producers were able to keep a portion of the surplus product for themselves – perhaps because of the shift from labor to money rents – some of them were able to accumulate capital. This further accelerated class formation and led to a small layer of rich peasants or *kulaks*, on the one hand, and a much larger layer of impoverished peasants, on the other (Dobb 1976b:167). Dobb viewed class conflict as an internal engine of feudal society during the fourteenth and fifteenth centuries. He further argued that, even though the feudal economy was disintegrating and a mode of petty production was crystallizing, English society continued to be dominated political by feudal lords, rather than merchant capitalists, until the mid-seventeenth century.

The medieval historian Rodney Hilton (b. 1916) took a slightly different tack in the debate that followed. The exploitative social relations of feudalism provided the direct producers – who retained control over their means of production, including the land – -with an incentive to improve the efficiency of their tools. This resulted in organizational changes and the enlargement of disposable surpluses (Hilton 1974, 1976a). He also argued that Dobb's view of feudal class conflict was one-sided, focusing too much attention on the pressures the lords exerted on the peasants and not enough attention on the efforts of the peasants to keep as much of the surplus as possible under the existing circumstances.

> . . . This peasant resistance was of crucial importance in the development of the rural communes, the extension of free tenure and status, the freeing of peasant and artisan economies for the development of commodity production and eventually the emergence of the capitalist entrepreneur (Hilton 1976b:27).

In his summary of the debate in 1962, Eric Hobsbawm pointed out that the transition from feudalism had been a highly uneven development on a world scale.

> The triumph of capitalism occurred fully in one and only one part of the world, and this region in turn transformed the rest. Consequently we have to explain primarily the special reasons which caused this to happen in the Mediterranean-European region and not elsewhere (Hobsbawm 1976:160).

In this view, the rise of industrial capitalism occurred in Western Europe alone because of a long, complex process that did not operate uniformly in every area or in each of the five or six historical phases that extended from the break-up of the Western Roman Empire to the triumph of capitalism during the Industrial Revolution. This 1,000-year span of European history was marked time and again by major crises. During each crisis, the most advanced sections of bourgeois development in Europe – like the Italian and Flemish textile industries, with their capitalist employers and workers in the fourteenth century – collapsed or were overtaken by backward areas – like England.

Thus feudalism was not replaced as a result of some steady unfolding or progression of stages that inevitably led to capitalism. Such a characterization was applicable, in his view, only to a limited extent outside Europe, where there were

> ... certain signs of comparable development under the impetus of the development of the world market after the 16th century, perhaps in the encouragement of textile manufactures in India. But these are more than offset by the *opposite* tendency, namely that which turned the other areas that came into contact with and under the influence of the European powers into dependent economies and colonies of the west. In fact, large parts of the Americas were turned into slave economies to serve the needs of European capitalism, and large parts of Africa were pushed back economically through the slave-trade; large areas of eastern Europe were turned into neo-feudal economies for similar reasons. . . . The net effect of the rise of European capitalism was therefore to intensify uneven development, and to divide the world ever more sharply into two sectors; the 'developed' and the 'under- developed' countries, in other words the exploiting and the exploited (Hobsbawm 1976:163–4).

The Brenner Debate, published in 1985, marked an end of sorts to this aspect of questions regarding the transition from feudalism to capitalism in Europe (Aston and Philpin 1985). In the mid-1970s, the historian Robert Brenner (b. 1943) reasserted Dobb's argument about the primacy of class struggle in the dissolution of feudal relations of production in Europe (Brenner 1985a). Medieval historians responded and variously reaffirmed their belief in the determinant roles played by trade or demography. Brenner (1985b) responded, arguing that the roots of capitalist development in Europe are to be found in class struggles that took place in the countryside. Brenner's argument represents the dialectical strand of Marxist historical thought, which gives primacy to historical contingency and agency in the class struggles that underpin social transformation. Another strand is represented by those scholars who claim that the motor for social change resides in unequal exchange relations between different societies.

Unequal Exchange, World Systems and Modes of Production

During the 1970s and 1980s, Marxist and Third World analysts critiqued, debated, and refined the theories of development and underdevelopment discussed earlier. They considered whether the agricultural sectors of the Third World and even the countries themselves were better described as capitalist, as articulations of different modes of production, or as a distinctive colonial mode of production. They explored the role overseas exchange played in the economic development of former colonies. They investigated how the conditions for capital accumulation were established in the Third World and how capitalism constrained development in those countries (Banerjee 1985).

Two opposing perspectives shaped the terrain of their discussions. One claimed that the impetus for change and development emanated from the capitalist countries, that the world capitalist system actively underdeveloped the Third World countries, and that no development was possible as long as capitalism survived. The other asserted that Third World countries were underdeveloped because of internal class struggles rather than their positions in the world capitalist system. The first emphasized the role of unequal exchange; the second stressed the importance of class structures and capital accumulation.

Ernesto Laclau (b. 1935) disagreed with Frank's assertion that colonial Latin American societies had been capitalist since the sixteenth century. However, if they were not capitalist, then how should they be conceptualized? He argued that the underdevelopment of the region resulted not only from the way the European countries appropriated surplus produced in the colonies, but also from the way they fixed '. . . their relations of production in an archaic mould of extra-economic coercion, which retarded any process of social differentiation and diminished the size of their internal markets' (Laclau 1971:35). The feudal social relations of the region would tend to impede or block capitalist development, even if more surplus were available. While the economic system described by Frank might have been capitalist in the sense that it was shaped by the need for profit and expansion of the productive forces, it also included different non-capitalist modes of production.

Social scientists concerned with rural class structures and forms of surplus extraction in the agricultural sector of modern India also rejected Frank's claim that a satellite became capitalist once it was linked to the world capitalist system through imperialism and unequal exchange (Alavi 1975; McEachern 1976; Patnaik 1972a, b). They argued instead that 'ex-colonial countries like India are characterised precisely by a limited and distorted development of capitalism which does not revolutionise the mode of production' (Patnaik 1971 quoted by A. Thorner 1982:1964). In their view, wage labor and the sale of a large portion of the produce on the market were not, by themselves, sufficient markers of capitalism. What was indispensable was the accumulation and reinvestment of surplus value on an ever-expanding scale – that is, capital intensification and changes toward a higher than average organic composition of capital that would yield greater productivity in land and labor.

While capitalist production was beginning to emerge in Indian agriculture as a result of the 'Green Revolution', the agrarian sector in particular and Indian society as a whole were neither capitalist nor feudal. They were structured instead by a distinctive, colonial mode of production that linked them through market relations to a world capitalist system.

> . . . [C]olonial modes of production were precisely the circuits through which capital was drained out of the colonies in the form of bullion, consumption goods, raw materials

and so on. The financing of primary accumulation outside the colonial world was their chief historical function and it was this fact which determined their peculiar retrograde logic. We can describe this in the following terms: the colonial modes of production transmitted to the colonies the pressures of the accumulation process in the metropolis without releasing any corresponding expansion in the forces of production (Banaji 1972:2500).

While Laclau argued that colonial societies were formed by the combination of capitalist and non-capitalist modes of production, the Indian analysts – Utsa Patnaik and Jairus Banaji, among others – viewed them as the product of a distinctive colonial mode of production that was shaped by unequal exchange. In a sense, they merged Laclau's insights about the distinctiveness of colonial societies with Frank's views about the importance of exchange relations.

The historical sociologist Immanuel Wallerstein (b. 1930) entered the debate in the mid-1970s with a different tack. He argued that there were significant differences between the feudal relations of production in medieval Europe and the feudal-like relations imposed on producers in Latin America by the capitalist world economy in the sixteenth century, which he referred to as forced or coerced cash-crop labor (Wallerstein 1974:126–7). Like Frank and in contrast to Laclau, he began with an analysis of unequal exchange.

In *The Origins of the Modern World System*, Wallerstein (1974, 1980, 1989) pointed out that states never exist in isolation, but rather that they participate in world economies of varying sizes in which each polity is linked to its contemporaries by exchange relations. Economic development was largely impossible in the world economies that existed before the sixteenth century, because the bureaucracies of the constituent states absorbed surplus and effectively precluded its accumulation for productive investment (Brenner 1977:29–33). The crisis of the medieval world economy was resolved when it was dissolved by the formation of a capitalist world economy centered in Western Europe; this occurred around 1500, and coincided with the

> . . . expansion of the geographical size of the world in question, the development of variegated methods of labor control for different products and different zones of the world-economy, and the creation of relatively strong state machineries in what would become the core-states of this capitalist world-economy (Wallerstein 1974:38).

Thus, a capitalist world system forged by the expansion of commerce and maintained by an enforced international division of labor shaped economic structures and directed change. The system as a whole rather than the constituent cultural-political units was the appropriate unit of analysis (Wallerstein 1974:xi).

The states of Northwestern Europe formed the core of the capitalist world system:

By a series of accidents – historical, ecological, geographic – northwest Europe was better situated in the sixteenth century to diversify its agricultural production and add to it certain industries (such as textiles, shipbuilding, and metal wares) than were other parts of Europe. Northwest Europe emerged as the core area of this world-economy, specializing in agricultural production of higher skill levels, which favored . . . tenancy and wage labor as the modes of labor control (Wallerstein 1979:18).

As a result, the states of Northwestern Europe were able to impose regional specialization on production – e.g. sugar in the Caribbean, bullion in the Andes and cereals in Eastern Europe. The increasingly powerful state machines of the core countries that controlled the division of labor were able to consolidate the accumulation of surplus and to ensure that it ultimately flowed into the core region; they were also able to enforce backwardness on the peripheries of Latin America and Eastern Europe and on the semi-periphery of Southern Europe, which had once been a core area but had turned in the direction of the periphery. While wage labor was the predominant form of labor control in Northwestern Europe, forced or coerced labor prevailed in the periphery, and sharecropping was dominant in the semi-periphery.

Semi-peripheries were geographical areas or states that fell between the core and the periphery, because of their in-between forms of labor control (Wallerstein 1974:101–8). They played a different role from the core and periphery, because

In part they act as a peripheral zone for core countries and in part they act as a core country for some peripheral areas. Both their internal politics and their social structure are distinctive, and it turns out that their ability to take advantage of the flexibilities offered by the downturns of economic activity is in general greater than that of either the core or the peripheral countries (Wallerstein 1979:97).

The semi-periphery of the post-war era consisted of states – like Canada, Mexico, Norway, Yugoslavia, the USSR, Saudi Arabia, Israel, Indonesia and the People's Republic of China – that have diverse economic and political regimes. Socialist states – like the USSR or China – had nationalized the means of production, while in others, like Canada, the major means of production were controlled by capitalists.

In Wallerstein's (1979b:117) view, neither the socialist countries nor those of the Third World constituted distinct world systems governed by non-capitalist economic relations. They occupied spaces in a single, hierarchically organized system driven by unequal exchange. The countries of the semi-periphery, both socialist and non-socialist, were sites where significant change would occur.

The political economist Samir Amin (b. 1931) rejected claims that the capitalist countries in the core extracted surplus from the periphery, and that the modern world system was shaped solely by the capitalist mode of production (Higgott 1981:83–5). Instead, the process of capital accumulation has taken place on a global scale in a world divided into a multitude of national societies in which the capitalist mode of production has combined with different precapitalist modes of production (S. Amin 1974; 1976). In his view, the process of accumulation did not produce uniformity across the globe, but rather led to the consolidation of two distinct categories of national societies – center and periphery. In the center, the accumulation process is *autocentric* – i.e. it is self-centered and governed by the internal dynamic described by Marx. Accumulation is *extraverted* in the periphery – i.e. it is dependent on the center-periphery relations and constrained by capitalist production relations. The peripheral societies are based on combinations of capitalist and precapitalist modes of production.

The distinction between the center and periphery had important implications:

> In an autocentric economy, there is an organic relation between the two terms of the social contradiction – bourgeoisie and proletariat – that they are both *integrated* into a single *reality*, the *nation*. In an extraverted economy, this unity of opposites is not to be grasped within the national context – this unity is broken and can only be rediscovered on the world scale. . . . Unequal exchange means that the problem of the class struggle must necessarily be considered on the world scale (S. Amin 1974:599–600, emphasis in the original).

The differences appeared because the countries in the center became capitalist earlier. Initially wages were held close to subsistence levels in both the center and periphery; however, the center gained a lead when wages began to rise in certain economic sectors and the precapitalist modes of production were eliminated. This established a pattern of unequal regional specialization. Unemployment and the continued existence of precapitalist modes of production, which held wages down on the periphery, fueled further unequal specialization and development. While the center was increasingly dominated by capitalist relations of production and reproduction, the societies on the periphery, with their disarticulated economic sectors, were based on combinations of capitalist and non-capitalist modes of production. Here, the capitalist export sectors, which were often foreign-owned, coexisted with various precapitalist modes of production (S. Amin 1980).

Amin focused attention on how different modes of production were combined in societies on the periphery. Since each class- divided mode of production was composed of pair of classes that are simultaneously linked and opposed to one another – e.g. feudal lord with peasant, capitalist with wage worker – peripheral societies that combine different modes of production have complex class structures. These might include, for instance, in a society manifesting tribute-paying and capitalist modes, foreign and national capitalists, feudal landlords, peasants, small commodity producers, merchants and tribal peoples. The class that controls state power and the bureaucracy determines the dominant mode of production, since the state plays a role in the production, accumulation and distribution of surplus in peripheral societies. As a result, class struggles are complex in peripheral societies, because they are taking place both within separate national frameworks and in the context of the world system.

Amin's views about the structure of peripheral societies echoed those of anthropologists concerned with the processes underpinning the development of linkages between capitalist and precapitalist modes of production in Third World countries (Binsbergen and Geschiere 1985; Clammer 1978; Davidson 1989; Goodman and Redclift 1982; Seddon 1978: Taylor 1979). The anthropologists were not concerned with whether particular societies were better described as capitalist, as having dual economies, or as manifestations of a colonial mode of production. They argued that *articulation* was in reality a relation of transformation, which specified the nature of the contradiction between the capitalist and precapitalist modes of production in a particular society as well as the nature of the class struggle they produced as the relations and institutions associated with the once-dominant precapitalist mode are dissolved, transformed, and reintegrated under the emerging dominance of the capitalist mode (Bettelheim 1972; Foster-Carter 1978a, b; Wolpe 1980, 1985).

The French anthropologist Pierre-Philippe Rey portrayed the articulation of capitalist and precapitalist modes of production in terms of a three-stage progression. He considered both the breakdown of feudalism and the rise of capitalism in Europe, and the subsequent linkages of capitalist and precapitalist modes of production in colonial countries. In the first stage, the capitalist and precapitalist modes of production are linked in the sphere of exchange, which reinforces the precapitalist structures. The capitalist mode of production subordinates the precapitalist modes of production after the advent of colonial settlement. In the third stage, the capitalist mode completes the destruction of the precapitalist modes, especially in the agricultural sector; peasant agriculture is transformed and handicrafts are eliminated as a wage-labor force and reserve army of labor are created. Rey further argued that articulation was an inherently violent process, since it destroyed communal social relations, intensified exploitation, and promoted class struggle. The violence of articulation led him to consider the relations between his three-stage scheme and earlier theories of imperialism elaborated by Marx, Lenin and Luxemburg (Rey 1982).

The South African anthropologist Harold Wolpe (1926–96) recommended that social analysts concerned with the process of articulation define the mode of production concept broadly in order to take account of individual production units, how they are linked and brought into relationships with one another, and how the units and their relationships are reproduced and transformed. Wolpe (1980:36) was concerned with other kinds of relations – the production of goods, their circulation and distribution, the market, the process of accumulation, and the role played by the state in securing the conditions required for capitalist accumulation to proceed (Wolpe 1980:36). He focused attention on what happens when different and potentially opposed labor forms, production priorities, and means of distribution are brought together and forcibly interrelated in contexts shaped by political and economic domination.

National Liberation and New Nations

Administrators and anthropologists influenced by Bronislaw Malinowski and A. R. Radcliffe-Brown during the inter-war years believed that social analyses of colonial settings should begin with the tribe, which they saw as the traditional unit of political authority. Colonial rule was only one outside force that impinged on tribal societies in culture contact situations. They focused on the integrative elements of social life, and treated conflict as a social pathology (Worsley 1961).

Nationalist leaders in the colonies believed that the colony itself, rather than the constituent societies and cultures, was the basic unit to which the idea of self-determination should be applied. The colony was a race- and class-stratified power structure dominated by Europeans, who were usually citizens of the metropolitan country or their descendants (Wallerstein 1966: 1–3). Since tribal societies were only one of the groupings that made up colonial society, it was essential to understand their relationship with the metropolitan power and the larger global society as well as with circumstances that were created within and by the colony (Balandier 1966:55; Gluckman 1966).

Nationalist writers were acutely aware of the power of nationalism after the Second World War. For Jawaharlal Nehru (1889–1964), Prime Minister of India, it was '. . . one of the most powerful urges that move a people, and round it cluster sentiments and traditions and a sense of living and common purpose' (Nehru 1946:41). While culture and tradition were arenas in which the struggle for national liberation would be waged, not every class would participate, because the

> . . . [Indian] middle class felt caged and circumscribed and wanted to grow and develop itself. Unable to do so within the framework of British rule, a spirit of revolt grew against this rule, and yet this spirit was not directed against the structure that crushed us. It sought to retain it and control it by displacing the British. These middle classes were too much the product of that structure to challenge it and seek to uproot it (Nehru 1946:45).

Nehru recognized three strands of thought critical of colonial regimes that fueled nationalist sentiments in the post-war years: cultural nationalism, the psycho-pathologies of the colonial experience, and socialism.

Cultural nationalists argued that identities were based on shared personal experiences, suffering, and struggles. The most fully developed cultural nationalist viewpoint after the war was Negritude, which originated in the writings of diasporic Africans, mostly from French West Africa and the French Caribbean, who described their experiences of racism and the subordinate relationships they had with whites in their quest for freedom and personal identity (Irele 1973a, b). They saw colonialism in terms of the relations between individuals or races rather than class structures, imperialism, and exploitation. Certain themes – exile, racial consciousness, alienation, African cultural heritage, and African personality – played prominent roles in the formation of these identities. Exile and the alienation of the colonial situation were oppressive, denying Blacks the capacity to achieve their full self-development and distorting or erasing altogether their true cultural heritage. Cultural nationalist thought appealed largely to the colonial middle classes; it provided a powerful but incomplete explanation for the oppression they felt. Many of the new elites that emerged after independence used cultural nationalism to justify not developing the productive forces or altering the distribution of wealth (McCulloch 1983a:5–9).[8]

In 1947, the French psychoanalyst Octave Mannoni wrote about the psychological effects of the colonial experience on both settlers and indigenous peoples in the wake of an unsuccessful Malagasy rebellion for political independence. He argued that not all people can be colonized, and not all people become colonizers. What was required, in his view, was that the personality type of the subject population was shaped by a dependency complex, while that of the settlers was based on individualism and self-dependency. The combination made European colonialism possible in Madagascar. He portrayed the situation in terms of the two personality types deployed in Shakespeare's *The Tempest*: Prospero, the omnipotent settler who became touchy whenever his authority was even remotely threatened, and Caliban, the slave whom he ruthlessly exploited and the unruly and incorrigible son whom he disowned. For Prospero, Caliban was the scapegoat on whom he projected his own evil intentions. Caliban responded by plotting against Prospero – not to gain his own freedom, but to become the 'foot-licker' of a new master (Mannoni 1964:105–6).

Mannoni's thesis had several implications. The settler mentalities were shaped in Europe rather than in the colonial experience, and the Europeans were drawn to the colony to resolve their own feelings of inferiority by expressing them in a desire for perfection, aggression, and escapism and by projecting them onto the native peoples whom they dominated and controlled. The personality type of the colonized Malagasy, manifested in their dependence on the authority of the dead, already

8. During the civil rights struggles of the 1960s in the United States, various groups – Black separatists, some Puerto Rican *independentistas*, Native Americans, and Chicanos of La Raza Unida, to name only a few – made cultural nationalist claims, which also appealed largely to the more class-conscious petite bourgeoisie, which was constituted in part because of those struggles (Marable 1995:194–5).

existed when the French colonizers arrived. Thus culture was a function of personality, and

> the other characteristic features of a colonial situation – domination of a mass by a minority, economic exploitation, paternalism, racialism, etc. – are either the direct outcome of the relationship between the two peoples, as, for instance, paternalism, or they are distinctly 'colonial' as a result of that relationship (Mannoni 1964:27).

Mannoni (1964:27) further argued that cultural change and acculturation could occur only if

> . . . the personality of the native is first destroyed through uprooting, enslavement, and the collapse of social structure, and this is in fact what happened – with debatable success – in the older colonies [like the French Antilles, which had been a slave-based society] (Mannoni 1964:27).

This meant isolating individuals from their natal communities and raising them in ways that allowed them to acquire a European personality or to superimpose one on their Malagasy personality. If they repressed their Malagasy personality, they sought out the company of Europeans but were not accepted as their equals. Since these individuals were uncomfortable in both societies, this only heightened their awareness of racial differences. Europeanized Malagasy who failed to integrate the European traits into their own personality grew increasingly resentful and hostile and were the ones who fomented and led the revolt (Mannoni 1964:74–80).

In the 1950s, the Martiniquan psychiatrist Frantz Fanon (1925–61), whose views were shaped by the Algerian struggles for independence, also examined the psychopathological underpinnings and consequences of the colonial situation. He was influenced by and critical of Mannoni's work. There was '. . . a connection between colonialism as a pathogenic social system and the incidence of mental disorders found among colonized peoples' (McCulloch 1983a:90). When the colonizers seized the productive forces and subordinated the indigenous population, conditions were created that led to the distortion and deformation of the personality and culture of both the colonized community and the settlers (Fanon 1967a:18, b; McCulloch 1983a:125). Fanon linked these conditions to the form racism took during different stages of colonial domination. When the colonists had just established their presence by force, they dehumanized native peoples and claimed their subordination was rooted in some physiological inferiority. After skilled indigenous peoples had been incorporated into the lower levels of the state apparatus, the colonizers claimed that the subordination of the natives was due to the inferiority of their culture. By contrast with Mannoni, Fanon believed that racism, exploitation, personality and other features of the colonial experience were forged in the colonial situation.

The colonial situation involved the suppression of the indigenous culture – the denigration of its traditional foods, dress, music, practices and beliefs, which gave meaning to everyday life. This affected the indigenous middle classes, the peasants, and the beggars, prostitutes and unemployed people who in different ways constituted lumpenproletariat. The members of the native middle class – the schoolteachers, policemen, government workers and shopkeepers – accepted the devaluation of the indigenous culture in order to acquire and maintain their position in the colonial society. Tragically, they came to see themselves, their kin and neighbors through the eyes of the colonizer; the result was the despair and self-loathing of the colonized middle classes. Alienated from the colonial society and mistrustful of its authority, the peasants and the lumpenproletariat withdrew into traditionalism in order to preserve some of the originality of their native culture; however, in the process, they were often unable to distinguish between the harmful aspects of the imperialist culture and those that might be beneficial – such as Western medicine – or lacked the opportunity to make use of them. The cultural withdrawal of the peasants and the lumpenproletariat and the oppositional national cultural identity they maintained made them, not the educated middle classes as Mannoni claimed, the potentially revolutionary classes in colonial situations (Fanon 1965:51, 1967c:101).

In *The Wretched of the Earth*, which was published in 1961, Fanon investigated the role national culture played in colonized societies and, more importantly, in struggles for national liberation. While colonialism actively distorted and destroyed the cultural traditions of colonized peoples, nationalism rehabilitated the idea of a national consciousness, promoted social unity, and provided hope for the creation of a national culture in the future. Nationalism could trigger anti-colonial struggles; however, if national consciousness did not acquire a social dimension after liberation, there was a very real danger that the history of repression and poverty of the colonial era would be repeated, especially if the national middle classes were able to seize power. In Fanon's (1967c:122) view, they would act as a '. . . transmission line between the nation and a capitalism, rampant though camouflaged, which today puts on the mask of neo-colonialism'.

Marxism in various forms also shaped post-war discussions of national liberation. Guinean agronomist Amílcar Cabral (1924–73) was one of its most articulate, influential spokesmen (Chabal 1983; Chilcote 1991; McCulloch 1983b). Cabral argued that people had a right to their own history, but that imperialism, colonialism, and neo-colonialism had interrupted the history of Third World peoples and impeded the formation of national consciousness and independence.[9] National liberation

9. Neo-colonialism, in Cabral's (1969:73) view, was the strategy of a post-Second World War phase of imperialism, characterized by monopoly capital and multinational corporations:

Neocolonialism is at work on two fronts – in Europe as well as in the underdeveloped countries. Its current framework in the underdeveloped countries is the policy of aid, and one of the essential

was the way they could recover their interrupted history. Once they regained control over their mode of production, they could overcome the condition of being a people without history (Cabral 1979:143).

Class structures, according to Cabral (1969:56–75), expressed the relation of various groups to the dominant pattern of ownership of productive wealth. The class structure of Guinea-Bissau was complex. There were four classes in the urban areas: a small class composed of high-ranking state officials and professionals; the petite bourgeoisie, made up of low-level officials, shopkeepers, and wage workers; a third consisting of workers without contracts, such as domestic servants or people employed in workshops; and *déclassés* – individuals from the petite bourgeoisie who did not work, peasants who had recently been uprooted from the countryside and the lumpenproletariat. The class structures were different among the twenty tribal groups in the countryside, ranging from the semi-feudal, class-stratified Fula to the primitive communism of Balanta society, where social stratification and ranking based on differential of wealth and privilege were absent, land was owned by the village, and day-to-day decisions were made by a council of elders.

Culture was the vital element in the process of national liberation, since colonial systems repressed the cultural life of colonized peoples. Culture was a product of the relationship between people and nature, on the one hand, and among people, on the other. It was a result of the tensions within economic and political activities. It provided individuals with a sense of identity that told them who they were in their own social milieu and how they were similar to and different from other people. While culture could not be deduced solely from class relations, any change in those relations would alter not only an individual's sense of himself but also the whole system of identities that had been forged and reproduced (Cabral 1973: 40–5; McCulloch 1983b:84–6).

The colonial system had different effects on the cultures of the various urban classes and tribal societies. In Cabral's view, the peasants retained a vibrant cultural life, since the colonizers had been unable to inhibit the cultural activity of the rural populations. As a result, their culture could serve as a basis for new forms of resistance to colonial domination. However, the tribal divisions in the countryside were a problem that could be overcome by proper political mobilization and organization. On the one hand, Fula chieftains resisted the idea of national liberation, because it would undermine their authority in the cultural realm; but Fula peasants who were exploited by their chiefs cooperated with the nationalists. On the other

---

aims of this policy is to create a false bourgeoisie to put a brake on the revolution and to enlarge the possibilities of the petty bourgeoisie as a neutraliser of the revolution; at the same time it invests capital in France, Italy, Belgium, England, and so on. In our opinion, the aim of this is to stimulate the growth of a workers' aristocracy, to enlarge the field of action of the petty bourgeoisie so as to block the revolution.

hand, the peasants of the stateless ethnic groups, like the Balanta, readily joined the nationalists, because they were acutely aware of how the colonial economy had already disrupted their own agricultural practices.

But the impetus for national liberation in Guinea-Bissau would come from the urban petite bourgeoisie, because its members were most acutely aware of the limitations on their privileges in the colonial system.

> The *petite bourgeoisie* is a new class created by foreign domination and indispensable to the operation of colonial exploitation. It is located between the working masses of the countryside and of the cities on the one hand, and on the other the local representatives of the foreign ruling classes. . . . The *petite bourgeoisie* usually aspires to emulate the life of the foreign minority while at the same time reducing its links with the masses. . . . But it can never integrate itself into the foreign minority however successful it might have been at overcoming the colonial hurdles. It is a prisoner of the cultural and social contradictions imposed on it by the colonial reality, which defines it as a marginal or marginalised class (Cabral quoted by Chabal 1983:174).

The weakness of the colonial system was that it engendered nationalism among the class it created to serve as collaborators. Thus, the major contradiction was between the colonized people as a nation-class and the colonial state. Nationalist movements required unity, and their leaders came from the urban petite bourgeoisie. The reason for this was the poorly developed, embryonic character of the native working class in Portuguese Guinea. For the revolution to succeed, the petite bourgoisie had to be capable of committing suicide as a class in order to be reborn as revolutionary workers (Cabral 1969:89).

Peasant men and women who had emigrated to the cities and who had ties with the petite bourgeoisie were an important group in national liberation movements. They carried political mobilization into the rural areas from which they came – areas where cultural traditions remained strong and the colonizers had been unable to inhibit the activity of the subject population (Chabal 1983:174–5). While the cultural traditions of the rural areas would be models for new economic, social, and political forms of resistance to challenge foreign domination, they would ultimately be crafted and implemented by the petite bourgeoisie (Chilcote 1991: 28–31).

Nationalist writers realized the importance of national cultures. Fanon and Cabral, for instance, recognized that peasants had important roles to play in national liberation movements. In Fanon's view, they played a leading role; in Cabral's, while they provided linkages and their cultures provided models, the urban petite bourgeoisie was the leading class in revolutionary nationalist movements, because its members were most aware of how limited their privileges were in the colonial system. The creative capacities and revolutionary potential of peasants in national liberation movements will be examined further in the next section.

Once nationalist movements succeeded, they had to confront the effects of primordial attachments on the constitution of the new civic or national identity (Geertz 1963b). These were the culturally assumed 'givens' of social existence – ethnicity, tribe, race, language, region, culture, or religion – that shaped the search for identity and the demands that those identities be acknowledged publicly in the new states. They were unleashed by the same forces that buttressed movements for political independence. They could be a motor for progress, rising standards of living, and a more effective political order; at the same time, they could impede or block the creation of new civic identities and values. As a result, school systems, social statistics, dress, official histories, and the official symbols of public authority often became sites of contestation between the traditional givens of social existence and the newly constituted civic values of the state.

It was often difficult to dissolve the tensions between primordial identities and civic politics. Nevertheless, some new states attempted to domesticate culturally prescribed identities instead of belittling them or denying their existence by aggregating primordial groups into larger, more diffuse units so that their governments could proceed without threatening the cultural frameworks that underpinned the issue of personal identity and without seriously distorting the political functioning of the state bureaucracy (Geertz 1963b).

Rural Development, Social Revolution and Peasant Communities

Rural communities appeared again at center stage in the post-war years. The role they had played in underwriting industrial development in Europe, the USSR, and Third World countries like Mexico was increasingly understood and endorsed as a viable strategy of economic and political development. By the time the Chinese Communists took power in 1949, peasantries were appreciated as potential forces of revolutionary change. This led ruling classes and progressive forces in a number of countries – e.g. Guatemala, Bolivia, and South Korea – to recognize the importance of land reform and a more equitable distribution of income and wealth as conditions for maintaining or transforming the existing balance of forces in those states. It also meant that social scientists, especially those from Europe and the Third World, began to pay attention to peasant communities and how they were integrated into national structures.

Peasantries perplexed liberal and Marxist theorists of change and development who predicted that the rural class structures would eventually disappear as industrialization progressed. What perplexed them was that peasant communities, the majority of the world's population, were not disappearing in various countries. For these theorists, this meant that there was a crisis – the rural production systems had been knocked out of kilter by the Second World War, colonialism, or the threat of socialist revolution. In this context,

The agrarian question was not only a set of political and economic questions, however; at another level, it was a political question that was given a primarily economic answer. To know who the peasants were and how they would act in a political upheaval, or how they could be incorporated within an urban-directed socialist movement, one had to analyze their class position, their role and fate in capitalist development, their relation to the state (Roseberry 1993:336).

In the process of analyzing rural class structures and their relation to national structures, social scientists slowly realized that they did not understand rural life.

While the anthropologist Robert Redfield (1955), whose work was discussed in the last chapter, was one of the first to study rural communities, he did not, in fact, use the concept of peasant until the mid-1950s. Up to that time, he referred to the non-literate peasant and tribal peoples in rural areas as 'folk'. He contrasted their lives and cultures with the urban values, beliefs, and social relations of city-dwellers (Redfield 1962e:176).

The anthropologist Sidney W. Mintz (b. 1922) challenged the utility of Redfield's folk–urban continuum. While he agree that typological characterizations were useful, the rural proletarian communities of the hennequen plantations that formed the backbone of the Yucatecan economy were not a social type that Redfield discussed. They were, in effect, outside the folk–urban continuum altogether. For Mintz, the plantations and the rural proletariats associated with them were a form of industrial organization, and that was an integral feature of modern urban society. The rural proletarians were '. . . a class isolate, its existence predicated on the existence of other classes who own the instruments of production, provide work opportunities, pay the wages, and sell the commodities to be bought' (Mintz 1953:141). They were molded by the same social forces that shaped urban societies, and their connections with wider structures needed to be investigated empirically, comparatively, and historically (Wolf and Mintz 1957; Rubin 1959).

The anthropologist Eric R. Wolf (b. 1923) examined these questions in comparative studies of closed corporate and open peasant communities (Wolf 1955, 1956, 1957). The members of closed corporate communities, like those found throughout the highlands of Latin America, were agricultural producers who retained effective control over their land through ownership, undisputed squatter rights, or customary rental or use agreements. They were concerned mainly with subsistence rather than agriculture as a business that required continual reinvestment. The closed corporate communities were formed during the colonial period, when peasantries were integrated into colonial structures in ways that inhibited direct contact between them and the outside world (Wolf 1955:456). These communities were often characterized as 'Indian'. The persistence of Indian cultural forms both shaped and depended on the maintenance and reproduction of the structural identity of the closed corporate community. The members of closed corporate communities defended the traditional rights and customs that perpetuated those subsistence imperatives and usages that protected them from memories of famine, risk, and the market.

The members of open communities engaged in the production of coffee, cocoa, and other cash crops for the market. Fifty to 75 per cent of their produce was sold in the market. As a result, their livelihoods were subject to fluctuations in market demand for the crops they grew, and they continually needed capital to invest in their businesses. The landowning middle peasants of the open communities had continuous interactions with the outside through the capitalist market. Their fortunes were tied to the larger market-based structures of which they were a part.

For Wolf (1955:466–8), ethnographic information, scanty as it was in the 1950s, suggested his preliminary survey of peasant types did not exhaust the diversity of the peasantries found in Latin America. He suggested the existence of other types: those who produced entirely for the market, those who sold their goods in local markets, those whose holdings were residual bits of earlier large-scale organizations, foreign colonists, and those who lived on the margins of capitalist markets and sold portions of their crops to obtain goods they could not produce for themselves. He also examined how the different types of peasantries were linked with wider national economic and political structures. In the process, he viewed peasants as rural cultivators whose surplus production was transferred to a politically dominant group as tribute or rent, and distinguished peasants from farmers, for whom agriculture was a business enterprise, and from tribal peoples, for whom agriculture was about subsistence and surplus to be exchanged with other groups (Wolf 1966:2–10; Mintz 1973).

Wolf and Mintz built on the Marxist tradition of class analysis. They did not view all peasantries as exploited producers left over from some precapitalist system of production, nor did they see them as a class that was disappearing in the wake of the expansion of capitalist social relations. They argued instead that the class structures and social relations of the more open-ended types of peasantries and rural proletarian communities were forged in the context of the expansion of capitalist market relations. They distinguished the theoretical underpinnings of their work from other approaches to understanding peasant societies. Their work can also be seen as a critique of the other approaches.

However, there were also other understandings of peasant communities at the time. Redfield's folk–urban continuum, which was the dominant one, was heavily influenced by the traditional–modern dichotomy employed by Durkheim and his generation. It viewed cultural change in terms of increasing complexity resulting from increased communication between folk communities and modern city-dwellers. George Foster (1967) argued that peasants were the rural representatives of earlier national traditions whose inertia prevented them from modernizing, industrializing, and adopting the modern, urban standards of rationality that would ultimately lead to their dissolution. A third approach built on Chayanov's (1986a, b) ahistorical theories of peasant farm organization and non-capitalist economic systems, which sought to show how autonomous family farms generated peasant social structures at the local level and dual economies at the national level (Shanin 1971:291–3; Silverman 1979).

One consequence of the intensification of armed conflict in Vietnam in the mid-1960s was that social scientists began to explore the relationship between peasants and social revolution. These efforts were important, because they paid close attention to the historical specificity and particularities of different cases at the same time that they attempted to provide empirically grounded generalizations about peasant wars.

The earliest was the sociologist Hamsa Alavi's (b. 1921) comparative study of '. . . the respective rôles of the so-called *middle peasants* and *poor peasants* and the pre-conditions that . . . are necessary for the revolutionary mobilization of the *poor peasants*' (Alavi 1965:243, emphasis in the original). He argued that the peasantries in Russia, China, and India were internally differentiated and that rich, middle, and poor peasants did not stand in a single hierarchical order, but rather belonged to three different sectors of the rural economy. In the first sector, the land owned by landlords was worked by sharecroppers – i.e. poor peasants. In the second, middle peasants owned the land they cultivated and did not rely on the labor of others. The third sector was constituted by capitalist farmers – i.e. rich peasants – who owned substantial amounts of land and relied on the waged work of a rural proletariat rather than sharecroppers or tenants (Alavi 1965:243–4).

Alavi's analysis of the literature available in the mid-1960s led him to conclude that the poor peasants were initially the least militant of the peasant classes, because they and their families were totally dependent on particular landlords for their livelihood and were often enmeshed in paternalistic patron–client relations. However,

> . . . this backwardness of the [poor] peasantry, rooted as it is in objective dependence, is only a relative and not an absolute condition. In a revolutionary situation, when anti-landlord and anti-rich-peasant sentiment is built up by, say, the militancy of the middle peasants, his morale is raised and he is ready to respond to calls to action. . . .
>
> The middle peasants, on the other hand, are initially the most militant element of the peasantry, and they can be a powerful ally of the proletarian movement in the countryside, especially in generating the initial impetus of peasant revolution. But their social perspective is limited by their class position. When the movement in the countryside advances to a revolutionary stage they may move away from the revolutionary movement unless their fears are allayed and they are drawn into a process of co-operative endeavour (Alavi 1965:275).

Thus, unlike Maoists, Alavi argued that the middle peasants were initially the leading force and then the main force of revolutionary change in the countryside, and further that, once the success of the revolution was no longer in doubt, their position was taken over by the poor peasants, whose revolutionary energies were set in motion by the militancy of the landowning middle peasants.

In *Peasant Wars of the Twentieth Century*, Eric Wolf (1969:295) remarked that the 'peasant rebellions of the twentieth century are no longer simple responses to local problems. . . . They are . . . parochial reactions to major social dislocations, set in motion by major societal changes' associated with the spread of Western capitalism, markets, and capitalist economic rationality. The intrusion of capitalism upset traditional social relations and ways of making a living, as well as the balance of force. As peasants lost control over their lands and were transformed into '. . . economic actors, independent of prior social commitments to kin and neighbors', a crisis in the exercise of power emerged (Wolf 1969:279). Peasant revolutions were one possible response to the crisis provoked by social change, and sometimes crystallized in these circumstances.

These revolutions, in Wolf's view, were launched by landholding peasants who had material and organizational advantages that sharecropping poor peasants and rural proletarians lacked. Since they controlled the disposal of their crops and were outside the direct control of landlords, they were neither as poor nor as vulnerable to repression as the poor peasants and rural waged workers. It was the middle peasants and tenants in villages outside the direct control of landlords, as well as the free peasants in frontier areas where landlords and state authorities exercised indirect and/or intermittent control at best, who possessed tactical advantages during these transitional phases. Furthermore, the middle peasant who remained on the land while he sent his children to town to work was also more exposed to the influences of the urban proletariat. As a result, he became the transmitter of urban unrest and political ideas. It was his attempt '. . . to remain traditional which makes him revolutionary' (Wolf 1969:292).

In Wolf's (1969:294) view, the battlefield of peasant revolutions in the twentieth century was society itself.

> Where the peasantry has successfully rebelled against the established order – under its own banner and with its own leaders – it was sometimes able to reshape the social structure of the countryside closer to its heart's desires; but it did not lay hold of the state, of the cities which house the centers of control, of the strategic nonagricultural resources of the society. . . . Thus a peasant rebellion which takes place in a complex society already caught up in commercialization and industrialization tends to be self-limiting, and, hence, anachronistic (Wolf 1969:294).

The peasant's role in these revolutions is both tragic and hopeful: tragic in the sense that '. . . his efforts to undo a grievous present only usher in a vaster, more uncertain future', and hopeful to the extent that '. . . theirs is the party of humanity' (Wolf 1969:301–2).

The historical sociologist Barrington Moore (b. 1913) examined the patterns of social relations that facilitated or suppressed peasant rebellion during the transformation from agrarian to industrial society. His thesis was that: 'The ways in which the landed upper classes and the peasants reacted to the challenge of commercial agriculture were decisive factors in determining the political outcome' (Moore 1966:xvii). The transformation from agrarian to industrial society proceeded along three different roads. Parliamentary democracies – England, France, and the United States – were the end-product of one route. They originated in instances in which the peasants were unable to resist successfully the efforts of the landed upper classes to promote commercialized agriculture and to benefit along with capitalist merchants and industrialists from the operation of markets in both the towns and the countryside. Fascism was the end-product of the second road; it appeared in Germany and Japan, because the capitalist groups in those countries were unable to challenge the landlord class, which held state power, and the social structure of the peasantry prevented the tenants, sharecroppers, and smallholders from mounting effective opposition. Communism in Russia and China was the end-product of the third road. Since the capitalist merchant and industrialist classes were weak, their repression and exploitation of the peasants could not stem the growth of peasant movements and rebellions.

Moore examined the interplay of factors that affected or altered the balance of force in particular historical instances. He argued that:

> ... the most important causes of peasant revolutions have been the absence of a commercial revolution in agriculture led by the landed upper classes and the concomitant survival of peasant social institutions into the modern era when they are subject to new stresses and strains. Where the peasant community survives, as in Japan, it must remain closely linked to the dominant class in the countryside if revolution is to be avoided. Hence an important contributing cause of peasant revolution has been the weakness of the institutional links binding peasant society to the upper classes, together with the exploitative character of this relationship. Part of the general syndrome has been the regime's loss of the support of an upper class of wealthy peasants because these have begun to go over to more capitalist modes of cultivation and to establish their independence against an aristocracy seeking to maintain its position through the intensification of traditional obligations, as in eighteenth-century France. When these conditions have been absent or reversed, peasants revolts have failed to break out or have been easily suppressed.
>
> The great agrarian bureaucracies of royal absolutism including China, have been especially liable to the combination of factors favoring peasant revolution. Their very strength enables them to inhibit the growth of an independent commercial and manufacturing class. . . . By taming the bourgeoisie, the crown reduces the impetus toward further modernization. . . . Furthermore, an agrarian bureaucracy, through its heavy demands for taxes, risks driving the peasants into an alliance with local élites in the

towns. . . . Finally, to the extent that it takes over the protective and judicial functions of the locally residing overlord, royal absolutism weakens the crucial links that the peasants to the upper classes (Moore 1966:477–9).

Moore examined the shifting relations within the entire class structure rather than those that affected mainly the rural classes. Peasant social structures did not always underpin effective forms of resistance. However, in the route leading to communism, the forces promoting the development of commercial agriculture and labor-repressive forms of agricultural exploitation were weak; as a result, peasants were able to mobilize and to collaborate with workers in affecting the structural transformation of Russia and China. Thus, *The Social Origins of Dictatorship and Democracy* extends the analyses of Alavi and Wolf by providing a clearer indication of the circumstances in which peasants were able to mobilize successfully against state-based structures of power.

Discussion

The Second World War weakened capitalism on a world scale. The industrial economies of most capitalist states were destroyed or badly damaged, and the power of the imperial centers over their colonial possessions was more limited than it had been a decade or so earlier. The appearance of socialist states in Eastern Europe and China, of civil wars, and of national liberation movements in a host of colonial countries further challenged their hegemony. The consequences and implications of these conditions demanded explanation and the formulation of plans.

Social analysts responded with richly textured theories of change and development in the post-war decades to account for the post-war conditions. Western arguments that proclaimed the superiority of capitalism, that portrayed capitalist growth as natural and equally beneficial to all, and that construed colonialism as benevolence, a burden to be assumed by the advanced countries, no longer had the explanatory power they had once held. New explanations of change and development ultimately had to take cognizance of nationalist sentiments and of rural communities as potential agents.

The economic growth and modernization theorists were boosters of capitalist development. They reiterated evolutionist accounts that proclaimed or implied that capitalism was the natural outcome of processes inherent in the core of society and that it could be promoted by investing either in the economic base or in groups whose members would benefit materially by its development. With sufficient investment and incentives, all countries would eventually converge and resemble the industrial capitalist states of the West, and their citizens would come to enjoy Western patterns of mass consumption.

The dependency theorists of Latin America recognized clearly that convergence had not and would not take place between the developed capitalist countries of the First World and the underdeveloped, economically dependent countries of the Third World given the political-economic conditions that were crystallizing rapidly in the post-war years. The economies of their countries were less like those of the First World than they had been forty or fifty years earlier. They recognized earlier and more clearly than most that not all countries benefited from capitalist development, and that the circumstances of the economically backward countries of the Third World were a consequence of unequal exchange. Moreover, the underdevelopment of vast portions of the world was, in fact, an integral, necessary feature of capitalist development itself.

From the 1970s onwards, world systems theorists have argued unequal exchange relations have shaped the world economy since the 1500s, dividing it into a core region where capital accumulation occurs, a vast periphery that produces surplus, and a semi-periphery that accumulates capital from parts of the periphery and produces it for the metropoles. The fundamental divisions in the world, from this perspective, are conceptualized less in terms of the capitalist countries, the socialist states, or the Third World than in terms of a position in a single world economy. In the process, the world systems theorists acknowledge the fundamental insight of the dependency writers: capitalist development has taken different trajectories in different parts of the world.

In spite of some obvious differences, these theorists of capitalist development held remarkably similar ideas about society and change (Brenner 1977). For the growth theorists, the development of the productive forces intensified agricultural production, which underwrote population growth and a steadily expanding division of labor, which, in turn, promoted exchange between groups producing more diverse and more specialized goods. Supervisors emerged to manage the production, distribution, and exchange of surplus in this increasingly complex social system. Once markets were established, the natural differences that existed between individuals, groups, or regions surfaced and inequality followed. The modernization theorists agreed, but argued that such inequalities would be diminished by the capitalist industrial development, urbanization, mass consumption, and convergence that would follow as a result.

Writers whose points of view were shaped by their experiences in ex-colonies or Third World countries rather than the capitalist states produced diverse explanations for a different set of concerns. These ranged from conceptualizing the social and political-economic structures of Third World countries to exploring the class structures, social relations, and conditions that would promote the success of national liberation movements. While some accepted the arguments of the theory of dual economies, others did not. The dependency theorists claimed that the economic structures of the colonial countries in Latin America had been capitalist since the sixteenth century, but that they were not quite the same as the structures that appeared in the core countries of the West. The theorists of articulation argued that these structures represented linkages between capitalist and precapitalist modes of production that were reproduced and developed over time. Theorists of colonial modes of production suggested that the social forms of the Third World countries are distinctive and do not represent the co-existence of capitalist and precapitalist social relations. Theorists realized that these historically contingent situations resembled in some general way the transition from feudalism to capitalism that had already occurred or was then taking place in Europe.

The critics of colonial rule stressed the need for decolonization and the right of a people to proclaim their national autonomy and independence – that every nation should have its own territory was the argument of the day. However, since the vast majority of the world's population were peasants or tribal peoples who lived in the countryside, nationalist movements repeatedly took cognizance of their sentiments. In China, the revolutionary nationalists were in fact from the countryside rather than the cities, and theorists as diverse as Fanon and Cabral pointed to the revolutionary potential of peasants and the importance of rural cultures as reservoirs for new forms of resistance. As a consequence, rural class structures and social relations were investigated in order to ascertain which rural classes were revolutionary and under what circumstances their revolutionary potential might be unleashed.

In the final chapter, we will consider the relationship between imperialism and globalization, and explore more fully globalization's relationships with states and its role in the dissolution of socialism. We will also examine transformations of rural class structures and the emergence of both nationalist and identity social movements in the late twentieth century. We will conclude with a brief assessment of postmodern and postcolonial efforts to explain these developments.

Globalization and Postmodernity

A severe economic and political crisis has racked most of the world's population since the mid-1970s, when industrial production in the developed capitalist countries dropped 10 per cent in a single year. The economic crashes of the 1970s and 1980s were as deep and widespread as the Great Depression of the 1930s. Economic growth has yet to reappear in much of Africa and Latin America; its absence has left nearly a billion people destitute and driven millions of others to the brink of abject poverty. When economic growth did reappear in the developed capitalist countries in the mid-1980s, it occurred at a much slower rate than before, except for a time in the newly industrialized countries of East Asia, which are now experiencing the crisis for the first time. The extent of the breakdown became apparent in the Soviet Union and the socialist countries of Eastern Europe in the late 1980s and early 1990s, when industrial production fell more than 20 per cent and national currencies collapsed. The political dimensions of the crisis were particularly apparent in Eastern Europe: State machines were dismantled; states disintegrated; and there was a resurgence of nationalism, ethnic conflict and civil wars (Hobsbawm 1994: 404–8).

The slowing rate of economic growth and the political crises it spawned have been accompanied and exacerbated by a restructuring of the world economy. This involved the proliferation of interlocked banking and business corporations that transcend national boundaries and increasingly regulate the accumulation of capital on a world scale. These transnational firms have forced national states to focus their attention on financial policies and debt collection, to assume responsibility on occasion for the private debts of the corporations, and to reduce through balanced budgets and structural adjustments the health care, retirement, social services and other benefits that citizens won from the states through ongoing struggles. This economic restructuring has led to the steadily increasing concentration of wealth in the hands of fewer and fewer individuals; as a result, the inequitable distribution of wealth that exists now is probably greater than it has been at any time in the last two centuries (Chossudovsky 1997a).

The current crisis, according to critic István Mészáros (b. 1930), has a number of features that distinguish it from earlier ones.

The historical novelty of today's crisis is manifest under four main aspects: 1. its character is universal rather than restricted to one particular sphere . . .; 2. its scope is truly global rather than confined to a particular set of countries; 3. its time scale is extended, continuous . . . rather than limited and cyclic; 4. its mode of unfolding might be called creeping – in contrast to the more spectacular and dramatic eruptions and collapses of the past . . . (Mészáros 1995:680–1).

The current crisis does indeed have new features – e.g. concerns about the destruction of ecosystems, the depletion of natural resources, and the transformation of the environment (Harvey 1996:120–206), However, many features are old familiar ones: imperialism, the accumulation of capital, nationalism, the agrarian question and the state as an agent of change.

Globalization or the Internationalization of Capitalism?

Since the mid-1980s, various analysts have claimed that the existing theories of change and development were no longer able to explain what was happening in the world (Booth 1985; Kiely 1994). While earlier phases in the internationalization of capitalism had involved imperialism and the relocation of production, the processes of globalization now taking place were transforming manufacturing, trade, and services within a global system. Transnational (multinational) corporations operating in a number of countries pursued the maximization of growth and profits across national frontiers. The rapid development of global financial markets in the 1980s as well as the adoption of strategies of flexible specialization and accumulation by these firms, buttressed by the emergence of the new information technologies and cheap transportation, were driving the globalization of the capitalist economy (Martinussen 1997:120).

Economic interdependence and interpenetration at a global level were merely two facets of the globalization process (Robertson 1991:282–3). The process was a much more pervasive one that also involved the consolidation of a new world order, new conceptions about the form of the global society that was emerging, and new ideas about what it means to be human in a world where culturally distinct communities that were once separated by distance have begun to interact with one another in regular, institutionalized ways (Lechner 1991). As important as the internationalization of finance and plant relocations were the movements of people as migrants, refugees, and tourists and the flows of images and information associated with global media and telecommunications.

Globalization, from this perspective, is also the spread of capitalist culture – i.e. the coming of modernity – to parts of the world that were previously underdeveloped. It blurred the distinction between the advanced, developed nations and their formerly undeveloped neighbors who have only recently begun to made the transition from backwardness to modernity. The modern world is steadily shrinking; it is being compressed into a global village, where the universalism and cosmopolitanism of capitalist modernity, as well as the aims and practices of the transnational corporations and states that control telecommunications and the media and dictate political-economic strategies, confront diverse local institutions, practices and discourses shaped by tradition. Both the global forces and the local cultural forms are reworked in the wake of these confrontations but not in the same ways (Giddens 1990; Gilroy 1993; Hall 1991; Nonini and Ong 1997; Pred and Watts 1992).

The process of globalization was launched during the economic crisis of the early 1970s, when transnational corporations adopted new strategies and more flexible forms of capital accumulation to remedy declining productivity and profitability (Hymer 1976). Early efforts to explain globalization focused mainly on the actions of the firms that were implemented about the same time that new export-oriented industrial economies were emerging in East Asia – i.e. Taiwan, South Korea, Hong Kong and Singapore.

The productivity of large-scale industrial enterprises manufacturing standardized, mass-produced goods slowed in core capitalist countries like the United States during the late 1960s. As fewer consumers purchased the commodities they produced, their profit rates also declined. Transnational corporations did not increase wages, and hence buying power, to create greater demand and a larger domestic market for their goods, because this would have adversely affected their already falling rates of profit. Instead, they closed factories with unionized workforces and outdated equipment in core industrial areas like Pennsylvania and opened modern production facilities in previously non-industrialized areas like the southern United States or in Third World countries, where tax incentives, subsidies, and the existence of large, unorganized reserve armies of labor ensured low wages and opportunities to maximize profits (Fröbel, Heinrichs and Kreye 1977, 1980).

The relocation of production facilities to new sites produced a *new international division of labor*. The effects of such actions varied significantly from one country or region to another and between different economic sectors. They led to deindustrialization and rising unemployment in old industrial areas like the British Midlands and the northern United States. The factories and assembly plants established along the US–Mexico border and in countries with small populations like Barbados or Singapore drew employees from reserve armies of labor and underwrote massive social and cultural changes in the areas that supplied and reproduced the labor force. The effects of the new international division of labor were hardly felt in vast parts of sub-Saharan Africa. The relocation of production facilities occurred mainly in industries like clothing or electronics, where increased mechanization was difficult or impossible given the existing technologies (Herold and Kozlov 1987; Jenkins 1984:43).

Sociologists Michael Piore and Charles Sabel (1984) offered a second explanation to account for the changes that occurred in the 1970s and 1980s: the organization of production shifted from an ideal system based on mass production to one based on craft production or *flexible specialization*. That is, mass production that involved the manufacture of large numbers of standardized items using special-purpose machinery and unskilled labor was replaced by a system of craft production that involved the manufacture of a wide variety of customized goods by skilled, adaptable workers using general-purpose machinery. The transnational firms intro-duced flexible forms of work organization, employment, and technology; they employed technical advances in computers and telecommunications to coordinate production with the maintenance of small inventories; and they decentralized manufacturing processes in ways that often linked highly efficient, hi-tech produc-tion systems with more traditional labor practices such as sweatshops or putting out systems (Harvey 1989:189–97). Flexible specialization developed, because the system of mass production had reached the limits of expansion. The markets for standardized goods were saturated and were giving way to fragmented markets that catered to rapidly changing demands for a greater variety of goods produced in smaller batches (Hirst and Zeitlin 1991:2).

Industrial regions like Tuscany or the Silicon Valley were seemingly built on flexibility. They used computers, robotics and other technological innovations to engage in specialized craft production for rapidly changing markets. They combined these with flexible forms of work organization, like flextime or team approaches, and with flexibility in employment that allowed managers to shift the size and composition of their workforces during the business cycle – i.e. to differentiate between the small core of technically skilled workers and the larger, peripheral workforce whose unskilled members were disposable (Curry 1993:100–1; Pollert 1988).

Social analysts focused on the new international division of labor and flexible specialization were concerned with the historical contingency of particular practices and their effects on localities or regions in a capitalist world economy. They were not concerned with the capitalist world economy as a totality or with structural transformations of that totality. However, other social analysts saw the changes they described as aspects of an epoch-making shift of global magnitude in the capitalist mode of production.

For some, the economic and social changes of the 1970s and 1980s marked a *global shift from Fordist to post-Fordist capitalism* (Harvey 1989; Lash and Urry 1987). In this perspective, the post-war capitalist world was dominated by Fordism – i.e. the manufacture of large quantities of standardized goods for mass markets in large factories located in urban areas, which took advantage of economies of scale and employed mostly male workers on a continuous, full-time basis. Fordist production was sustained by the continued existence of mass markets and by Keynesian economic policies that stabilized the production system and enabled the capitalist class to exploit its full potential (Hirst and Zeitlin 1991:9–14).[1] The shift to a post-Fordist society occurred because of changes in the market, when the demand for standardized mass-produced goods diminished as customized goods became more available.

For the French *regulation theorists*, many of whom were state officials, the shift from mass to flexible production combined with the relocation of production to the periphery constituted an entirely new regime of intensive capital accumulation on a world scale – one characterized by high rates of exploitation in the Third World export platforms and by the exportation of their products to the markets located primarily in the core. Although production was moved to the periphery, engineering and financial decision-making remained in the corporate offices located in the core capitalist countries (Aglietta 1979; Boyer 1988, 1990; Lipietz 1986).

The regulation theorists based their explanation of the development of the capitalist mode of production on an analysis of the US economy that was extended to other parts of the world. They portrayed it in terms of a progression of phases, each of which was characterized by the combination of a particular regime of capital accumulation and a particular mode of regulation. The regime of accumulation was a relatively stable relation between production and consumption that was reproduced for a limited period of time at the level of the international economy. The mode of regulation was an historically contingent network of institutions that ensured the reproduction of the capitalist property relations guiding the regime of accumulation. Each national economy has its own distinctive mode of development, depending on how it is inserted into the international division of labor (Brenner and Glick 1991:47–8).

The regulation theorists distinguished three phases of development in the US economy since 1920. From 1920 to 1940, a regime of extensive accumulation was regulated by the institutions of competitive capitalism; it witnessed the beginnings of mass production, the rationalization of the production process, and under-consumption, because low wages did not permit workers to purchase many of the

---

1. The theorists who claimed that we live in a post-Fordist world borrowed the idea of Fordism from Antonio Gramsci (1971c) and deployed a much-simplified version of it. Gramsci's notion was not only more specific but also more inclusive, as he subsumed a series of problems, besides purely economic ones, under the title of 'Americanism and Fordism'. These included: (1) whether Fordism constituted a new revolutionary historical epoch or merely the gradual evolution of the already existing one; (2) whether the old ruling stratum been replaced by an emergent class whose wealth and power derived from a new mechanism for the accumulation and distribution of finance capital based on industrial production; (3) whether Fordism, which was based on rationalized industry and high wages, was the ultimate attempt of capital to overcome the tendency of the rate of profit to fall; (4) the impact of this rationalization; (5) whether psychoanalysis was an expression of the increased moral coercion exercised by both the state apparatus and society on single individuals; and (6) sex and the appearance of new concepts of masculinity and femininity that were linked with the formation of the new society.

goods they produced. From 1945 through to 1967, a Fordist regime of accumulation regulated by monopoly institutions was shaped by the capitalists' management of capitalist–worker relations through collective bargaining, regular wage increases, and new forms of credit that allowed workers to purchase standardized, mass-produced commodities. By becoming a major consumer of the means of production, the state prevented crises of underconsumption during this phase of development. This Fordist regime disintegrated in the mid-1960s as a result of the uneven development of different sectors of the economy, insufficient working-class consumption, the tendency of the rate of profit to fall, a decline in productivity and the appearance of a crisis of overaccumulation. Firms increased their productivity by installing new machines, moving to new locations, fragmenting the workforce, and producing smaller batches of goods to meet particular market demands (M. Davis 1978; Brenner and Glick 1991).

The views discussed above represent different positions in a debate about the nature and direction of change since the 1970s. They imply that the social and economic changes that have occurred since the early 1970s are of a different order from any changes that occurred earlier in the historical development of capitalism. The mostly Marxist critics of these viewpoints rejected their functionalist theorization of history, their assertion that change was path-dependent, and their effort to discern the rules governing the transition from one epoch to the next (A. Amin 1994:2–3).

The economist Paul Sweezy described globalization not as a new phase of capitalist development but rather as a process that has been taking place since capitalism emerged four or five centuries ago. In his view, the three most important trends underlying the globalization of capitalism since the recession of 1974–5 have been

> ... the reassertion and intensification of trends dating back to the turn of the century: retarded growth, increasing monopolization, and the financialization of the accumulation process.
>
> These three trends are intricately interrelated. Monopolization has contradictory consequences: on the one hand it generates a swelling flow of profits, on the other it reduces the demand for additional investment in increasingly controlled markets: more and more profits, fewer and fewer profitable investment opportunities, a recipe for slowing down capital accumulation and therefore economic growth which is powered by capital accumulation (Sweezy 1997:3–4).

Sweezy (1997:4) pointed out that monopolization and the financialization of capital accumulation, which were dominant trends in the capitalist world economy from the 1890s through to the collapse of 1929–33, reappeared as the motor force of capital accumulation on an increasingly world scale in the mid-1970s; he further argued that the context of globalization '. . . puts its imprint on the way the various processes play themselves out'. It also put its stamp on where accumulation and the concentration of capital takes place; today, these processes are no longer confined to the capitalist countries of the West, as they were a century ago. In Sweezy's view, the term 'globalization' masks the uneven development of capitalism, makes it difficult to study the processes that have produced that unevenness, and obscures the particular ways in which many local communities have responded to those circumstances.

Other critics distinguish between the *international* and the *global* dimensions of the world economy in order to assess the extent and impact of globalization (e.g. Wade 1996; Hirst and Thompson 1996). The political scientist Robert W. Cox (1997:22) describes the difference in the following way:

The international economy [was concerned with] movements in trade, investments, and payments crossing national frontiers that were regulated by states and by international organizations that were created by states. The world economy, in contrast, was the sphere in which production and finance were being organized in cross-border networks that could very largely escape national and international regulatory powers.

The critics do not dispute the globalists' claims about the movement of goods, people, capital, and money across national borders at the present time. They ask instead whether the current volume is without historical precedent, whether it is truly world-wide in scope, and whether it retains significant national and regional dimensions. Linda Weiss (1997:13) concludes

. . . while national economies may in some ways be highly integrated with one another, the result – with the partial exception of money markets – is not so much a globalized world (where national differences virtually disappear), but rather a more internationalized world (where national and regional differences remain substantial and national institutions remain significant).

Social analysts who argue that the late twentieth century is witnessing the internationalization of the world economy rather than its globalization support their conclusions with the same kinds of statistical arguments that the boosters of globalism use to buttress their claims (e.g. Gordon 1988; Jenkins 1987:13, 132; Kiely 1994:140; L. Weiss 1997:4–14). For example,

1. The ratio of export trade to gross domestic product and the ratio of capital flows to output for the industrialized countries in 1913 exceeded those of the inter-war years and resembled those of the 1980s.
2. The ratio of world trade to output, which grew during the 1960s and 1970s, weakened in the 1980s and 1990s.

3. The percentage of direct foreign investment in manufacturing in Third World countries declined between 1960 and the early 1980s, which means that the proportion of foreign investment in First World countries actually increased during the same period.
4. While the Third World's share of total global manufacturing increased from 12.2 per cent in 1964 to 13.9 per cent in 1984, both figures were actually lower than the 14 per cent share these countries had in 1948.
5. Employment in the export processing zones of the various Third World countries, where transnational firms have tended to invest most heavily, rarely constituted more than 5 per cent of the total industrial employment in those states.
6. The importance of direct foreign investment varies from one country to another; it was important in Singapore, for example, and less so in Taiwan, where foreign firms accounted for less than 6 per cent of the capital formation between 1962 and 1975.
7. Most foreign direct investment goes toward existing ventures – mainly non-productive ones, like real estate or golf courses, and, to a lesser extent, mergers and acquisitions.
8. Domestic investment in Europe is nearly double the figure for direct foreign investment.
9. More than 80 per cent of foreign direct investment in 1991 was in highly industrialized, high-wage countries like the United States, England, Germany or Canada.
10. Production, trade and investment are concentrated in the industrialized countries of the North; roughly 85 per cent of the trade and 90 per cent of the investment occur in these countries, and about 90 per cent of the production in the United States, Japan and Europe is destined for domestic markets.
11. Intra-regional trade – which now accounts for about two-thirds of the total exports in North America, Europe, and Asia – has been growing more rapidly than trade between the three regions.

These data indicate that the Third World's share of global manufacturing peaked during the Second World War. They show that the percentages of foreign investment by industrialized countries in the 1980s were more similar to those at the beginning of the century than they were to those of the inter-war years and the Second World War. They also indicate that most foreign investment is concentrated in industrialized countries of the First World. They further show that North America, Europe, and East Asia constitute three semi-autonomous regions of production, trade, and investment that are linked together by financial markets.

Samir Amin (1990:100; 1992:49–52; 1997:67) took a slightly different position on the relation between globalization and the internationalization of capitalism. Globalization, in his view, meant the crystallization of capitalist production around regional growth poles. As a result, countries on the periphery – i.e. the Third World reconceptualized as the South – have different possibilities for change and development from those in the core. Globalization creates difficulties for countries on the periphery, because these states have different capacities to isolate capital and their citizens from the effects of being integrated into a world capitalist system.

Arif Dirlik (1997:70–2) points out that the internationalization of production has simultaneously unified and fragmented the history of capitalism. While the consumption of commodities produced by transnational corporations has forged economic, social, and cultural linkages across the globe, the formation or increased importance of supranational regional organizations – like NAFTA – manifests the fragmentation of capitalism, as does the fact that localities and regions within national states now compete with each other and bypass the state altogether in order to gain access to transnational capital.

Critics, like the anthropologist Peter Worsley (1990), would undoubtedly agree that it is impossible to understand the processes of globalization taking place today without a concept of culture. Since the cultural changes taking place in the world today correspond in complex ways to underlying economic and political realities, a clear understanding of globalization can only be gained by appreciating the significance of the interrelations between the contemporary cultural changes and the economic and political conditions that fuel their expression and nourish the development of new forms and practices. In other words, uneven development, the juxtaposition of modern and seemingly archaic practices in a single setting, and localized responses are as characteristic of these clashes in the late twentieth century as they were in the 1890s and early 1900s.

Globalization and the State

Writers with diverse theoretical perspectives have claimed that the globalization of capitalism has provoked crises of the national state. The sociologist Daniel Bell (1987:14) has written that the nation-state was '. . . too small for the big problems of life, and too big for the small problems of life'. Social critic Fredric Jameson (1991:319, 412) has suggested that it no longer plays a central role in the expansion of capitalism in its multinational stage. The flow of people, capital, and goods across national boundaries threatens the autonomy and authority of the state as well as its capacity to implement and enforce policies both at home and abroad. As international organizations like the World Bank or the European Community become more influential, states must relinquish old functions and assume new ones in order to ensure the smooth operation of the market. The advocates of globalism argue that the power of the state is steadily eroding as a result of the power of the market.

Predictions of the demise of the national state appeared with increasing frequency after 1969, when the economist Charles Kindleberger (1969:207) remarked that 'the nation-state is just about through as an economic unit'. The internationalization of monetary policy and innovations in transportation and communications had facilitated the movement of people, materials, and ideas across frontiers.[2] During the 1980s, the neo-liberal proponents of globalization used this argument to buttress claims about the steady erosion of state power – i.e. the 'myth of the powerless state' (L. Weiss 1998). They made these claims at about the same time that banks and transnational corporations began to portray themselves as the primary agents of economic development and depict globalization as the inevitable end-product of the monetarist policies, currency speculation and market forces at work. As a result, theories of globalization also have a significant ideological component.

For example, Kenicki Ohmae (1990) asserts that transnational corporations and global market forces are erasing national boundaries and eroding the power of state officials. Jean-Marie Guéhenno (1995) argues that recent innovations in telecommunications are undermining legal and political systems, so that power no longer operates from the top down but rather from the sheer number of connections individuals have in complex communications networks. Matthew Horsman and Andrew Marshall (1994:ix-xi) assert that the traditional nation-state is threatened by changes in the structure of the international economy, the end of the Cold War, and technological advances, which have facilitated the deregulation and integration of financial and commercial markets and made national borders obsolete, and will force a realignment between states and the international economy, as well as new relations between citizens and their governments.

Neo-liberal theorists aligned with the World Bank hinted that the apparent success of the late industrializing countries of East Asia during the 1970s and 1980s was due to the fact that their governments did not intervene in significant ways in the economies.[3] The high rates of economic growth they achieved resulted from

2. Robert Wade (1996:60) points out that Kindleberger recycled an older argument made by Norman Angell in *The Great Illusion*, which appeared in 1911. Angell claimed that the world's economy, especially its financial markets, had become so interdependent that national independence had become anachronistic. Science, technology, and economics – not governments – were the forces of modernity driving this increased interdependence.

3. Walden Bello (1998) and other critics of neo-liberal arguments showed that the governments of all the industrialized countries of East Asia intervened repeatedly to promote economic development (Appelbaum and Henderson 1992; Deyo 1987). The governments of Japan, South Korea, and Taiwan implemented land reform policies after the Second World War that created in each country a class of small landowners whose members allied themselves with the state; these policies also leveled income distribution and promoted savings. The states also enacted tariffs to protect domestic markets and provided subsidies to promote technology, exports, and technical linkages among industries. In South Korea, the state-owned bank, which was awash with savings, subsidized firms with loans and reviewed their progress each year. The state initiated price controls to curb the formation of monopolies and

the fact that their export industries produced steel, supertankers, textiles, and other commodities at prices that were competitive in the world market. In the eyes of these theorists, the strategy of export-oriented industrialization pursued by the firms in these countries was superior to the import-substitution strategies launched a decade or so earlier by many economic ministries in Latin America. Import substitution was an inefficient failure, because the firms never generated domestic or foreign markets. Furthermore, since the countries imported more than they exported, they quickly incurred large international debts. The moral they drew from this account was that export platform strategy should be emulated by other countries on the verge of industrialization (Balassa 1981).

Only the liberal version of the myth of the powerless state expounded by Robert Reich (1991) suggests that globalization might have negative or unintended consequences. In his view, the globalization of financial markets, driven by technological advances and political forces like the demise of communism, is irreversibly eroding national economies, diluting national sovereignty, and disempowering national political processes. As a result, not all the citizens of a particular state will experience this decline in the same way. While a small number who own or possess capital and knowledge will benefit from globalization, the vast majority of the population will experience chronic economic insecurity and steadily increasing immiseration (Bienefeld 1994:98–116).

The state, as Robin Murray (1971) and others have repeatedly shown, has always been an economic instrument of capitalism, even during those periods of territorial expansion when liberal and neo-liberal analysts claim it is not. The state, in Murray's view, is an objective structure in the capitalist international economy that underwrites capitalist production, on the one hand, and the reproduction of the system, on the other. It guarantees property rights, the standardization of weights and measures, and the free movement of goods; it ensures the availability of low-cost inputs, like land and labor, so that an economic infrastructure is available; it assures the existence and training of workers, controls their wages, and ameliorates the effects of their exploitation; it regulates business cycles, provides aid to ailing firms, and absorbs surplus; it collects taxes to support its activities; it enacts and enforces laws; and it manages external relations through military power, foreign aid, and commercial and financial sanctions. Furthermore, during periods of capitalist expansion, the state also acts as the political agent of capitalist firms, especially dominant ones, and cooperates with other states to protect property, exploit resources, and coordinate economic functions through its participation in international agencies like the International Monetary Fund.

---

enacted laws that limited overseas investment and capital flight (Amsden 1990:24–5, 1991). All the East Asian states provided indirect support to companies through relatively inexpensive public education and through legislation that disciplined and subordinated labor (Deyo 1989).

Linda Weiss (1997) has pointed out that capitalism is structured differently in different countries. This diversity of national capitalisms is paralleled by states with varying capacities or abilities to pursue domestic economic policies. Further-more, states did not act in the same way or even in accord with neo-liberal dicta during the 1980s and 1990s. Germany and Japan, for instance, found new ways to pursue programs of industrial transformation, while Australia used deficit spending to fund welfare and industrial policies. What distinguishes strong states from weaker ones is their ability to promote new conditions and relations or to make use of them once they appear. The bureaucracies of strong states with robust domestic economies – like Japan – have promoted the internationalization of their firms either through direct assistance or as a way of balancing trade deficits.

Catalytic states that seek to be indispensable to the success of strategic coalitions are able to consolidate national and regional networks of trade and investment through international agreements. The United States has accomplished this through the promotion of NAFTA; Germany or Japan used their leverage in domestic affairs to gain advantageous positions in regional coalitions. The ability of modern states to adapt is, according to Weiss (L. Weiss 1997:17) '. . . embedded in a dynamic economic and inter-state system'. Thus, states, like people, operate with structures not entirely of their own making and under circumstances that are not entirely of their own choice. They are integral elements in the development and reproduction of capital, and their autonomy is both conditional and historically contingent.

The perspectives of Murray, Weiss and Marxist scholars contrast with the arguments of neo-Weberians like the sociologist Theda Skocpol, who insists that states are autonomous. She describes this autonomy in the following way: 'States conceived as organizations claiming control over territories and people may formu-late and pursue goals that are not simply reflective of the demands or interests of social groups, classes, or society' (Skocpol 1985:9). Thus, states have the capacity or power to pursue and achieve particular goals, even '. . . over domestic and international nonstate agents and structures, especially economically dominant ones' (Skocpol 1985:19). Skocpol also insists:

> . . . the political expression of class interests and conflicts is never automatic or economic-ally determined [but] depends on the capacities classes have for achieving consciousness, organization, and representation. Directly or indirectly, the structures and activities of states profoundly condition such class capacities (Skocpol 1985:25).

The irony of assertions about state autonomy, as Leo Panitch (1997:84–5) notes, is that they coincided with the rise of the Reagan–Thatcher neo-liberal political regimes, whose officials deregulated industries and financial institutions, broke trade unions and impoverished the poor as they '. . . enveloped themselves in an ideology that proclaimed the necessity of state subordination to the requirements of capital accumulation and markets and even to the norms and opinions of capitalists themselves'. In other words, pronouncements about the autonomy of states were made at a time when the political minions of the capitalist classes were moving even more of the economy from the public to the private sphere and, by so doing, were further reinforcing the separation of the economic and political realms in contemporary nation-states.

Globalization and the Dissolution of Socialism

The disintegration of the Soviet state, the elections in the Eastern Bloc countries, and the development of export industries in southern China heralded by the Western media in the 1980s and 1990s have been interpreted in different ways. For many, they mark not only the restoration of capitalism but also its globalization. For Rightwing writers, they signal the death of Communism and Marxism. For neo-liberal convergence theorists, they indicate that the industrial countries of the world are once again following the same path of global capitalist development. For mainstream political scientists, they reveal the triumph of market democracy, in which elites compete for power to govern society and maintain social order. By the 1960s, Marxist scholars were already examining the conditions that would promote the 'restoration of capitalism' in the socialist states and the changes they would unleash (Esherick 1979). In this section, let us briefly review the forces that precipitated these changes and then consider four more significant consequences – renewed discussions of civil society and the state, the resurgence of nationalism, class formation, and the rise of organized crime.

The increased oil prices of the early 1970s combined with the inefficiency of the industrial planning and production bureaucracies in the socialist countries underwrote the widely acknowledged decline in economic growth that was apparent by the end of the decade (Mandel 1989:56–67). The economic stagnation of the USSR and the socialist countries of East Europe was exacerbated by the enormous military expansion of the United States and its NATO allies and by the technology boycotts orchestrated by the United States in the early 1980s. The Soviet President Mikhail Gorbachev was convinced that any attempt to match the Star Wars initiatives and other military expenditures would do irreparable harm to the Soviet economy (Alexander 1995:30, 54 n.36). Further economic and political havoc was wreaked on the socialist countries as a result of National Security Council Decision Directive 54 of 1982, which stated that the objectives of the US government were to overthrow the Communist governments and parties of Eastern Europe and to reintegrate those countries into the capitalist world market (Chossudovsky 1997b:2). The structural adjustments and reforms demanded by the International Monetary Fund and World Bank in return for extensive loans in the 1980s imposed austerity measures and immiserated the populations of the socialist countries. They also provided a further rationale for the top-down, conservative revolutions promoted by the central governments of the socialist states that dismantled the institutions of their command economies and replaced them with the market (e.g. Meisner 1996:343).

One consequence of these changes has been the renewed discussions about the meaning of civil society, democracy and the state since the late 1980s (Cohen and Arato 1992; Keane 1988). However, there are significant differences between how civil society was conceptualized historically and how it is being used in these current debates. In the eighteenth century, civil society

> ... represent[ed] a separate sphere of human relations and activity, differentiated from the state but neither public nor private or perhaps both at once, embodying not only a whole range of social interactions apart from the private sphere of the household and the public sphere of the state, but more specifically a network of distinctively *economic* relations, the sphere of the market-place, the arena of production, distribution and exchange. A necessary but not sufficient condition for this conception of civil society was the modern idea of the state as an abstract entity with its own corporate identity . . . [and] the emergence of an autonomous 'economy', separated out of the unity of the 'political' and 'economic' which still characterized the absolutist state (Wood 1990:61, emphasis in the original).

The development of the concept of civil society in the eighteenth century was intimately linked with the development of capitalism. In the current discussions, it refers to the non-economic realm of public and personal life outside the state where autonomy, voluntary association, and plurality are presumed to be guaranteed by the kind of democracy that exists in the West. In other words, the current usage opposes the freedom and pluralism supposedly characteristic of civil society with state oppression. Moreover, it presumes that capitalism already exists and asserts that the exploitative social relations resulting from increased dependence on market relations are the same as those that shape participation in voluntary associations (Wood 1990:63–5).

The debates about civil society were linked with the dissemination and adoption of a peculiarly US notion of democracy, one rooted in the market and totally devoid of the egalitarian and moral ideals that had been central to liberal-democratic discourse since the middle of the nineteenth century. This equilibrium-market theory of democracy treats citizens as a mass of apathetic consumers with conflicting, individual political interests who attempt to optimize them by purchasing political goods from one of a small number of self-appointed entrepreneurs who are compelled to perform social functions in order to sell their commodities in a competitive market, where a balance is maintained between the supply and demand of these items. Such a model does not require high levels of citizen participation, only a majority or plurality of the votes cast in an election. Numerous critics have pointed out that the equilibrium produced in such a market, where purchasing power is based largely on money, is one of inequality, since people are neither equally wealthy nor always rational in their behavior. The political theorist Crawford B. Macpherson (1973:170–194; 1977:77–92) suggested that a political theory based on utilitarian and equilibrium market assumptions can thrive only in capitalist democracies with expanding economies, and that it can be no more than an academic luxury in those countries where political parties reflect real class interests rather than false consciousness.

One striking feature of the introduction of the market and the dissolution of socialist ideals in the late 1970s and 1980s was the resurgence of nationalist sentiments and movements. For example, the export processing zones created by Deng Xiaoping in 1979 in Guangdong province and elsewhere on the south coast of China opened the areas to capitalist investment, foreign-owned enterprises, and capitalist labor markets; consequently, the distinction between Chinese nationals and foreigners quickly became marked in these zones (Meisner 1996:516–7). When Boris Yeltsin and his contemporaries weakened or dissolved the federated socialist states – the USSR, Yugoslavia, and Czechoslovakia – in the early 1990s without referenda, they left in place various national republics – Russia, Latvia, and Croatia, for instance – whose existence was already recognized in the federal constitutions. After the federations were dissolved, the leaders of the dominant national groups in each of the successor states continued to exercise power. Where there were multinational populations, as in Latvia or Russia, the members of the dominant ethnic or national group used their identity to secure preferential treatment and access to scarce resources in a system marked by organized shortages (Verdery 1991:126–7; 1996:85–8).

The resurgence of nationalism in the formerly socialist countries, as Maurice Meisner (1996) pointed out with reference to China, supported the political status quo. Nationalist sentiments also reinforced the capitalist market as the best means to achieve national goals, such as rapid economic growth, the accumulation of wealth through privatization of state property and entrepreneurial activity, and, most importantly, the maintenance of existing power relations.

Thus, the national question came to center stage again because of the upswell of nationalist sentiments in the 1980s, particularly in Eastern Europe. What is interesting about the current discussions of the national question is that they are not particularly concerned with the issues of national integration and national liberation that dominated the inter-war years and the period following the Second World War (see Chapters 4 and 5). They focus instead on the issues that were current at the turn of the last century – e.g. the cultural vs. political foundations of nationalist thought, the relation between class and state formation and national education, the interconnections of nationalism and capitalist expansion, and the relation between the collapse of absolutist regimes and mass movements calling for creation of bourgeois-democratic states (see Chapter 3). Furthermore, many writers concerned with nationalism today seem to have reinvented the wheel in the sense that they make little or no reference to the contributions made by critics nearly a century ago. That the current debate over nationalism resembles the one that flourished before the First World War is perhaps not so surprising, when one considers that both are periods marked by capitalist expansion into new lands as well as by class and state formation.

The rise of nationalism in the context of class and state formation in Eastern Europe has also sparked intense discussions about the role that the institutions of civil society play in securing civil rights. Katherine Verdery has shown the diverse ways in which alternative visions of civil society and national identity that have been counterposed in Romania involve substantially different conceptualizations of citizenship. At issue is whether constitutional rights are guaranteed equally to individuals resident in Romania, or whether they are granted to autonomous communities, which allows their members '. . . to resolve without external interference any matters relating to community identity: education, language maintenance, culture, and so on' (Verdery 1996:119). In this context, guaranteeing civil rights to individuals implied a strong central state that enforces the law and dispenses justice equally to all its residents; it assumed that the population of the state was homogeneous – i.e. composed of citizens, all of whom had the same rights and obligations before the law. Vesting these rights in autonomous communities rather than the individual redressed the grievances resulting from the homogenizing practices of the central state; it implied the decentralization and reconfiguration of state power – ultimately an erosion and weakening of the power of the central state.

Class formation and class struggle, as Iván Szelényi and his associates have shown, also shaped social development in the USSR and the socialist states of Eastern Europe from the 1970s onward. These processes, which emerged in the wake of the Second World War, gained momentum in the 1960s, especially after the revelations about Stalin's abuse of power. These disclosures threatened the legitimacy of state bureaucracies, composed mainly of Communist party members, both in the USSR and in the other socialist states of Eastern Europe. They forced the party bureaucracies to share power, at least temporarily, with technocrats and other members of the intelligentsia (Konrád and Szelényi 1979). However, in the 1970s and 1980s, the bureaucrats were increasingly disinclined to make concessions to the intelligentsia or to share power with them; at the same time, they were more flexible in their dealings with private business, and allowed second economies based on market production and exchange to flourish (Szelényi 1988: 216–8).

The second economies emerged in response to the industrialization policies imposed during the 1950s. Rapid industrialization was achieved by simultaneously creating as many industrial jobs as possible, collectivizing agriculture, and reducing personal consumption and infrastructural investments, such as housing, schools, or shops, but not public transportation. As a result, many of the first generation of industrial workers were forced to leave agriculture for urban industry. However, they retained control over their farm plots and continued to live in the countryside, traveling back and forth between their homes and job sites on public transportation. Since they retained control over their lands, they enjoyed relatively high living standards and a degree of autonomy from their employers. By the 1970s, workers had stopped leaving the rural villages, and some of those who had immigrated to the cities earlier returned to their natal communities because of the entrepreneurial opportunities afforded by selling the agricultural commodities their families produced. By 1981, the 1.5 million family farms in Hungary, which had a population of 10 million, grew one quarter of the agricultural commodities produced in the country (Szelényi 1988:29–31).

By 1990, two class hierarchies co-existed in the socialist states: the old established hierarchy, with party members and bureaucrats at the top and waged workers at the bottom, and the emerging new hierarchy based on integration with the capitalist market. In the new hierarchy, where social mobility was tied to the possession of wealth and entrepreneurial skills, owners and entrepeneurs occupied the upper rungs of the social ladder, with waged workers again at the bottom.

The result was a complex class structure. The ruling elite was fragmented, composed of a declining number of old-style bureaucrats and an increasing number of intellectuals with technical skills. The entrepreneurial class was also fragmented: the petite bourgeoisie whose members emerged out of the second economy, where they sold agricultural produce, services, and other commodities; members of the old Communist Party elite who had converted their political assets into economic capital by purchasing state firms or entering into joint ventures with Western firms; and professionals who were employed by foreign firms as capitalist investment began to play an increasingly important role in the economy. The working class was also divided between those who gained some income from the second economy and those who did not (Szelényi and Szelényi 1991:123–6).

While the major enterprises in the Eastern European economies are run in a thoroughly capitalist manner, privatization has not led to the formation of a capitalist class. These firms are run not by shareholders, but rather by technocrats and financial managers who subscribe to a neo-liberal, monetarist ideology (Szelényi and Martin 1988). The technocrats and managers of the new economic elite, more than 70 per cent of whom had been managers or members of the party-bureaucratic apparatus before 1989,

> ... are well-endowed with all *three* of post- communism's defining capitals. They are not only well endowed with cultural capital, the ideology of monetarism. Managers also own substantially more wealth than other groups. They are also the best endowed with social capital among the fractions of the new power elite: technocrats and managers

appear to have particularly successful in converting former political capital into social capital, that is, social networks which are particularly important in getting things done under post-communism (Eyal, Szelényi, and Townsley 1997:79, emphasis in the original).

Szelényi and his associates consider the possibilities of alternative pathways of class formation in Eastern Europe in the near future. While a propertied bourgeoisie may not emerge, the post-communist managerial elite may constitute itself, alongside significant foreign ownership, as a capitalist managerial class. And, together with the more successful entrepreneurs, they may eventually constitute a new bourgeoisie (Eyal, Szelényi and Townsley 1997:92).

Class formation combined with the shift from command to market economies has intensified criminal activity in the post- communist countries. A number of the high-level bureaucrats who facilitated marketization and privatization during the 1980s as well as their close kin – for example, Deng Xiaoping's children – have profited directly or indirectly from the emerging capitalist market economy. They have done so by plundering the state, influence-peddling, bribery, graft, profiteering, embezzlement, currency manipulation, receiving kickbacks and expropriating both state firms and property (R. Smith 1997:11).

In another context, Pino Arlacchi (1979:60) argued that the development of capitalist markets – combined with the weakness or absence of state control over violence and state regulation of economic relations and with intense competition or conflict between individuals or groups – underwrites the formation of organized crime syndicates. In Russia, for example, the 6,000 criminal organizations spawned between 1992 and 1995 emerged in a milieu in which law enforcement and government officials were poorly paid and, hence, susceptible to bribes, and where laws regulating contracts and criminal penalties for fictitious businesses or phoney bankruptcies were absent.

The Russian criminal organizations range in size from a few dozen to several thousand members. They are often distinguished by the nationality of their members or by place. Many are highly specialized; some focus their criminal activities on gambling, loans, drug-dealing, exporting stolen petroleum and cars, or trading stolen metals and weapons, while other organizations control transportation, undertake contract killings, or engage in burglary and hostage-taking. For example, one organization that controls truck transportation in agricultural areas creates shortages in the Moscow market by controlling both the quantity and distribution of agricultural produce entering the city from outlying agricultural areas; at times, the gang has been able to ensure the scarcity of certain commodities by preventing crops from being harvested. The effects of its activities have been to drive up the prices of those goods that do reach the city's markets. Furthermore, many of the organizations have close ties with government officials or members who are officials, and many have infiltrated banking and other business enterprises. In 1995, according to recent studies, the 8,000 or so major crime gangs in Russia in 1995 controlled more than 50,000 companies and an estimated 25 to 40 per cent of the gross national product (Dunn 1997; Voronin 1997).

Criminal organizations, like those in Russia and other countries with emerging capitalist markets, came into existence as market forces became more important; their steady growth has been fueled by scarcity, competition, and the weakness of the state. These highly entrepreneurial organizations accumulate wealth by discouraging competition in the market, by reducing wages scales, by promoting flexible conditions of employment, by evading health insurance and other workers' benefits, and by providing financial security and flexibility to those activities in which they are involved.

Reassessing Rural Class Structures and the Potential for Peasant Protest

In the 1970s, Claude Meillassoux (1981:89–137), Sidney Mintz (1973, 1974), and others examined the complexity of the class relations that developed in diverse ways in rural areas in the wake of imperialist expansion in the late nineteenth and early twentieth centuries. Different classes of peasants concerned primarily with subsistence lived side-by-side with farmers who produced exchange values for the market, fully waged workers and a diverse groups of semi- or sub-proletarian laborers whose members toiled daily or seasonally for wages in order to supplement their subsistence production, and who were neither peasants, nor urban folk, nor an agricultural proletariat that gained its livelihood by toiling in capitalist agricultural enterprises (Mintz 1974:298). Rural class structures were complex, and representations of rural life were further complicated by the uneven penetration of capitalism into the countryside. Social relations typical and characteristic of one region might be absent or exist only in nascent form in an adjacent area. As a result, the appearance of different rural class structures in the capitalist world system depended both on the part of the system that was being described and on the time when the observations were made.

From the inter-war years through to the 1970s, Maoist activists, social scientists like Eric Wolf, and others had examined rural class structures. They concluded that peasants had on occasion mobilized themselves for collective political action and participated in revolutionary or reformist political movements. One of their aims was to assess the revolutionary potential of different groups living in the countrysides of underdeveloped countries. They sought to identify those classes that would mobilize themselves for collective action and to specify the historically contingent circumstances in which they had done or might do so.

Since the mid-1980s, several authors have re-examined the effects that imperialism has had on peasantries and on their capacity for collective political action.

They have constructed a questionable baseline against which they measure change. In their view, peasant communities were relatively homogeneous and closed before they were enveloped by market forces, and, once enmeshed in social relations structured by the market and the state, their social structures simultaneously became more differentiated and fragmented. They suggest that individual acts of resistance directed against wealthy elites and the state have been and are more common among the rural poor than collectively organized protest. These studies mark a retreat or a reversal from the 1970s in the ways that social scientists understand the political capacities of rural communities whose members still constitute the vast majority of the world's population in this time of an expanding capitalist economy.

Michael Kearney's (1996) *Reconceptualizing the Peasantry* is one of the more extended reassessments. His views have been shaped in significant ways by the experiences of the Mixtec peasants he investigated in the 1970s, who now move back and forth between Mexico and California. From his perspective, definitions of peasants that focus exclusively on their lives and activities in the countryside and that stress their partial independence from other social types do not capture the complexities of everyday life that his Mixtec friends and informants, whom he calls postpeasants, have to confront. For example, in the 1980s, the effects of global economic transformations forced a number of peasants into new social contexts outside the closed corporate communities in which they lived in southern Mexico. The Mixtec became migrant workers in the agribusinesses of northwestern Mexico and California; vendors and semi-skilled or unskilled workers who dwelled in urban shantytowns on both sides of the border; and entrepreneurs, small merchants, professionals, and civil servants in the larger towns of the region. Moreover, individuals repeatedly moved in and out of these contexts, assumed different identities as they move from one context to another, and typically had close kin in other positions on both sides of the border at any given moment (Kearney 1996:23–41, 174–80).

The issue does not seem to be whether the complexities of postpeasant life described by Kearney are in fact new features linked with the processes of globalization, as he implies, or whether they are typical of peasantries that have become increasingly enmeshed in the social relations generated by imperialist expansion, as Meillassoux and Mintz suggested. There are certainly some striking similarities between the experiences of Mixtec people in and from southern Mexico in the 1980s and 1990s, on the one hand, and the complex class structures linking peasants and rural and urban enterprises in Russia and the Yangzi delta of southern China at the turn of the century, on the other (e.g. K. Walker 1999). However, as I suggested above, what is now called globalization is capitalist imperialism by another name.

What is at stake is Kearney's characterization of the quintessential peasant: they are organically linked to the countryside; they are partially autonomous from other social classes; they retain effective control over the land; they engage primarily in subsistence agricultural production; they pursue social status gained through a narrow set of social relations; and they render part of their surplus to non-peasants – i.e. to landlords, merchants, or the state. His essentialized peasant seems to be similar to the middle peasants discussed earlier by V. I. Lenin and more recently by Eric Wolf. If this is true, then he deploys a much narrower conception of both different peasant strata and the other rural social classes with whom they interact.

There have also been efforts since the late 1960s to reassess the capacity of middle peasants as agents of social change and to examine the kinds of political movements promoted by their actions. As Tom Brass (1991) observed and as you will recall from previous chapters, Lenin (1960a, 1966) argued that the peasantry played a dual role in the revolutionary transformation of the countryside. During the transition to capitalism, rich peasants overwhelmed the feudal landowning class. During the transition to socialism, the small peasants and rural wage workers challenged the capitalist layer of the peasantry. In other words, the middle peasants – those who frequently hired labor and who held enough land to provide both subsistence for the family and a small surplus – did not, in Lenin's view, participate in the transformation of rural class relations.

By contrast, Wolf (1969:291–2) suggested that the traditional, culturally conservative middle peasants who had secure access to land and who were only marginally controlled from the outside played a central role in transforming rural class structures. They were not only the layer most vulnerable to changes wrought by the market, but also the stratum that was most dependent on the mutual aid of kin and neighbors. Furthermore, they were the layer that was most exposed to influences emanating from the urban proletariat, as well as the group that sent its children to work in the cities. The middle peasant

> . . . is caught in a situation in which one part of the family retains a footing in agriculture, while the other undergoes 'the training of the cities'. . . . This makes the middle peasant a transmitter of urban unrest and political ideas. This point bears elaboration. It is probably not so much the growth of an urban proletariat as such which produces revolutionary activity, as the development of an industrial work force still closely geared to life in the villages.
>
> Thus it is the very attempt of the middle and free peasant to remain traditional which makes him revolutionary (Wolf 1969:292).

In other words, middle peasants protest when their moral economy – the precapitalist relations and cultural practices that protect them from hardship and starvation – is threatened or destroyed by capitalist development in the countryside. For Wolf (1969:290) '. . . the decisive factor in making a peasant rebellion possible lies in the relation of the peasantry to the field of power which surrounds it. A rebellion cannot start from a situation of complete impotence.' In other words, the middle peasants of Mexico, Russia, China, Vietnam, India, Algeria and Cuba organized and reacted against capitalism in order to restore the *status quo*, and their collective action had unintended consequences.

The political scientist James Scott (1977:289) takes a slightly different tack, although he agrees with Wolf that the peasants most likely to resist the penetration of capitalism and the colonial state are those who have property, entrenched precapitalist values, and social networks that promote local communal solidarity; they typically reside in areas that are only marginally incorporated into the state. In the *Moral Economy of the Peasant*, Scott (1976:3–7) merges Wolf's self-sufficient middle peasant with Chayanov's (1986b) family-labor farmer. This has several consequences. First, it suggests that all peasants share the same economic rationality regardless of whether they live in Latin America or Southeast Asia. Second, it assumes that the producer–consumer balance of the peasant household rather than surplus appropriation by landlords or the state determines work organization on the farm. Third, it argues that changes in the subsistence needs of the peasant household are related to the domestic cycle of the group rather than its place in wider capitalist or socialist class structures. As a result, peasants everywhere tend to share the same ethic: avoid undue risks, make use of a wide variety of social arrangements that redistribute produce to assure a minimum income to everyone, and work the system to minimize disadvantage. What is important is not how product or labor is appropriated by landlords or the state, but rather how much the peasants are able to retain for their own use or consumption.

As a consequence, Scott blurs the specificity of the various ways in which surplus is pumped out of peasant communities – e.g. capitalist wages, feudal rents, or socialist redistribution. Scott (1976:57) also argues that the commercialization of agriculture and the growth of the colonial state complicated the security of the peasants by threatening their subsistence base. They exposed an ever-widening sector of the peasantry to market forces, eroded the risk-sharing values of the village, reduced or eliminated subsidiary occupations that buffered the peasant villagers from bad harvests, and allowed landlords to extract more rent from the peasants. The growth of state power allowed the state to stabilize tax revenues.

Scott notes that peasants do in fact revolt on occasion; however, in *Weapons of the Weak* (1985) he argues that individual acts of resistance that require little or no formal organization and do not directly confront authority are more common than peasant rebellions that seek to restore the traditional balance of social forces in the community or peasant-inspired revolutions that strive to overthrow the existing social order and the state that guarantees its continued existence (Scott 1985:xvi–xvii). As a result, it is the clandestine, spontaneous, small-scale acts of resistance by individuals – such as theft, arson, sabotage, false compliance, feigned ignorance, lying, desertion, or foot-dragging – rather than organized rebellions that protect the traditional practices and institutions that underpin the moral economy of the peasant community. These weapons of the weak are the normal or routine forms of resistance that peasants wield to thwart those who seek to extract goods, rents, labor, or taxes from them. They act individually, spontaneously, and anonymously, unlike Wolf's middle peasants, who organized themselves collectively to resist capitalist penetration into the countryside.

Scott's conclusions in *Weapons of the Weak* were buttressed by an analysis of class relations and resistance in a Malaysian village whose residents were in the process of being ensnared in social relations created by the Green Revolution and the intensification of large-scale capitalist agriculture. This was a monumental, transformative event on a par with the advent of British colonial rule at the turn of the century and the Japanese occupation in the early 1940s. While Scott recognized the texture of the social diversity that was emerging in the village, and perhaps could have said more about intraclass struggles within the community, commentators following his lead have glossed over both class differentiation among peasantries and its significance. For example,

> For the sake of convenience the rural poor are described as peasants. Numerous discussions about what constitutes a peasant remain inconclusive. At times it is important to acknowledge the heterogeneity of the rural poor. Not so here. Thus the definition adopted is broad, with only two easily satisfied characteristics: (1) the peasant works in agriculture, and (2) he or she has a subordinate position in a hierarchical economic and political order (Colburn 1989:ix).

Thus, class struggle, as Brass (1991:180) notes, is reduced to the opposition between the elite and the state, on the one hand, and the rural poor or weaker party, on the other. In a later work, *Domination and the Arts of Resistance*, Scott (1990) treats the rural poor as merely one kind of subordinated or powerless group, and extends his conclusions about resistance and rebellion to other groups that he portrays as powerless.

Identities, Grievances and New Social Movements

Social commentators re-examined the diverse forms collective action has taken in modern industrial capitalist society. This, of course, is a well-established interest of social theorists since the time of Marx, Durkheim, and Weber. In recent years, they have devoted a good deal of attention to the forms of social protest that appeared in the Western countries during the 1960s and 1970s in response to the structural formations of industrial capitalist society. They claimed that the *new social movements* – e.g. the women's, gay men's and lesbians', anti-war, peace, environmental, anti-nuclear, anti-tax, religious fundamentalist, and White power groups – were not rooted in class conflict as earlier movements had been. Instead, these largely urban-based, decentralized movements drew their members from various social classes and expressed diverse political and theoretical perspectives, ideas, and values. They often gave voice to the grievances and sentiments of individuals and collectivities whose identities were weakly developed, blurred, subordinated, or suppressed by the dominant cultural, social, and political systems. Their grievances and the identities they sought to construct focused on cultural and social issues that often involved the expression of personal, intimate aspects of everyday life – such as sexual preference. They used non-violent forms of civil disobedience drawn from Gandhi and Thoreau to organize and to mobilize popular sentiment against the existing structures of power (Johnston, Laraña, and Gusfield 1994).

Theorists of the new social movements were concerned with Durkheim's notion of *conscience collective*. They were exploring how and why people in a society based on individualism and alienation mobilize for collective action. They offered '. . . the concept of "collective identities" as a way of explaining how people act in concert with the object of achieving a new, distinct, or semiautonomous kind of presence and cultural recognition . . . in the process of political activity' (Stephen 1997:20).

What distinguished the new social movements from earlier forms of social protest was that they were not concerned with the economic grievances of the working class. Their support did not come from political parties, trade unions, or subordinated social strata, but rather from middle-class individuals who opposed the institutions and practices of the welfare state. The aims of the new social movements were to articulate and defend certain values and to mobilize their participants for political action to reappropriate civil society from the state. Their members frequently circumvented established political institutions, since they felt marginalized or disenfranchised by political parties, trade unions, and other organizations as they struggled to influence and control the policies of the state. Theorists of the new social movements have offered three different accounts of their rise (Assies 1990:44–50).

In the earliest account, the sociologist Alain Touraine (1974, 1977, 1981) argued that the new social movements are merely the first manifestations of a new unified movement that reflected the appearance of Daniel Bell's (1973) post-industrial society. The distinctive features of this post-industrial society were that services had eclipsed the production of goods in the economic sphere, that a professional and technical class had become pre-eminent, and that theoretical knowledge was the basis for innovation and policy formulation. Since this modern, post-industrial society was also characterized by a high degree of reflexivity, its political institutions, organizational practices and cultural arrangements were often contested. While the members of the pre-eminent classes shared the same cultural orientation, which ultimately shapes their views about productivity, they disagree over how this model should be deployed. The new social movements are the expression of this structural conflict. They not only reproduce conflict in post-industrial society but also explain the appearance of this new social type.

In the second version, the critical theorist Jürgen Habermas (1981) portrays the contemporary West as late capitalism. This means that the state exercises regulatory functions over the economy and that it is concerned with rationality, which it defines narrowly as the instrumentalization of reason. The late capitalist state also suffers from a crisis of legitimization, since it has become disconnected from the communicatively constructed life world, which contains both the public and private spheres. The public sphere, as the arena of open debate, has already been invaded and remodeled by commercial interests and shapers of public opinion, and political issues are increasingly treated as technical problems, and have become depoliticized in the process. The new social movements arose as the same fate threatened the private sphere. They appeared in those areas of society that were concerned with cultural reproduction, social integration, and socialization. These extra-parliamentary forms of protest focused on issues concerning the quality of life, self-realization, and human rights rather than economic, domestic, or military security. These highly particularistic movements seek to block formal, organized spheres of action by forging new structures of communication.

Ernesto Laclau and Chantal Mouffe (1985) provide the third account. In their view, '. . . the new social movements express antagonisms that emerged in response to the hegemonic formation that was fully installed in the Western countries after World War II' (Mouffe 1988:91). This formation was based on the articulation of assembly-line production, an interventionist state and new cultural forms that unleashed complex processes. The state intervened to ensure capitalist reproduction by taming the capitalists' urge to lower wages and using regular cost-of-living wage increases to tie workers' demands to increased productivity. Capitalist relations penetrated almost every sphere of social life, commodifying and homogenizing culture, transforming people into consumers, destroying the environment, and underwriting new forms of subordination and resistance. The state's increasing intervention in all aspects of social life underwrote the steady growth of a bureaucracy and of the antagonisms that underpinned the appearance of new forms of protest. Groups also resisted the growing uniformity of everyday life that resulted from a media-imposed mass culture.

What is new about the new social movements for Laclau and Mouffe is that they emerged in spheres of everyday life that had only recently come under the domination of capital and the state. What the new social movements have in common is that they are not rooted in the class position of their participants. They are rooted instead in the appearance of antagonisms that are '. . . always discursively constructed' (Mouffe 1988:95). In other words, the collective subjects constituted by particular discourses (1) find that their identities and rights are negated by the emergence of new discourses and practices, or (2) that they are constituted as subordinates by some discourses and as equals by others. Mouffe (1988:95–6) suggests that:

> People struggle for equality not because of some ontological postulate but because they have been constructed as subjects in a democratic tradition that puts those values at the center of social life. . . . Democratic discourse questions all forms of inequality and subordination.

As a result, opposition to subordination and inequality and efforts to democratize social life have taken diverse forms in the present situation. In this milieu, progressive movements are the ones whose members are capable of linking their own interests with those of other collective groups.

In a carefully argued response to their claims, Ellen Wood (1986:47, 62–8) pointed out that Laclau and Mouffe had dissolved social reality into discourse and politics into struggles for control over those discourses. Since the collective identities constituted in these discourses are autonomous from the relations of exploitation and domination rooted in the political economic structures of capitalist society – i.e. they are not organically linked to the members of a particular class – they can be delinked from the ideology of one class and assimilated to that of another. In other words, these free-floating, class-neutral identities have no necessary relation to exploitation and domination. Thus, Laclau and Mouffe stripped these identities from the class relations and contexts in which they developed. Moreover, their liberal-democratic reconceptualization of the economic sphere displaced exploitation from its central position in capitalist social relations and separated the economic and political levels of society. Politics, in the process, became limited to the relations among free and equal individuals.

Finally, Wood raises another issue. If these identities are not related to class struggle and class position, then who really constitutes them: a plural subject, a popular force, no one, everyone or some external agent or agency, like intellectuals standing partly or wholly outside the struggle? Class is central, and Laclau and Mouffe's perspective is a retreat. For Wood (1986:99–100), the economic sphere does have a bearing on the structure of social and political domination; the exploitative relations between capital and labor have had tangible effects on the working class; people who are exploited have an interest and benefit from the abolition of exploitation; the destruction of the structures of domination is an essential part of the struggle for human emancipation; and the groups most exploited by capitalist accumulation and exploitation are the ones best situated to understand those relations.

By the early 1990s, scholars from Third World regions were beginning to explore social movements emerging in response to the impact of capitalism on the internal crises of their countries (Wignaraja 1993). Unlike some of their counterparts in the West, they retained a much clearer awareness of the relations between those movements and the political and economic structures that gave rise to them.

Subaltern Studies and Postcolonial Theory

Dissatisfaction with various nationalist, Marxist and revisionist accounts of Indian history, especially those that privileged global capitalist modernization and denied agency to subordinated groups, led a number of Calcutta-based scholars, known as the Subaltern Studies collective, to reconceptualize Indian history (Bahl 1999; Prakash 1994; Sivaramakrishnan 1995). In their view, Indian society was composed of elite and subaltern layers. The dominant elite layer was a heterogeneous group composed of British colonial officials; foreign industrialists, merchants, bankers, planters, landlords and missionaries; and indigenous feudal magnates, merchants, industrialists and recruits to the upper levels of the bureaucracy. The subaltern layer was composed of the rest of '. . . the total Indian population', whose subordination was manifested in myriad ways: class, caste, age, gender or office (Guha 1982:8). Furthermore, uneven regional economic and social development meant that an elite group which was dominant in one area might be subordinate in another; this created contradictions and ambiguities, especially for the lower strata of the rural gentry, rich peasants or impoverished landlords.

The Subaltern Studies collective derived the concept of the subaltern from the research plan that Antonio Gramsci (1971a:52) sketched in 'Notes on Italian History'. Since subalterns, for Gramsci, were not unified and could not be unified until they became a state, their history and development were intimately intertwined with those of civil society and the state. They were not autonomous nor were they self-determining, rational human subjects (Arnold 1984; O'Hanlon 1988:191). The political formation of the dominant and subaltern classes was interdependent. The subaltern groups attempted to influence the dominant classes and to establish their own autonomous organizations at the same time that the politically dominant groups sought to gain their support and acquiescence. One of the goals of the Subaltern Studies collective was '. . . to demonstrate how, in the political transformation occurring in colonial and postcolonial Indian society, subalterns not only developed their own strategies of resistance but actually helped define and refine elite options' (Mallon 1994:1494).

Unlike Gramsci, the Subaltern Studies collective argued that subaltern groups were autonomous and, further, that their autonomy resulted from the fact that the processes of class formation were incomplete and aborted during the colonial period; this autonomy resided not in a common class position, but rather in the shared consciousness and sense of community that was forged as a result of their subordinate position (Chakrabarty 1992; Chatterjee 1984). They argued, following

Durkheim and Geertz, that this shared consciousness was manifested in myth, religion, and other cultural beliefs that surfaced during periods when the rural subalterns opposed the hegemonic practices of the elite. These moments of resistance often pitted kin and neighbors against outsiders and strangers until the hegemony of the elite was restored.

The Subaltern Studies collective examined a range of topics to demonstrate the autonomy of subaltern communities – e.g. peasant revolts, nationalism, the prose of counter-insurgency, tribal protest, the production of knowledge about workers' conditions, the politics of drinking or how elite histories deny the agency of subaltern groups. They attempted to show that the subalterns were autonomous historical persons who acted on their own rather than because they were led by some elite group. In order to discover what subalterns thought and did in particular circumstances, they had to 'read against the grain', since the subalterns did not and could not speak for themselves – i.e. the documents used to recuperate the history of Indian society during the colonial period were written by members of the elite.

The Subaltern Studies scholars accepted Michel Foucault's (1978: 95–6) idea that power and resistance were continually reconfigured (Chatterjee 1983). Power, in this view, is diffused throughout society, and resistance is constituted as its opposite. Resistance becomes the homogenized everyday response of people striving to recapture what they have lost, to cope with their daily needs, and to deal with forces that emanate from both inside and outside the community. What this perspective fails to acknowledge is that power is not diffused throughout the society, but rather that it is unevenly distributed in time and space; it tends to be concentrated at particular places and times. As a consequence, resistance is also unevenly distributed; it also is manifested at particular times and places (Cooper 1994:1533).

As the Subaltern Studies group sought to find the voices of subaltern people, their research took a decidedly linguistic turn – i.e. it assigned priority to mind over matter, and viewed reality as a representation rather than the product of social relations (Wolfe 1997:409). Their focus shifted first toward an exploration of what constituted subalternity and then toward an investigation of how historical knowledge was produced and a critique of Enlightenment thought. By the early 1990s, their project had shifted to challenging and decentering Europe and its history, both of which they saw as resting on the universal claims of Enlightenment thought. To accomplish this, they emphasized the constitution of difference, which not only described the situations in which subalterns acted, but also shaped both language and the meaning of the identities that were produced in the interrelations between these rational human subjects. In the process, they incorporated the insights of Edward Said's *Orientalism*, which argued that

Orientalism [is] a Western style for dominating, restructuring and having authority over the Orient . . . [It is an] enormously systematic discipline by which European culture was able to manage – and even produce – the Orient politically, sociologically, militarily, ideologically, scientifically and imaginatively during the post-Enlightenment period (Said 1978:3).

It was here that the arguments of some subalternists merged with those of the postcolonial theorists. Ella Shohat (1992:101–2) described postcoloniality in the following manner:

Echoing 'postmodernity,' 'postcoloniality' marks a contemporary state, situation, condition or epoch. The prefix 'post,' then, aligns 'postcolonialism' with a series of other 'posts' – 'poststructuralism,' 'postmodernism,' 'post-Marxism,' 'postfeminism,' 'post-deconstructionism' – all sharing the notion of a movement beyond. Yet while these 'posts' refer largely to the supersession of outmoded philosophical, aesthetic and political theories, the 'postcolonial' implies both going beyond anti-colonial nationalist theory as well as movement beyond a specific point in history, that of colonialism and Third World nationalist struggles. In that sense, the prefix 'post' aligns the 'postcolonial' with another genre of 'posts' – 'postwar,' 'post-Cold War,' 'post-independence,' 'post-revolution' – all of which underline a passage into a new period and a closure of a certain historical event or age, officially stamped with dates. Although periodizations and the relationships between theories of an era and the practices which constitute that era always form contested terrains, it seems to me that the two genres of the 'post' are nonetheless distinct in their referential emphasis, the first on disciplinary advances characteristic of intellectual history, and the latter on the strict chronologies of history *tout court*. The unarticulated tension between the philosophical and the historical teleologies in the 'postcolonial' . . . underlies some of the conceptual ambiguities of the term.

The distinction between the philosophical and historical genres of the concept of the postcolonial, as Arif Dirlik (1997:165) remarks, allows us to understand '. . . postcolonality as a product of the conjuncture between a EuroAmerican temporality . . . and the societies formerly subject to EuroAmerican domination'. As former colonial societies are incorporated into an increasingly capitalist world where the Second World has dissolved and the Third World no longer bears the same meaning it had in the 1960s, postcolonial theorists are attempting to rewrite the history of colonialism and its aftermath from a postmodernist perspective. They have accomplished this by erasing alternative histories of colonialism rooted in political economy and revolution and by privileging textuality over other sources of information.

Postcolonial theorists have observed, correctly and unremarkably, that much of the literature describing former colonies reproduces Eurocentric viewpoints, that colonial subjects had an instrumental role in shaping postcolonial culture, and that colonial and postcolonial cultures were hybrids produced by the dialectical relationship between the colonizer and the indigenous. In other words,

> . . . postcolonialism was not merely a passive recipient of 'postmodernism,' but has made a contribution to it by explicitly bringing within its scope the Third and Fourth Worlds as active ingredients. If postmodernism opened up a new space for criticism by questioning an earlier Eurocentric conceptualization of the world (and all that went with it in the questioning of identities, etc.), postcolonialism was to globalize that space (more by opening up the rest of the world to postmodernist critique than by making postmodernism acceptable to the rest of the world, although that too has happened) (Dirlik 1997: 173–4).

Dirlik (1997:175) agrees with Aijaz Ahmad (1995:16), a critic of postcolonial thought, who wrote that 'postcoloniality is . . . a matter of class'. This class is a transnational capitalist class composed of academics, business executives, computer experts, and professionals from the Third World countries for whom cultural hybridity rather than some reified ethnic identity is an aspect of everyday life that crystallized with the globalization of capitalism in the 1980s and 1990s.

Discussion

The social commentators discussed in this chapter have argued that the world has undergone an epochal shift since the late 1960s or early 1970s. They have sought to characterize that shift and to explain why it took place. Some portrayed it as the appearance of a new form of capitalism. The imperialist monopoly capitalism that shaped the post-war years was suddenly transformed or displaced by a new multinational, global capitalism that affected all parts of the world but in different ways. The neo-liberals among them suggested that the socialist regimes of the Second World were dismembered by the advance of global capitalism, the free market and democracy, and that this marked the death of socialism, communism, and Marxism. They also claimed that the futures of Third World countries were now more tightly tied to the industrial capitalist states as a result of export industrialization in East Asia, massive debts, international organizations like the World Bank, NAFTA-like trade agreements, and the dissolution of a viable socialist alternative. As a result, they believe that Third World peasants, who still constitute the vast majority of the world's population, are no longer capable of collective political action and are now reduced to carrying out individual acts of resistance against powerholding elites whose demands threaten their ability to satisfy certain minimal needs.

Postmodernism, they argued, is the cultural logic of this new stage of capitalist development. While the postmodern condition has been portrayed in myriad ways, four claims stand out. The first is a technological determinist assertion that computers, telecommunications and data banks play new transformative roles in the everyday lives of those institutions, individuals and that small but growing portion of the world's population which has access to them. Knowledge has been transformed into information that can be purchased and consumed like other commodities.

The second claim builds on the ideas of Smith, Durkheim, and Weber that social relations are forged in the market. It asserts that individuals and groups are characterized and defined by the commodities they consume. In these circumstances, logos, brand names, and copies take on new meanings as they are deployed to create and refine identities. Thus, we find individuals clad in Italian suits who drive their German cars to eat *nouveau* Mexican cuisine in a Philadelphia restaurant, where they drink Chinese beer and watch World Cup soccer matches played in France in real time before attending a reggae concert or a meeting of their favorite new social movement. At the same instant that cultural differences are emphasized, cultural distinctions are also blurred.

The third claim is that people are very mobile at the present time. Each year, millions of them travel across national borders in search of work, to sample culture in museums, or to find pleasure in Disney-like theme parks. However, by focusing exclusively on the movement of people and ignoring the specificity and contingency underlying their circumstances and motives, they conflate the mishaps and adventures of the tourist in a foreign country with the very real constraints that undocumented immigrants encounter when they attempt to find wage work in a new cultural milieu. They do not explain the differences between the experiences of the Japanese CEO's wife in San Francisco and those of teenage girls brought from remote farming villages in Thailand to toil as sex workers in Kuwait or those of Mixtec women who crossed the US–Mexico border illegally and now sew clothing with real and fake designer labels in Los Angeles sweatshops.

The fourth claim is that it is impossible to know the past as it actually happened, because it does not exist independently of historians and their rhetorical uses of language as they construct narratives to represent it (Munslow 1997). Since these written texts are contemporary products, they are obviously influenced not only by the ideological (theoretical) concerns of their authors, but also by the current disposition of power. Since one historical account is almost as good as any other, they say, the only possible way of distinguishing a good narrative from a poor one is to compare the rhetorical skills of their authors. Since historical knowledge is subjective, truth is ultimately based on the coherence of the argument rather than on a correspondence between the argument and independent evidence or on a consensus among experts. This leads quickly to anti-foundationalism and radical relativism: since truth and meaning are culturally constructed, and neither has objective foundations, as empiricists and Marxists claim, different cultures are ultimately incommensurate. As a result, postmodernists repudiate any quest for a ('master') narrative and have no faith in foundational categories, like modes of production, that transcend the modern era.

Alex Callinicos (1990:170–1) has argued that the increased influence of post-modernist thought in the 1980s and 1990s

> . . . is best seen as the product of a socially mobile intelligentsia in a climate dominated by the retreat of the Western labour movement and the 'overconsumptionist' dynamic of capitalism in the Reagan–Thatcher era. From this perspective the term 'postmodern' would seem to be a floating signifier by means of which this intelligentsia has sought to articulate its political disillusionment and its aspiration to a consumption-oriented lifestyle. The difficulties involved in identifying a referent for this term are therefore beside the point, since talk about postmodernism turns out to be less about the world than the expression of a particular generation's sense of ending.

The cynicism and despair of this postmodernist intelligentsia, their out-of-hand rejection of any project of radicalized Enlightenment or even the possibility of more egalitarian, more democratic alternatives to capitalism, is emulated often uncritically by students who believe that embracing postmodernist claims will somehow guarantee them a future in the academy.

The Keynesian policies adopted by capitalist countries from the 1930s onward kindled discussions about the nature of the state, state power and state intervention in the economy. The participants brought diverse perspectives to bear on the capitalist state – its form, functions, and limitations, as well as the centrality of its role in capital accumulation. In the 1970s, Marxist analysts who rejected the reductionist, economic determinist arguments of the social evolutionists and econ-omic growth theorists produced a variety of alternative perspectives (Jessop 1990:24–47). They argued that the capitalist state was relatively autonomous from the economy and from the dominant classes. It was a system of domination that intervened to regulate or mediate crises and class conflict in order to ensure the continued movement and reproduction of capital. Since the maintenance of the capitalist system rests on repression and persuasion, the organization of the capitalist state must be historically contingent and fluid in order to confront and resolve crises.

Antonio Gramsci, whose writings were being published in English for the first time, was the most influential Marxist theorist of the state in the 1970s. While Marxists dominated discussions about the state and state power in the 1970s, liberals and postmodernists were prominent in those of the 1980s. Some minimized or ignored altogether the fact that Gramsci wrote from prison during the rise of fascism in Italy as they attempted to appropriate and subsume his work. They were fascinated by his critique of economism, by his concerns with civil society and with strategies for exercising power, by the roles he assigned to intellectuals and by the ways he dealt with language, folklore, culture and diversity. In their view, he seemed to argue that the political realm was the mediating moment of the social totality. They saw his discussions of hegemony as a way of understanding the roles intellectuals played in building coalitions of diverse groups or new social movements whose distinctive, culturally constituted identities already existed and were sealed from those of other groups. In other words, the post-Marxists misused Gramsci in their denial of the relevance of theories that emphasized the primacy of structural contradictions, social classes, and crises in determining the collective identities of social actors.

At the same time Gramsci's writings were being transmuted, other liberal theorists resurrected Durkheim's view that the state and society constituted separate spheres. Some focused on the state and argued that it was autonomous. The state had its own internal causality, and it was not derivative from the economic or social realms. For this reason, state leaders could resist pressures from society in order to pursue the interests of the state even when its interests were opposed to those of the dominant classes. They were concerned with how the managers of the state's administrative and legal apparatus ruled and controlled diverse social actors as they pursued the distinctive aims of the state. However, one implication of state autonomy arguments was that the interests of groups or classes that might have a real stake in the decisions made by the state might be regularly excluded from the political process.

Others, like the sociologist Alaine Touraine, focused on civil society or the social realm of the totality. They argued that the social movements of the 1970s and 1980s were struggles by social actors to realize the full potential of the cultural patterns of modern post-industrial society. Thus the new social movements had the capacity to create new forms of social and cultural life and, hence, to alter the orientation of society itself. Civil society rather than the economy or the state was the arena where these contests occurred. They believed that it was crucial to democratize civil society; however, they downplayed the fact that the economy and the state still influenced civil society. They also minimized the possibility that such struggles might actually facilitate the expansion of the state or the economy into new realms of everyday life. This, of course, would diminish rather than expand civil society and confine the democracy they postulate to steadily smaller domains. It also suggests that civil society can ultimately exist only as a reflection of political society or the economy.

While the state autonomy and new social movement theorists were proclaiming the separation of the state from the economy and society, neo-liberals were busily re-organizing state apparatuses in countries around the world in order to facilitate the processes of capital accumulation. At the extreme, they denied the existence of the social realm, arguing that society was merely an aggregate of individuals linked together by exchange in the market. They further argued that the state forms best suited to the emerging global economy were those that lifted constraints on the operation of the market and on the processes of capital accumulation. This meant, for example, repealing or ignoring provisions of the Environmental Protection Act, intensifying class struggle by crushing labor unions like the air traffic controllers in the United States or the coal miners in England, and looting the former East Germany after unification.

Other critics have suggested that announcements of the death of Marxist social thought, the end of history, or the ultimate impossibility of socialism or communism are premature. Their curiosity has been fueled by events like the Zapatista rebellion in Chiapas and the massive changes that occurred in the socialist countries during the 1980s and 1990s. In the wake of these and other events, they produced impressive analyses of capitalist expansion, the rise of criminal organizations, class formation, the resurgence of nationalism, and the changing role of the state in the late twentieth century.

In sum, the arguments of the social theorists surveyed in this book, from the earliest ones to the most recent, indicate that we continually need to examine whose interests are served by championing theories that reductively locate motors for change exclusively in the economic, political, social or cultural realms of society. They also suggest that we need to refine accounts that consider the diversity of these interconnections both abstractly and in specific instances. Finally, they also point out that we continually need to consider how people have collectively gone about making their own history.

Bibliography

Aglietta, Michel 1979 *A Theory of Capitalist Regulation: The US Experience* [1976]. London, UK: Verso.

Ahmad, Aijaz 1995 The Politics of Literary Postcoloniality. *Race and Class*, vol. 36, no. 3, pp. 1–20. London.

Alavi, Hamsa 1965 Peasants and Revolution. In *The Socialist Register, 1965*, edited Ralph Miliband and John Saville, pp. 241–77. New York: Monthly Review Press.

—— 1975 India and the Colonial Mode of Production. *Economic and Political Weekly*, vol. X, no. 33–5, pp. 1235–62. Bombay.

Alavi, Hamza and Teodor Shanin 1988 Introduction to the English Edition: Peasantry and Capitalism. In *The Agrarian Question* [1899], by Karl Kautsky, Vol. 1, pp. xi–xxxix. London, UK: Zwan Publications.

Alexander, Jeffrey 1982 *Theoretical Logic in Sociology*, Vol. 2, *The Antinomies of Classical Thought*. Berkeley, CA: University of California Press.

—— 1983a *Theoretical Logic in Sociology*, Vol. 3, *The Classical Attempt at Theoretical Synthesis: Max Weber*. Berkeley, CA: University of California Press.

—— 1983b *Theoretical Logic in Sociology*, Vol. 4, *The Modern Reconstruction of Classical Thought: Talcott Parsons*. Berkeley, CA: University of California Press.

—— 1986 Rethinking Durkheim's Intellectual Development I: On 'Marxism' and the Anxiety of Being Misunderstood. *International Sociology*, vol. 1, no. 1, pp. 91–107. Cardiff.

—— 1995 *Fin de Siècle Social Theory: Relativism, Reduction, and the Problem of Reason*. London, UK: Verso.

Amin, Ash 1994 Post-Fordism: Models, Fantasies and Phantoms of Transition. In *Post-Fordism: A Reader*, edited by Ash Amin, pp. 1–40. Oxford, UK: Blackwell Publishers.

Amin, Samir 1974 *Accumulation on a World Scale: A Critique of the Theory of Underdevelopment* [1972]. New York: Monthly Review Press.

—— 1976 *Unequal Development: An Essay on the Social Formations of Peripheral Capitalism* [1973]. New York: Monthly Review Press.

—— 1980 *Class and Nation, Historically and in the Current Crisis* [1979]. New York: Monthly Review Press.

—— 1990 *Maldevelopment: Anatomy of a Global Failure*. London, UK: Zed Books. 1992 *Empire of Chaos*. New York: Monthly Review Press.

Bibliography

—— 1997 *Capitalism in the Age of Globalization: The Management of Contemporary Society*. London, UK: Zed Books.

Amsden, Alice 1990 Third World Industrialization: 'Global Fordism' or New Model? *New Left Review*, no. 182, pp. 5–32. London.

—— 1991 Diffusion of Development: The Late-Industrializing Model of Greater East Asia. *The American Economic Review*, vol. 81, no. 2, pp. 282–6. Princeton.

Appelbaum, Richard P. and Jeffrey Henderson 1992 *States and Development in the Asian Pacific Rim*. Newbury Park, CA: Sage Publications.

Aristotle 1984 Politics. In *The Complete Works of Aristotle*, edited by Jonathan Barnes, Vol. 2, pp. 1986–2129. Princeton, NJ: Princeton University Press.

Arkush, R. David 1981 *Fei Xiaotong and Sociology in Revolutionary China*. Cambridge, MA: Council on East Asian Studies, Harvard University.

Arlacchi, Pino 1979 From Man of Honour to Entrepreneur: The Evolution of the Mafia. *New Left Review*, no. 118, pp. 53–72. London.

Arnold, David 1984 Gramsci and Peasant Subalternity in India. *Journal of Peasant Studies*, vol. 11, no. 2, pp. 155–77. London.

Arrighi, Giovanni 1978 *The Geometry of Imperialism: The Limits of Hobson's Paradigm*. London, UK: Verso.

Assies, Willem 1990 Of Structure Moves and Moving Structures: An Overview of Theoretical Perspectives on Social Movements. In *Structures of Power, Movements of Resistance: An Introduction to the Theories of Urban Movements in Latin America*, CEDLA Publication 55, edited by Willem Assies, Gerrit Burgwal and Ton Salman, pp. 9–98. Amsterdam.

Aston, T. H. and C. Philpin, editors 1985 *The Brenner Debate: Agrarian Class Structure and Economic Development in Pre-Industrial Europe*. Cambridge, UK: Cambridge University Press.

Augustine, Saint (Aurelius Augustinus, bishop of Hippo) 1984 *Concerning the City of God against the Pagans* [c. 427], with an introduction by John O'Meara. London, UK: Penguin Books.

Avineri, Schlomo, editor 1969 *Karl Marx on Colonialism and Modernization: His Dispatches and Other Writings on China, India, Mexico, the Middle East and North Africa*. Garden City, NY: Anchor Books.

Bahl, Vinay 1999 The Relevance or Irrelevance of Subaltern Studies to the Study of Working Class History. In *After Three Worlds: The Crisis of Historical Consciousness*, edited by Vinay Bahl, Arif Dirlik and Peter Gran. Totowa, NJ: Rowman and Allanheld.

Balandier, Georges 1966 The Colonial Situation: A Theoretical Approach [1951]. In *Social Change: The Colonial Situation*, edited by Immanuel Wallerstein, pp. 34–62. New York: John Wiley and Sons.

Balassa, Bela 1981 *The Newly Industrializing Countries in the World Economy*. New York: Pergamon Press.

Balibar, Etienne 1977 *On the Dictatorship of the Proletariat*. London, UK: Verso.

Banaji, Jairus 1972 For a Theory of Colonial Modes of Production. *Economic and Political Weekly*, vol. VII, no. 52, pp. 2498–502. Bombay.

—— 1976a Summary of Selected Parts of Kautsky's *The Agrarian Question*. *Economy and Society*, vol. 5, no. 1, pp. 2–49. London.

—— 1976b Chayanov, Kautsky, Lenin: Considerations toward a Synthesis. *Economic and Political Weekly*, vol. XI, no. 40, pp. 1594–607. Bombay.

—— 1990 Illusions about the Peasantry: Karl Kautsky and the Agrarian Question. *Journal of Peasant Studies*, vol. 17, no. 2, pp. 288–307. London.

Banerjee, Diptendra 1985 In Search of a Theory of Pre-capitalist Modes of Production. In *Marxian Theory and the Third World* edited by Diptendra Banerjee, pp. 13–40. New Delhi: Sage Publications.

Baran, Paul A. 1957 *The Political Economy of Growth*. New York: Monthly Review Press.

Barnard, F. M. 1965 *Herder's Social and Political Thought*. Oxford, UK: Oxford University Press.

Barnett, Homer G., Leonard Broom, Bernard J. Siegel, Evon Z. Vogt and James B. Watson 1954 Acculturation: An Exploratory Formulation. *American Anthropologist*, Vol. 56, no. 1, pp. 973–1002. Menasha.

Baron, Hans 1959 The *Querelle* of the Ancients and the Moderns as a Problem for Renaissance Scholarship. *Journal of the History of Ideas*, Vol. XX, no. 1, pp. 3–22. Lancaster, PA.

Bauer, Otto 1979 *La cuestión de las nacionalidades y la socialdemocracia* [1907]. Mexico, DF: Siglo Veintiuno Editores.

Beetham, David 1985 *Max Weber and the Theory of Modern Politics*, 2nd edn. Cambridge, UK: Polity Press.

Beiser, Frederick C. 1992 *Enlightenment, Revolution, and Romanticism: The Genesis of Modern German Thought, 1790–1800*. Cambridge, MA: Harvard University Press.

Bell, Daniel 1973 *The Coming of Post-Industrial Society*. New York: Basic Books.

—— 1987 The World and the United States in 2013. *Daedalus*, Vol. 116, no. 3, pp. 1–32. Boston.

Bello, Walden 1998 The End of the Asia Miracle. *The Nation*, Vol. 266, no. 2, January 12/19, pp. 16–21. New York.

Benedict, Ruth 1961 *Patterns of Culture* [1934]. London, UK: Routledge & Kegan Paul.

Bernstein, Eduard 1961 *Evolutionary Socialism: A Criticism and Affirmation* [1899], with an introduction by Sidney Hook. New York: Schocken Books.

Bernstein, Henry 1972 Modernization Theory and the Sociological Study of Development. *The Journal of Development Studies*, vol. 7, no. 2, pp. 141–60. London.

Bettelheim, Charles 1972 Theoretical Comments. In *Unequal Exchange: A Study of the Imperialism of Trade*, by Arghiri Emmanuel, pp. 271–322. New York: Monthly Review Press.

Bienefeld, Manfred 1994 Capitalism and the Nation State in the Dog Days of the Twentieth Century. In *The Socialist Register 1994*, edited by Ralph Miliband and Leo Panitch, pp. 94–129. London, UK: Merlin Press.

Binsbergen, Wim van and Peter Geschiere, editors 1985 *Old Modes of Production and Capitalist Encroachment: Anthropological Explorations in Africa*. London, UK: Routledge and Kegan Paul.

Birnbaum, Pierre 1976 La conception durkheimienne de l'Etat: l'apolitisme des fonctionnaires. *Revue Française de Sociologie*, tome XVII, no. 2, pp. 247–58. Paris.

Blömstrom, Magnus and Björn Hettne 1984 *Development Theory in Transition: The Dependency Debate and Beyond: Third World Responses*. London, UK: Zed Books.

Boas, Franz 1887a The Occurrence of Similar Inventions in Areas Widely Apart. *Science*, vol. IX, May 20, pp. 485–6.Washington.

—— 1887b Museums of Ethnology and Their Classification. *Science*, vol. IX, June 17, pp. 587–9. Washington.

—— 1894 The Half-Blood Indian, An Anthropometric Study. *Popular Science, Monthly*, vol. 45, no. 10, pp. 761–70. Washington.

—— 1911a Changes in the Bodily Form of Descendents of Immigrants. *Senate Document 208, 1911, 61st Congress, 2d Session*. Washington, DC: Government Printing Office.

—— 1911b *The Mind of Primitive Man*. New York: Macmillan. 1940a The Aims of Ethnology [1888]. In *Race, Language, and Culture*, by Franz Boas, pp. 626–38. New York: Macmillan.

—— 1940b Review of William Z. Ripley, 'The Races of Europe' [1899]. In *Race, Language, and Culture*, by Franz Boas, pp. 155–9. New York: Macmillan.

—— Bock, Kenneth E. 1956 The Acceptance of Histories: Toward a Perspective for Social Science. *University of California Publications in Sociology and Social Institutions*, vol. 3, no. 1, pp. 1–132. Berkeley, CA. 1963 Evolution, Function, and Change. *American Sociological Review*, vol. 28, no. 2, pp. 229–37. Chicago.

Bodin, Jean 1945 *Method for the Easy Comprehension of History* [1586], translated by Beatrice Reynolds. New York: Columbia University Press.

Boeke, Julius H. 1953 *Economics and Economic Policy of Dual Societies as Exemplified by Indonesia*. New York: Institute of Pacific Relations.

Booth, David 1975 Andre Gunder Frank: An Introduction and Appreciation. In *Beyond the Sociology of Development*, edited by Ivar Oxaal, Tony Barnett and David Booth, pp. 50–85. London, UK: Routledge and Kegan Paul.

—— 1985 Marxism and Development Sociology: Interpreting the Impasse. *World Development*, vol. 13, no. 7, pp. 761–87. Oxford.

Bottomore, Tom 1978 Introduction. In *Austro-Marxism*, edited by Tom Bottomore and Patrick Goode, pp. 1–44. Oxford, UK: Clarendon Press.

—— 1984 *Sociology and Socialism*. New York: St Martin's Press.

—— 1985 *Theories of Modern Capitalism*. London, UK: Allen and Unwin.

—— 1988 Introduction. In *Interpretations of Marx*, edited by Tom Bottomore, pp. 1–42. Oxford, UK: Basil Blackwell.

Bottomore, Tom and Patrick Goode, editors 1978 *Austro-Marxism*. Oxford, UK: Clarendon Press.

Boyer, Robert 1988 Technical Change and the Theory of 'Régulation'. In *Technical Change and Economic Theory*, edited by Giovanni Dosi, Christopher Freeman, Richard Nelson, Gerald Silverberg and Luc Soete, pp. 67–94. London, UK: Pinter Publishers.

—— 1990 *The Regulation School: A Critical Introduction* [1981]. New York: Columbia University Press.

Brass, Tom 1991 Moral Economists, Subalterns, New Social Movements, and the (Re-) Emergence of a (Post-) Modernised (Middle) Peasant. *The Journal of Peasant Studies*, Vol. 18, no. 2, pp. 173–205. London.

Brenner, Robert 1977 The Origins of Capitalist Development: A Critique of Neo-Smithian Marxism. *New Left Review*, no. 104, pp. 25–92. London.

—— 1978 Dobb on the Transition from Feudalism to Capitalism. *Cambridge Journal of Economics*, vol. 2, no. 2, pp. 121–40. London.

—— 1985a Agrarian Class Structure and Economic Development in Pre-Industrial Europe. In *The Brenner Debate: Agrarian Class Structure and Economic Development in Pre-Industrial Europe*, edited by T. H. Aston and C. H. E. Philpin, pp. 10–63. Cambridge, UK: Cambridge University Press.

—— 1985b The Agrarian Roots of European Capitalism. In *The Brenner Debate: Agrarian Class Structure and Economic Development in Pre-Industrial Europe*, edited by T. H. Aston and C. H. E. Philpin, pp. 213–327. Cambridge, UK: Cambridge University Press.

Brenner, Robert and Mark Glick 1991 The Regulation Approach: Theory and History. *New Left Review*, no. 188, pp. 45–119. London.

Brewer, Anthony 1990 *Marxist Theories of Imperialism: A Critical Survey*, 2nd edn. London, UK: Routledge.

Brinton, Daniel G. 1890 *Races and Peoples: Lectures on the Science of Ethnography*. New York: N. D. C. Hodges.

Brown, Richard 1973 Anthropology and Colonial Rule: Godfrey Wilson and the Rhodes–Livingstone Institute, Northern Rhodesia. In *Anthropology and the Colonial Encounter*, edited by Talal Asad, pp. 173–98. Atlantic Highlands, NJ: Humanities Press.

Brubaker, Rogers 1984 *The Limits of Rationality: An Essay on the Social and Moral Thought of Max Weber*. London, UK: Allen and Unwin.

Bukharin, Nicolai I. 1971 *Economics of the Transformation Period, with the Critical Remarks by Lenin* [1920]. New York: Bergman Publishers.

—— 1972 *Imperialism and the Accumulation of Capital* [1924], edited by Kenneth J. Tarbuck. New York: Monthly Review Press.

—— 1973 *Imperialism and the World Economy* [1929]. New York: Monthly Review Press.

—— 1982 *Selected Writings on the State and the Transition to Socialism*, edited by Richard B. Day. Armond, NY: M. E. Sharpe.

Byres, Terence J. 1991 The Agrarian Question and Differing Forms of Capitalist Agrarian Transition: An Essay with Reference to Asia. In *Rural Transformation in Asia*, edited by Jan Breman and Sudipto Mundle, pp. 3–76. New Delhi: Oxford University Press.

—— 1996 *Capitalism from Above and Capitalism from Below: An Essay in Comparative Political Economy*. New York: St Martin's Press.

Cabral, Amílcar 1969 *Revolution in Guinea: Selected Texts*. New York: Monthly Review Press.

—— 1973 *Return to the Source: Selected Speeches*. New York: Monthly Review Press.

—— 1979 *Unity and Struggle: Speeches and Writings*. New York: Monthly Review Press.

Callinicos, Alex 1990 *Against Postmodernism: A Marxist Critique*. New York: St Martin's Press.

Cardoso, Fernando H. and Enzo Faletto 1979 *Dependency and Development in Latin America* [1971]. Berkeley, CA: University of California Press.

Carneiro, Robert L. 1981 Leslie White. In *Totems and Teachers: Perspectives on the History of Anthropology*, edited by Sydel Silverman, pp. 208–52. New York: Columbia University Press.

Carr, Edward H. 1953 *A History of Soviet Russia*, Vol. 3, *The Bolshevik Revolution, 1917–1923*, vol. 3. London, UK: The Macmillan Press.

—— 1964 *A History of Soviet Russia*, Vol. 7, *Socialism in One Country, 1924–1926*, vol. 3, pt. 1. London, UK: The Macmillan Press.

Chabal, Patrick 1983 *Amilcar Cabral: Revolutionary Leadership and People's War*. Cambridge, UK: Cambridge University Press.

Chakrabarty, Dipesh 1992 Postcoloniality and the Artifice of History: Who Speaks for 'Indian' Pasts? *Representations*, no. 37, pp. 1–26. Berkeley.

Chatterjee, Partha 1983 More on Modes of Power and the Peasantry. In *Subaltern Studies II: Writings on South Asian History and Society*, edited by Ranajit Guha, pp. 311–50. Delhi: Oxford University Press.

—— 1984 Gandhi and the Critique of Civil Society. In *Subaltern Studies III: Writings on South Asian History and Society*, edited by Ranajit Guha, pp. 153–95. Delhi: Oxford University Press.

Chayanov, Alexander V. 1986a On the Theory of Non-Capitalist Economic Systems [1924]. In *The Theory of Peasant Economy*, edited by Daniel Thorner, Basile Kerblay and R. E. F. Smith, with a foreward by Teodor Shanin, pp. 1–28. Madison, WI: The University of Wisconsin Press.

—— 1986b Peasant Farm Organization [1926]. In *The Theory of Peasant Economy*, edited by Daniel Thorner, Basile Kerblay and R. E. F. Smith, with a foreward by Teodor Shanin, pp. 29–270. Madison, WI: The University of Wisconsin Press.

Chilcote, Ronald H. 1991 *Amilcar Cabral's Revolutionary Theory and Practice: A Critical Guide*. Boulder, CO: Lynne Rienner Publishers.

Childe, V. Gordon 1942 *What Happened in History*. Harmondsworth, UK: Penguin Books.

Chossudovsky, Michel 1997a *The Globalisation of Poverty: Impacts of IMF and World Bank Reforms*. London, UK: Zed Books.

—— 1997b Dismantling Former Yugoslavia: Recolonising Bosnia. *Capital and Class*, no. 62, pp. 1–12. London.

Cirese, Alberto Maria 1982 Gramsci's Observations on Folklore. In *Approaches to Gramsci*, edited by Anne Showstack Sassoon, pp. 212–48. London, UK: Writers and Readers Publishing Cooperative Society.

Clammer, John, editor 1978 *The New Economic Anthropology*. New York: St Martin's Press.

Clarke, Simon 1982 *Marx, Marginalism and Modern Sociology from Adam Smith to Max Weber*. London, UK: The Macmillan Press.

Cohen, Jean and Andrew Arato 1992 *Civil Society and Political Theory*. Cambridge, MA: The MIT Press.

Colburn, Forrest D. 1989 Introduction. In *Everyday Forms of Peasant Resistance*, edited by Forrest D. Colburn, pp. vii–xv. Armonk, NY: M. E. Sharpe.

Colby, William M. 1977 *Routes to Rainy Mountain: A Biography of James Mooney, Ethnologist*. Ph.D. Dissertation in History, University of Wisconsin, Madison. Ann Arbor, MI: University Microfilms 78–4851.

Collins, Randall 1980 Weber's Last Theory of Capitalism: A Systematization. *American Sociological Review*, Vol. 45, no. 4, pp. 925–42. Chicago.

Cooper, Frederick 1994 Conflict and Connection: Rethinking Colonial African History. *The American Historical Review*, vol. 99, no. 5, pp. 1516–45. Washington.

Coser, Lewis 1956 *The Functions of Social Conflict*. London, UK: Routledge and Kegan Paul.

Cox, Robert W. 1997 A Perspective on Globalization. In *Globalization: Critical Reflections*, edited by James A. Mittelman, pp. 21–30. Boulder, CO: Lynne Rienner Publishers.

Cox, Terry 1984 Class Analysis of the Russian Peasantry: The Research of Kritsman and his School. In *Kritsman and the Agrarian Marxists*, edited by Terry Cox and Gary Littlejohn, pp. 11–60. London, UK: Frank Cass.

—— 1986 *Peasants, Class, and Capitalism: The Rural Research of L. N. Kritsman and His School*. Oxford, UK: Clarendon Press.

Curry, James 1993 The Flexibility Fetish: A Review Essay on Flexible Specialization. *Capital and Class*, no. 50, pp. 99–126. London.

Dahrendorf, Ralf 1957 *Class and Class Conflict in Industrial Society*. London, UK: Routledge and Kegan Paul.

Darwin, Charles 1874 *The Descent of Man and Selection in Relation to Sex*. London: Murray.

Davidson, Andrew 1989 Mode of Production: Impasse or Passé? *Journal of Contemporary Asia*, vol. 19, no. 3, pp. 243–78. Ann Arbor.

Davis, Horace B. 1976 Introduction: Right of National Self-Determination in Marxist Theory – Luxemburg vs. Lenin. In *The National Question: Selected Writings by Rosa Luxemburg*, edited by Horace B. Davis, pp. 9–59. New York: Monthly Review Press.

Davis, Mike 1978 'Fordism in Crisis: A Review of Michel Aglietta's *Régulation et crises: L'expérience des Etats-Unis. Review*, vol. II, no. 2, pp. 207–69. Binghampton.

Deane, Herbert A. 1963 *The Political and Social Ideas of St. Augustine*. New York: Columbia University Press.

Deutsch, Karl 1961 Social Mobilization and Political Development. *American Political Science Review*, vol. 60, no. 3, pp. 463–515. New York.

Deutscher, Isaac 1954 *The Prophet Armed – Trotsky: 1879–1921*. Oxford, UK: Oxford University Press.

Deyo, Frederic C., editor 1987 *The Political Economy of the New Asian Industrialism*. Ithaca, NY: Cornell University Press.

Deyo, Frederic C. 1989 *Beneath the Miracle: Labor Subordination in the New Asian Industrialism*. Berkeley, CA: University of California Press.

DiMaggio, Paul 1982 Cultural Entrepreneurship in Nineteenth-Century Boston: The Creation of an Organizational Base for High Culture in America. *Media, Culture and Society*, vol. 4, no. 1, pp. 33–50. London.

Dirlik, Arif 1997 *The Postcolonial Aura: Third World Criticism in the Age of Global Capitalism*. Boulder, CO: Westview Press.

Dobb, Maurice 1947 *Studies in the Development of Capitalism*. New York: International Publishers.

—— 1966 *Soviet Economic Development since 1917*, 6th edn. London, UK: Routledge and Kegan Paul.

—— 1976a A Reply [1952]. In *The Transition from Feudalism to Capitalism*, edited by Rodney H. Hilton, pp. 57–67. London, UK: New Left Books.

—— 1976b From Feudalism to Capitalism [1962]. In *The Transition from Feudalism to Capitalism*, edited by Rodney H. Hilton, pp. 165–9. London, UK: New Left Books.

Du Bois, W. E. B. 1898 The Study of Negro Problems. *Annals of the American Academy of Political and Social Science*, vol. XI, no. 219, pp. 1–23. New Haven, CT.

—— 1903 *The Souls of Black Folk: Essays and Sketches*. Chicago, IL: A. C. McClurg.

Duggett, Michael 1975 Marx on Peasants. *Journal of Peasant Studies*, vol. 2, no. 2, pp. 159–82. London.

Dunn, Guy 1997 Major Mafia Gangs in Russia. In *Russian Organized Crime: The New Threat?* edited by Phil Williams, pp. 63–87. London, UK: Frank Cass.

Durkheim, Émile 1886 Les études de science sociale. *Revue Philosophique*, tome XXII, pp. 61–80. Paris.

—— 1887 La science positive de la morale en Allemagne. *Revue Philosophique*, tome XXIV, pp. 33–58, 113–43, 275–84. Paris.

—— 1888 Cours de science social: leçon d'ouverture. *Revue Internationale de L'Enseignement*, tome XV, pp. 23–48. Paris.

—— 1898 Préface. *L'Année Sociologique*, tome I, pp. i–vii. Paris.

—— 1938 *The Rules of Sociological Method* [1895], edited by George E. G. Caitlin. New York: The Free Press.

—— 1951 *Suicide: A Study in Sociology* [1897], edited by George Simpson. Glencoe, IL: Free Press.

—— 1958 *Socialism and Saint-Simon* [1895–6], edited by Alvin W. Gouldner. Yellow Springs, OH: The Antioch Press.

—— 1964 *The Division of Labor in Society* [1893], translated by George Simpson. New York: The Free Press.

—— 1965 *The Elementary Forms of Religious Life* [1912], translated by Joseph W. Swain. New York: The Free Press.

—— 1977 *The Evolution of Educational Thought: Lectures on the Formation and Development of Secondary Education in France* [1938]. London, UK: Routledge and Kegan Paul.

—— 1978 Review: Albert Schaeffle, *Bau und Leben des sozialen Körpers: Erster Band* [1885]. In *On Institutional Analysis*, edited by Mark Traugott, pp. 93–114. Chicago, IL: The University of Chicago Press.

—— 1992 *Professional Ethics and Civic Morals* [1898–1900], with a preface by Bryan S. Turner. London, UK: Routledge.

Eisenstadt, Shmuel N. 1973 Social Change and Development. In *Readings in Social Evolution and Development*, edited by Shmuel N. Eisenstadt, pp. 3–33. Oxford, UK: Pergamon Press.

Emmanuel, Arghiri 1972 *Unequal Exchange: A Study of the Imperialism of Trade* [1969]. New York: Monthly Review Press.

Engels, Frederick 1972 *The Origin of the Family, Private Property and the State:*

In the Light of the Investigations of Lewis H. Morgan [1884], edited by Eleanor B. Leacock. New York: International Publishers.

—— 1974 Democratic Pan-Slavism [1849]. In *Karl Marx Political Writings*, Vol. 1, *The Revolutions of 1848*, edited by David Fernbach, pp. 226–45. New York: Vintage Books.

—— 1990a On the Decline of Feudalism and the Emergence of the National States [1884]. In *Karl Marx and Frederick Engels Collected Works*, Vol. 26, pp. 556–65. New York: International Publishers.

—— 1990b The Peasant Question in France and Germany [1894]. In *Karl Marx and Frederick Engels Collected Works*, Vol. 27, pp. 481–502. New York: International Publishers.

Erlich, Alexander 1960 *The Soviet Industrialization Debate, 1924–1928*. Cambridge, MA: Harvard University Press.

Esherick, Joseph W. 1979 On the 'Restoration of Capitalism': Mao and Marxist Theory. *Modern China*, vol. 5, no. 1, pp. 41–78. London.

Eyal, Gil, Iván Szelényi and Eleanor Townsley 1997 The Theory of Post-Communist Managerialism. *New Left Review*, no. 222, pp. 60–92. London.

Fanon, Frantz 1965 *A Dying Colonialism* [1959]. London, UK: Pelican Books.

—— 1967a *Black Skin, White Masks* [1952]. London, UK: MacGibbon and Kee.

—— 1967b Racism and Culture [1956]. In *Toward an African Revolution (Political Essays)*, by Frantz Fanon, pp. 29–44. New York: Monthly Review Press.

—— 1967c *The Wretched of the Earth* [1961]. London, UK: Penguin Books.

Fei, Xiaotong 1939 *Peasant Life in China: A Field Study of Country Life in the Yangtze Valley*. New York: Dutton.

Filloux, Jean-Claude 1993 Inequalities and Social Stratification in Durkheim's Sociology. In *Émile Durkheim: Sociologist and Moralist*, edited by Stephen P. Turner, pp. 211–28. London, UK: Routledge.

Fisher, Donald 1988 The Scientific Appeal of Functionalism: Rockefeller Philanthropy and the Rise of Social Anthropology. *Anthropology Today*, Vol. 2, no. 1, pp. 5–8. London.

—— 1993 *Fundamental Development of the Social Sciences: Rockefeller Philanthropy and the United States Social Science Research Council*. Ann Arbor, MI: The University of Michigan Press.

Foley, Duncan 1991 Commodity. In *A Dictionary of Marxist Thought*, 2nd edn, edited by Tom Bottomore, pp. 100–2. Oxford, UK: Basil Blackwell.

Fortes, Meyer 1938 Culture Contact as a Dynamic Process. In *Methods of Study of Culture Contact in Africa*, edited by Lucy P. Mair, pp. 60–91. Oxford, UK: Oxford University Press.

Foster, George M. 1967 Introduction: What Is a Peasant? In *Peasant Society: A Reader*, edited by Jack M. Potter, May N. Diaz, and George M. Foster, pp. 15–24. Boston, MA: Little, Brown and Company.

Foster-Carter, Aidan 1978a The Modes of Production Controversy. *New Left Review*, no. 107, pp. 47–78. London.

—— 1978b Can We Articulate 'Articulation'? In *The New Economic Anthropology*, edited by John Clammer, pp. 210–39. New York: St Martin's Press.

Foucault, Michel 1978 *The History of Sexuality*, Vol. 1, *An Introduction*. New York: Vintage Books.

Frank, André G. 1967 *Capitalism and Underdevelopment in Latin America: Historical Studies of Chile and Brazil*. New York: Monthly Review Press.

—— 1969 The Development of Underdevelopment [1966]. In *Latin America: Underdevelopment or Revolution*, by André G. Frank, pp. 3–17. New York: Monthly Review Press.

—— 1972a Sociology of Development and Underdevelopment of Sociology [1969]. In *Dependence and Underdevelopment: Latin America's Political Economy*, edited by James D. Cockcroft, Andrée G. Frank, and Dale L. Johnson, pp. 321–98. Garden City, NY: Doubleday and Company.

—— 1972b *Lumpenbourgeoisie: Lumpendevelopment* [1970]. New York: Monthly Review Press.

Fried, Morton H. 1967 *The Evolution of Political Society*. New York: Random House.

Fröbel, Folker, Jürgen Heinrichs, and Otto Kreye 1977 The Tendency Towards a New International Division of Labor. *Review*, vol. I, no. 1, pp. 73–88. Binghamton. 1980 *The New International Division of Labour*. Cambridge, UK: Cambridge University Press.

Furtado, Celso 1964 *Development and Underdevelopment: A Structural View of the Problems of Developed and Underdeveloped Countries* [1961]. Berkeley, CA: University of California Press.

Gayton, Anna H. 1932 The Ghost Dances of 1870 in South-Central California. *University of California Publications in American Archaeology and Ethnology*, vol. XXVIII, pp. 57–82. Berkeley.

Geertz, Clifford 1956 The Development of the Javanese Economy: A Socio- cultural Approach. *Massachusetts Institute of Technology, Center for International Studies, Economic Development Program, Document* C/56–18. Cambridge, MA.

—— 1963a *Agricultural Involution; The Processes of Ecological Change in Indonesia*. Berkeley, CA: University of California Press.

—— 1963b The Integrative Revolution: Primordial Sentiments and Civil Politics in the New States. In *Old Societies and New States: The Quest for Modernity in Asia and Africa*, edited by Clifford Geertz, pp. 105–57. Glencoe, IL: The Free Press.

—— 1971 After the Revolution: The Fate of Nationalism in the New States. In *Stability and Social Change*, edited by Bernard Barber and Alex Inkeles, pp. 357–76. Boston, MA: Little, Brown and Company.

—— 1973a Ritual and Social Change: A Javanese Example [1959]. In *The Inter-pretation of Cultures; Selected Essays*, by Clifford Geertz, pp. 142–69. New York: Basic Books.

—— 1973b Religion as a Cultural System [1966]. In *The Interpretation of Cultures; Selected Essays*, by Clifford Geertz, pp. 87–125. New York: Basic Books.

Geras, Norman 1976 *The Legacy of Rosa Luxemburg*. London, UK: Verso.

Gerth, Hans H. and C. Wright Mills 1946 Introduction: The Man and His Work. In *From Max Weber: Essays in Sociology*, edited by Hans H. Gerth and C. Wright Mills, pp. 1–74. New York: Oxford University Press.

Giddens, Anthony 1987 Weber and Durkheim: Coincidence and Divergence. In *Max Weber and his Contemporaries*, edited by Wolfgang J. Mommsen and Jürgen Osterhammel, pp. 182–9. London, UK: Allen and Unwin.

—— 1990 *The Consequences of Modernity*. Stanford, CA: Stanford University Press.

Gilroy, Paul 1993 *The Black Atlantic: Modernity and Double Consciousness*. Cambridge, MA: Harvard University Press.

Girvan, Norman 1973 The Development of Dependency Economics in the Carib-bean and Latin America: Review and Comparison. *Social and Economic Studies*, vol. 22, no. 1, pp. 1–33. Kingston.

Gluckman, Max 1966 Malinowski's 'Functional' Analysis of Social Change [1947]. In *Social Change: The Colonial Situation*, edited by Immanuel Wallerstein, pp. 25–33. New York: John Wiley and Sons.

Gobineau, Joseph A. 1915 *The Inequality of Human Races* [1853–5], translated by A. Collins. London, UK: Heinemann.

Goldthorpe, John 1971 Theories of Industrial Society: Reflections on the Recru-descence of Historicism and the Future of Futurology. *Archives Européenes de Sociologie*, vol. 12, no. 2, pp. 263–88. Paris.

Goodman, David and Michael Redclift 1982 *From Peasant to Proletarian: Capital-ist Development and Agrarian Transitions*. New York: St Martin's Press.

Gordon, David 1988 The Global Economy: New Edifice or Crumbling Foundation. *New Left Review*, no. 168, pp. 24–65. London.

Gramsci, Antonio 1967 The Southern Question [1926]. In *The Modern Prince and Other Writings*, pp. 28–51. New York: International Publishers.

—— 1971a Notes on Italian History [1933]. In *Selections from the Prison Note-books*, edited by Quintin Hoare and Geoffrey N. Smith, pp. 44–120. New York: International Publishers.

—— 1971b The Intellectuals [1933]. In *Selections from the Prison Notebooks*, edited by Quintin Hoare and Geoffrey N. Smith, pp. 3–23. New York: Inter-national Publishers.

—— 1971c Americanism and Fordism [1931]. In *Selections from the Prison Notebooks*, edited by Quintin Hoare and Geoffrey N. Smith, pp. 277–318. New York: International Publishers.

—— 1992 Types of Periodicals [1929]. In *Antonio Gramsci Prison Notebooks*, edited by Joseph A. Buttigieg and Antonio Callari, Vol. 1, pp. 125–36. New York: Columbia University Press.

Gran, Peter 1979 *Islamic Roots of Capitalism: Egypt 1760–1840*. Austin, TX: University of Texas Press.

Guéhenno, Jean-Marie 1995 *The End of the Nation-State* [1993]. Minneapolis, MN: University of Minnesota Press.

Guha, Ranajit 1982 On Some Aspects of the Historiography of Colonial India. In *Subaltern Studies I: Writings on South Asian History and Society*, edited by Ranajit Guha, pp. 1–8. Delhi: Oxford University Press.

Habermas, Jürgen 1981 New Social Movements. *Telos*, no. 49, pp. 33–7. St Louis.

Hagen, Everett E. 1962 *On the Theory of Social Change: How Economic Growth Begins*. Homewood, IL: Dorsey Press.

Hall, Stuart 1991 The Local and the Global: Globalization and Ethnicity. In *Culture, Globalisation, and the World System: Contemporary Conditions for the Representation of Identity*, edited by A. D. King, pp. 19–39. London, UK: Macmillan.

Harman, Chris 1992 The Return of the National Question. *International Socialism*, no. 56, pp.3–62. London.

Harvey, David 1989 *The Condition of Postmodernity: An Enquiry into the Origins of Cultural Change*. Oxford, UK: Basil Blackwell. 1996 *Justice, Nature and the Geography of Difference*. Oxford, UK: Basil Blackwell.

Haupt, Georges, Michael Löwy and Claudie Weill, editors 1974 *Les marxistes et la question nationale, 1848–1914: études et textes*. Paris, FR: François Maspero.

Havighurst, Alfred F., editor 1958 *The Pirenne Thesis: Analysis, Criticism, and Revision*. Boston, MA: D. C. Heath and Company.

Hegel, George Friedrich 1952 *Philosophy of Right* [1821], translated by T. M. Knox. Oxford, UK: Oxford University Press.

—— 1964 The German Constitution. In *Hegel's Political Writings*, edited by T. M. Knox, pp. 153–64. Cambridge, UK: Cambridge University Press.

—— 1975 *Lectures on the Philosophy of World History: Introduction* [1830], with an introduction by Duncan Forbes. Cambridge, UK: Cambridge University Press.

Held, David 1991 Crisis in Capitalist Society. In *A Dictionary of Marxist Thought*, 2nd edn, edited by Tom Bottomore, pp. 118–21. Oxford, UK: Basil Blackwell.

Hennis, Wilhelm 1988 *Max Weber: Essays in Reconstruction*. London, UK: Allen and Unwin.

Herold, Marc W. and Nicholas Kozlov 1987 A New International Division of Labor: The Caribbean Case. In *The Year Left 2: An American Socialist Yearbook*, edited by Mike Davis, Manning Marable, Fred Pfeil and Michael Sprinker, pp. 218–41. London, UK: Verso.

Herskovits, Melville J. 1938 *Acculturation: The Study of Culture Contact*. New York: J. J. Augustin Publisher.

Hewitt de Alcántara, Cynthia 1984 *Anthropological Perspectives on Rural Mexico.* London, UK: Routledge and Kegan Paul.

Higgott, Richard A. 1981 Beyond the Sociology of Underdevelopment: An Historiographical Analysis of Dependencia and Marxist Theories of Underdevelopment. *Social Analysis*, no. 7, pp. 72–98. Adelaide.

Hilferding, Rudolf 1981 *Finance Capital: A Study of the Latest Phase of Capitalist Development* [1910], edited by Tom Bottomore. London, UK: Routledge and Kegan Paul.

Hill, Christopher 1971 *Lenin and the Russian Revolution.* London, UK: Penguin Books.

Hilton, Rodney 1974 Warriors and Peasants. *New Left Review*, no. 83, pp. 83–94. London.

—— 1976a A Comment [1953]. In *The Transition from Feudalism to Capitalism*, edited by Rodney Hilton, pp. 109–17. London, UK: New Left Books.

—— 1976b Introduction. In *The Transition from Feudalism to Capitalism*, edited by Rodney Hilton, pp. 9–30. London, UK: New Left Books.

Hinsley, Curtis M., Jr. 1981 *Savages and Scientists: The Smithsonian Institution and the Development of American Anthropology, 1846–1910.* Washington, DC: Smithsonian Institution Press.

Hirschman, Albert O. 1958 *The Strategy of Economic Development.* New Haven, CT: Yale University Press.

Hirst, Paul and Grahame Thompson 1996 *Globalization in Question: The International Economy and the Possibilities of Governance.* Cambridge, UK: Polity Press.

Hirst, Paul and Jonathan Zeitlin 1991 Flexible Specialization versus Post-Fordism: Theory, Evidence and Policy Implications. *Economy and Society*, vol. 20, no. 1, pp. 1–56. London.

Hobbes, Thomas 1968 *Leviathan* [1651], edited by C. B. Macpherson. London, UK: Penguin Books.

Hobsbawm, Eric J. 1965 Introduction. In *Pre-capitalist Economic Formations* by Karl Marx, pp. 9–65. New York: International Publishers.

—— 1976 From Feudalism to Capitalism [1962]. In *The Transition from Feudalism to Capitalism*, edited by Rodney Hilton, pp. 159–64. London, UK: New Left Books.

—— 1979 *The Age of Capital, 1848–1875.* New York: Mentor Books.

—— 1987 *The Age of Empire, 1875–1914.* New York: Pantheon Books.

—— 1996 *The Age of Extremes: A History of the World, 1914–1991.* New York: Vintage Books.

Hobson, John A. 1965 *Imperialism: A Study*, 1st edn [1902]. Ann Arbor, MI: University of Michigan Press.

Hodgen, Margaret T. 1964 *Early Anthropology in the Sixteenth and Seventeenth*

Centuries. Philadelphia, PA: University of Pennsylvania Press.

Horsman, Matthew and Andrew Marshall 1994 *After the Nation-State: Citizens, Tribalism and the New World Disorder*. New York: HarperCollins Publishers.

Howard, Michael C. and J. E. King 1989 *A History of Marxian Economics*, Vol. I, *1883–1929*. Princeton, NJ: Princeton University Press.

Hunter [Wilson], Monica 1936 *Reaction to Conquest: Effects of Contact with Europeans on the Pondo of South Africa*. Oxford, UK: Oxford University Press.

—— 1938 Contact between European and Native in South Africa: 1. In Pongoland. In *Methods of Study of Culture Contact in Africa*, edited by Lucy Mair, pp. 9–24. Oxford, UK: Oxford University Press.

Huntington, Samuel P. 1976 The Change to Change: Modernization, Development, and Politics [1971]. In *Comparative Modernization: A Reader*, edited by Cyril E. Black, pp. 25–61. New York: The Free Press.

Hussain, Athar and Keith Tribe 1981a *Marxism and the Agrarian Question*, Vol. 1, *German Social Democracy and the Peasantry, 1890–1907*. Atlantic Highlands, NJ: Humanities Press.

—— 1981b *Marxism and the Agrarian Question*, Vol. 2, *Russian Marxism and the Peasantry, 1861–1930*. Atlantic Highlands, NJ: Humanities Press.

Hutchinson, John and Anthony D. Smith 1994 Introduction. In *Nationalism*, edited by John Hutchinson and Anthony D. Smith, pp. 3–13. Oxford, UK: Oxford University Press.

Hymer, Stephen 1976 *International Operations of National Firms: A Study of Direct Foreign Investment*. Cambridge, MA: The MIT Press.

Ibn Khaldun 1967 *The Muqaddimah: An Introduction to History*, edited by N. J. Dawood. Princeton, NJ: Princeton University Press.

Ionescu, Ghita 1976 Introduction. In *The Political Thought of Saint-Simon*, edited by Ghita Ionescu, pp. 1–57. Oxford, UK: Oxford University Press.

Irele, Abiola 1973a Negritude or Black Cultural Nationalism. *The Journal of Modern African Studies*, vol. 3, no. 3, pp. 321–48. London.

—— 1973b Negritude: Literature and Ideology. *The Journal of Modern African Studies*, vol. 3, no. 4, pp. 499–526. London.

Jameson, Fredric 1991 *Postmodernism or the Cultural Logic of Late Capitalism*. London, UK: Verso.

Jenkins, Rhys 1984 Divisions over the International Division of Labor. *Capital and Class*, no. 22, pp. 28–57. London.

—— 1987 *Transnational Corporations and Uneven Development*. London, UK: Methuen.

Jessop, Bob 1982 *The Capitalist State*. New York: New York University Press.

—— 1990 *State Theory: Putting Capitalist States in Their Place*. University Park, PA: The Pennsylvania State University Press.

Johnston, Hank, Enrique Laraña and Joseph R. Gusfield 1994 Identities, Grievances, and New Social Movements. In *New Social Movements: From Ideology to Identity*, edited by Enrique Laraña, Hank Johnston and Joseph R. Gusfield, pp. 3–35. Philadelphia, PA: Temple University Press.

Jones, Greta 1980 *Social Darwinism and English Thought: The Interaction between Biological and Social Theory*. Brighton, UK: Harvester.

Kahn, Charles H. 1960 *Anaximander and the Origins of Greek Cosmology*. New York: Columbia University Press.

—— 1979 *The Art and Thought of Heraclitus: An Edition of the Fragments with Translation and Commentary*. Cambridge, UK: Cambridge University Press.

Katz, Claudio J. 1989 *From Feudalism to Capitalism: Marxian Theories of Class Struggle and Social Change*. New York: Greenwood Press.

Kautsky, Karl 1887 Die moderne Nationalität. *Die Neue Zeit*, Jahrgang V, pp. 442–51. Stuttgart.

—— 1908 Nationalität und Internationalität. *Die Neue Zeit, Erganzunghefte* 1, 18 Januar 1908, pp. 1–25. Stuttgart.

—— 1988 *The Agrarian Question* [1899], with an introduction by Hamza Alavi and Teodor Shanin, 2 vols. London, UK: Zwan Publications.

Keane, John 1988 *Democracy and Civil Society: On the Predicaments of European Socialism, the Prospects for Democracy, and the Problem of Controlling Social and Political Power*. London, UK: Verso.

Kearney, Michael 1996 *Reconceptualizing the Peasantry: Anthropology in Global Perspective*. Boulder, CO: Westview Press.

Keesing, Felix M. 1934 The Changing Life of Native Peoples in the Pacific Area: A Sketch in Cultural Dynamics. *The American Journal of Sociology*, vol. XXXIX, no. 4, pp. 443–58. Chicago.

Keynes, John M. 1936 *General Theory of Employment, Interest, and Money*. New York: Harcourt, Brace and Company.

Kiely, Ray 1994 Development Theory and Industrialisation: Beyond the Impasse. *Journal of Contemporary Asia*, vol. 24, no. 2, pp. 133–60. Stockholm.

Kindleberger, Charles 1969 *American Business Abroad: Six Lectures on Direct Investment*. New Haven, CT: Yale University Press.

Kluckhohn, Clyde 1943 Covert Culture and Administrative Problems. *American Anthropologist* Vol. 45, no. 2, pp. 213–27. Menasha.

Knei-Paz, Baruch 1978 *The Social and Political Thought of Leon Trotsky*. Oxford, UK: Oxford University Press.

Konrád, György and Iván Szelényi 1979 *The Intellectuals on the Road to Class Power* [1974]. New York: Harcourt Brace Jovanovich.

Krader, Lawrence 1974 Introduction. In *The Ethnological Notebooks of Karl Marx* [1880–1882], edited by Lawrence Krader, pp. 1–90. Assen, The Netherlands: Van Gorcum.

Kritsman, L. N. 1984 Class Stratification in the Soviet Countryside [1926]. In *Kritsman and the Agrarian Marxists*, edited by Terry Cox and Gary Littlejohn, pp. 85–143. London, UK: Frank Cass.

Laclau, Ernesto 1971 Feudalism and Capitalism in Latin America. *New Left Review*, no. 71, pp. 19–38. London.

Laclau, Ernesto and Chantal Mouffe 1985 *Hegemony and Socialist Strategy: Towards a Radical Democratic Politics*. London, UK: Verso.

Lash, Scott and John Urry 1987 *The End of Organized Capitalism*. Cambridge, UK: Polity Press.

Leacock, Eleanor B. 1963 Introduction. In *Ancient Society: Or, Researches in the Lines of Human Progress from Savagery through Barbarism to Civilization* [1877], by Lewis H. Morgan. Cleveland, OH: The World Publishing Company.

—— 1982 Marxism and Anthropology. In *The Left Academy: Marxist Scholarship on American Campuses*, edited by Bertell Ollman and Edward Vernoff, pp. 242–76. New York: McGraw-Hill Book Company.

Lechner, Frank J. 1991 Religion, Law, and Global Order. In *Religion and Global Order*, edited by Roland Robertson and William R. Garrett, pp. 263–80. New York: Paragon House Publishers.

Lee, George 1971 Rosa Luxemburg and the Impact of Imperialism. *The Economic Journal*, vol. 81, no. 324, pp. 847–62. London.

Lenin, Vladimir I. 1960a The Development of Capitalism in Russia: The Process of the Formation of a Home Market for Large-scale Industry [1899]. In *Collected Works*, Vol. 3, pp. 21–607. Moscow, USSR: Progress Publishers.

—— 1960b New Economic Developments in Peasant Life (On V. Y. Postnikov's *Peasant Farming in South Russia*) [1893]. In *Collected Works*, Vol. 1, pp. 11–74. Moscow, USSR: Progress Publishers.

—— 1960c The Agrarian Question and the 'Critics of Marx' [1903]. In *Collected Works*, Vol. 5, pp. 103–222. Moscow, USSR: Progress Publishers.

—— 1961 What Is to Be Done? Burning Questions of Our Movement [1902]. In *Collected Works*, Vol. 5, pp. 347–530. Moscow, USSR: Progress Publishers.

—— 1962 The Agrarian Program of Social-Democracy in the First Russian Revolution, 1905–1907 [1907]. In *Collected Works*, Vol. 13, pp. 217–431. Moscow, USSR: Progress Publishers.

—— 1963 The Agrarian Question in Russia Towards the Close of the Nineteenth Century [1908]. In *Collected Works*, Vol. 15, pp. 69–147. Moscow, USSR: Progress Publishers.

—— 1964a Imperialism, The Highest Stage of Capitalism: A Popular Outline [1917]. In *Collected Works*, Vol. 22, pp. 185–304. Moscow, USSR: Progress Publishers.

—— 1964b The Right of Nations to Self-Determination [1914]. In *Collected Works*, Vol. 20, pp. 393–454. Moscow, USSR: Progress Publishers.

—— 1964c Critical Remarks on the National Question [1913]. In *Collected Works*, Vol. 20, pp. 17–51. Moscow, USSR: Progress Publishers.

—— 1964d The Socialist Revolution and the Right of Nations to Self-Determination, *Theses* [1916]. In *Collected Works*, Vol. 22, pp. 143–56. Moscow, USSR: Progress Publishers.

—— 1964e New Data on the Laws Governing the Development of Capitalism in Agriculture, Part One. *Capitalism and Agriculture in the United States of America*. In *Collected Works*, Vol. 22, pp. 13–102. Moscow, USSR: Progress Publishers.

—— 1964f State and Revolution: The Marxist Theory of the State and the Tasks of the Proletariat in the Revolution [1917]. In *Collected Works*, Vol. 25, pp. 385–498. Moscow, USSR: Progress Publishers.

—— 1965a The Trade Unions, The Present Situation and Trotsky's Mistakes [1920]. In *Collected Works*, Vol. 32, pp. 19–42. Moscow, USSR: Progress Publishers.

—— 1965b The New Economic Policy and the Tasks of the Political Education Departments [1921]. In *Collected Works*, Vol. 33, pp. 60–80. Moscow, USSR: Progress Publishers.

—— 1965c The Tax in Kind [1921]. In *Collected Works*, Vol. 32, pp. 329–65. Moscow, USSR: Progress Publishers. 1966 Preliminary Draft Theses on the Agrarian Question. In *Collected Works*, Vol. 31, pp. 144–51. Moscow, USSR: Progress Publishers.

—— 1968 Notebooks on Imperialism [1915–1916]. In *Collected Works*, Vol. 39. Moscow, USSR: Progress Publishers.

Lerner, Ralph and Muhsin Mahdi 1963 *Medieval Political Philosophy: A Source-book*. Glencoe, IL: The Free Press of Glencoe.

Lewin, Moshe 1968 *Russian Peasants and Soviet Power: A Study of Collectiviza-tion*. New York: W. W. Norton.

—— 1974 *Political Undercurrents in Soviet Economic Debates: From Bukharin to the Modern Reformers*. Princeton, NJ: Princeton University Press.

—— 1985 *The Making of the Soviet System: Essays on the Social History of Interwar Russia*. New York: Pantheon Books.

Linton, Ralph, editor 1940 *Acculturation in Seven American Indian Tribes*. New York: D. Appleton-Century Company.

Lipietz, Alain 1986 New Tendencies in the International Division of Labor: Regimes of Accumulation and Modes of Regulation. In *Production, Work, Territory: The Geographical Anatomy of Industrial Capitalism*, edited by Allen Scott and Michael Storper, pp. 16–40. Boston, MA: Allen and Unwin.

Littlejohn, Gary 1977 Peasant Economy and Society. In *Sociological Theories of the Economy*, edited by Barry Hindess, pp. 118–56. New York: Holmes and Meier Publishers.

—— 1984 The Agrarian Marxist Research in its Political Context: State Policy and the Development of the Soviet Rural Class Structure in the 1920s. In *Kritsman and the Agrarian Marxists*, edited by Terry Cox and Gary Littlejohn, pp. 61–84. London, UK: Frank Cass.

Llobera, Josep R. 1981 Durkheim, the Durkheimians and their Collective Misrepresentation of Marx. In *The Anthropology of Pre-Capitalist Societies*, edited by Joel S. Kahn and Josep R. Llobera, pp. 214–40. London, UK: The Macmillan Press.

—— 1994 Durkheim and the National Question. In *Debating Durkheim*, edited by W. S. F. Pickering and H. Martins, pp. 134–58. London, UK: Routledge.

Lock, Grahame 1977 Introduction. In *Dictatorship of the Proletariat* by Etienne Balibar, pp. 7–33. London, UK: Verso.

Löwith, Karl 1982 *Max Weber and Karl Marx* [1960], edited by Tom Bottomore and William Outhwaite. London, UK: Allen and Unwin.

Löwy, Michael 1974 Le problème de l'Histoire. In *Les marxistes et la question nationale, 1848–1914: études et textes*, edited by Georges Haupt, Michael Löwy and Claudie Weill, pp. 370–91. Paris: François Maspero.

—— 1981 *The Politics of Combined and Uneven Development: The Theory of Permanent Revolution*. London, UK: Verso.

Lukes, Steven 1977 *Émile Durkheim: His Life and Work: A Historical and Critical Study*. London, UK: Penguin Books.

Luxemburg, Rosa 1951 *The Accumulation of Capital* [1913], edited by Joan Robinson. London, UK: Routledge and Kegan Paul.

—— 1970a Reform or Revolution [1900]. In *Rosa Luxemburg Speaks*, edited by Mary-Alice Waters, pp. 33–90. New York: Pathfinder Press.

—— 1970b The Mass Strike, the Political Party, and the Trade Unions [1906]. In *Rosa Luxemburg Speaks*, edited by Mary-Alice Waters, pp. 153–218. New York: Pathfinder Press.

—— 1971 Speech to the Hanover Congress [1899]. In *Selected Political Writings of Rosa Luxemburg*, edited by Dick Howard, pp. 44–51. New York: Monthly Review Press.

—— 1972 *The Accumulation of Capital – An Anti-Critique* [1915], edited by Kenneth J. Tarbuck. New York: Monthly Review Press.

—— 1976 The National Question and Autonomy [1908–9]. In *The National Question: Selected Writings by Rosa Luxemburg*, edited by Horace B. Davis, pp. 101–287. New York: Monthly Review Press.

Machiavelli, Niccolò 1988 *Florentine Histories* [1525], translated by Laura F. Banfield and Harvey C. Mansfield, Jr. Princeton, NJ: Princeton University Press.

Macpherson, Crawford B. 1973 *Democratic Theory: Essays in Retrieval*. Oxford, UK: Oxford University Press.

—— 1977 *The Life and Times of Liberal Democracy*. Oxford, UK: Oxford University Press.

Mair, Lucy, editor 1938 *Methods of Study of Culture Contact in Africa*. Oxford, UK: Oxford University Press.

Malinowski, Bronislaw 1938 Introductory Essay: The Anthropology of Changing African Cultures. In *Methods of Study of Culture Contact in Africa*, edited by Lucy P. Mair, pp. vii–xxxviii. Oxford, UK: Oxford University Press.

—— 1945 *The Dynamics of Culture Change: An Inquiry into Race Relations in Africa*. New Haven, CT: Yale University Press.

Mallon, Florencia E. 1994 The Promise and Dilemma of Subaltern Studies: Perspectives from Latin American History. *The American Historical Review*, vol. 99, no. 5, pp. 1491–1515. Washington.

Mandel, Ernest 1989 *Beyond Perestroika: The Future of Gorbachev's USSR*. London, UK: Verso.

Mannoni, Octave 1964 *Prospero and Caliban: The Psychology of Colonization* [1950]. New York: Frederick A. Praeger.

Mao Zedong 1965a Analysis of the Classes in Chinese Society [1926]. In *Selected Works of Mao Tse-tung*, Vol. 1, pp. 13–22. Peking: Foreign Languages Press.

—— 1965b How to Differentiate the Classes in the Rural Areas [1933]. In *Selected Works of Mao Tse-tung*, Vol. 1, pp. 137–40. Peking: Foreign Languages Press.

—— 1965c Report on an Investigation of the Peasant Movement in Hunan [1927]. *Selected Works of Mao Tse-tung*, Vol. 1, pp. 23–62. Peking: Foreign Languages Press.

—— 1990 *Report from Xunwu* [1930], with an introduction by Roger R. Thompson. Stanford, CA: Stanford University Press.

Marable, Manning 1995 *Beyond Black and White: Transforming African-American Politics*. London, UK: Verso.

Marcuse, Herbert 1960 *Reason and Revolution: Hegel and the Rise of Social Theory* [1941]. Boston, MA: Beacon Press.

Mariátegui, José Carlos 1971 *Seven Interpretive Essays on the Peruvian Reality* [1928], with an introduction by Jorge Basadre. Austin, TX: University of Texas Press.

Markus, György 1991 Culture: The Making and the Make-up of a Concept. *Dialectical Anthropology*, vol. 18, no. 1, pp. 3–31. Dordrecht.

Martinussen, John 1997 *Society, State and Market: A Guide to Competing Theories of Development*. London, UK: Zed Books.

Marx, Karl 1963 *The Eighteenth Brumaire of Louis Bonaparte* [1852]. New York: International Publishers.

—— 1964a *The Economic and Philosophic Manuscripts of 1844* [1844], edited by Dirk J. Struik. New York: International Publishers.

—— 1964b *Class Struggles in France 1848–1850* [1848–50]. New York: International Publishers.

—— 1968 *Theories of Surplus-Value* [1862–3], edited by S. Ryazanskaya, Vol. 2. Moscow, USSR: Progress Publishers.

—— 1970 *A Contribution to the Critique of Political Economy* [1859], edited by Maurice Dobb. New York: International Publishers.

—— 1971 The Civil War in France [1871]. In *On the Paris Commune* by Karl Marx and Frederick Engels, pp. 102–81. Moscow, USSR: Progress Publishers.

—— 1973 *Grundrisse: Foundations of the Critique of Political Economy* [1857–8], with an introduction by Martin Nicolaus. New York: Vintage Books.

—— 1974a *The Ethnological Notebooks of Karl Marx* [1880–2], edited by Lawrence Krader. Assen, The Netherlands: Van Gorcum.

—— 1974b The Civil War in France [1871]. In *Karl Marx Political Writings*, Vol. 3, *The First International and After*, edited by David Fernbach, pp. 187–268. New York: Vintage Books.

—— 1977 *Capital: A Critique of Political Economy* [1867], Vol. 1, with an introduction by Ernest Mandel. New York: Vintage Books.

—— 1978 *Capital: A Critique of Political Economy* [1884], Vol. 2, with an introduction by Ernest Mandel. London, UK: Penguin Books.

—— 1981 *Capital: A Critique of Political Economy* [1894], Vol. 3, with an introduction by Ernest Mandel. New York: Vintage Books.

—— 1982 *Critique of Hegel's 'Philosophy of Right'* [1843], edited by Joseph O'Malley. Cambridge, UK: Cambridge University Press.

—— 1983a Letter to Frederick Engels, 2 June 1853. In *Karl Marx and Frederick Engels Collected Works*, Vol. 39, pp. 330–5. New York: International Publishers.

—— 1983b Marx-Zasulich Correspondence: Letters and Drafts [1881]. In *Late Marx and the Russian Road: Marx and 'The Peripheries of Capitalism'*, edited by Teodor Shanin, pp. 97–126. New York: Monthly Review Press.

—— 1985 Letter to Frederick Engels, 19 December 1860. In *Karl Marx and Frederick Engels Collected Works*, Vol. 41, pp. 231–3. New York: International Publishers.

—— 1987 Letter to Ludwig Kugelmann, 29 November 1869. In *Karl Marx and Frederick Engels Collected Works*, Vol. 43, pp. 390–1. New York: International Publishers.

Marx, Karl and Frederick Engels 1970 *The German Ideology* [1845–6], edited by C. J. Arthur. New York: International Publishers.

—— 1974 Manifesto of the Communist Party [1848]. In *Karl Marx Political Writings*, Vol. 1, *The Revolutions of 1948*, edited by David Fernbach, pp. 62–98. New York: Vintage Books.

—— 1989 Preface to the Second Russian Edition of the *Manifesto of the Communist Party* [1882]. In *Karl Marx and Frederick Engels Collected Works*, Vol. 24, pp. 425–6. New York: International Publishers.

Mason, Otis T. 1894 Ethnological Exhibit of the Smithsonian Institution at the

World's Columbian Exposition. *Memoirs of the International Congress of Anthropology*, edited by C. Staniland Wake, pp. 208–16. Chicago, IL: Schute Publishing Company.

Mauss, Marcel 1958 Introduction to the First Edition [1928]. In *Socialism and Saint-Simon*, edited by Alvin W. Gouldner, pp. 1–4. Yellow Springs, OH: The Antioch Press.

McClelland, David C. 1961 *The Achieving Society*. Princeton, NJ: Van Nostrand.

McCulloch, Jock 1983a *Black Soul, White Artifact: Fanon's Clinical Psychology and Social Theory*. Cambridge, UK: Cambridge University Press.

—— 1983b *In the Twilight of Revolution: The Political Theory of Amílcar Cabral*. London, UK: Routledge and Kegan Paul.

McEachern, Doug 1976 The Mode of Production in India. *Journal of Contemporary Asia*, vol. 6, no. 4, pp. 444–57. Stockholm.

Meek, Ronald L. 1976 *Social Science and Ignoble Savage*. Cambridge, UK: Cambridge University Press.

Meillassoux, Claude 1981 *Maidens, Meal and Money: Capitalism and the Domestic Community* [1975]. Cambridge, UK: Cambridge University Press.

Meisner, Maurice 1996 *The Deng Xiaoping Era: An Inquiry into the Fate of Chinese Socialism 1978–1994*. New York: Hill and Wang.

Mészáros, István 1995 *Beyond Capital: Toward a Theory of Transition*. New York: Monthly Review Press.

Mintz, Sidney W. 1953 The Folk–Urban Continuum and the Rural Proletarian Community. *American Sociological Review*, vol. LIX, no. 2, pp. 136–43. Chicago.

—— 1973 A Note on the Definition of Peasantries. *Journal of Peasant Studies*, vol. 1, no. 1, pp. 91–106. London. 1974 The Rural Proletariat and the Problem of Rural Proletarian Consciousness. *The Journal of Peasant Studies*, vol. 1, no. 4, pp. 291–325. London.

Molina Enríquez, Andrés 1978 *Los grandes problemas nacionales* [1909], edited by Arnaldo Córdoba. Mexico, DF: Ediciones Era.

Mommsen, Wolfgang J. 1971 Discussion on Max Weber and Power-politics. In *Max Weber and Sociology Today*, edited by Otto Stammer, pp. 109–16. Oxford, UK: Basil Blackwell.

—— 1974 *The Age of Bureaucracy: Perspectives on the Political Sociology of Max Weber*. Oxford, UK: Basil Blackwell.

—— 1982 *Theories of Imperialism* [1977], translated by P. S. Falla. Chicago, IL: The University of Chicago Press.

—— 1984 *Max Weber and German Politics, 1890–1920* [1979]. Chicago, IL: University of Chicago Press.

—— 1987 Introduction. In *Max Weber and his Contemporaries*, edited by Wolfgang J. Mommsen and Jürgen Osterhammel, pp. 1–21. London, UK: Allen and Unwin.

—— 1989 *The Political and Social Theory of Max Weber*. Chicago, IL: The University of Chicago Press.

Mooney, James E. 1896 The Ghost-Dance Religion and the Sioux Outbreak of 1890. In *Fourteenth Annual Report of the Bureau of Ethnology, 1892–93*, pt. 2, pp. 653–1136. Washington, DC: Government Printing Office.

Moore, Barrington, Jr. 1966 *Social Origins of Dictatorship and Democracy: Lord and Peasant in the Making of the Modern World*. Boston, MA: Beacon Press.

Morgan, Lewis Henry 1963 *Ancient Society: Or, Researches in the Lines of Human Progress from Savagery through Barbarism to Civilization* [1877]. Cleveland, OH: The World Publishing Company.

Moses, Lester G. 1984 *The Indian Man: A Biography of James Mooney*. Urbana, IL: University of Illinois Press.

Mouffe, Chantal 1988 Hegemony and New Political Subjects: Toward a New Concept of Democracy. In *Marxism and the Interpretation of Culture*, edited by Cary Nelson and Lawrence Grossber, pp. 89–104. Urbana, IL: University of Illinois Press.

Moulder, Frances V. 1977 *Japan, China and the Modern World Economy: Toward a Reinterpretation of East Asian Development, ca. 1600 to ca. 1918*. Cambridge, UK: Cambridge University Press.

Munck, Ronaldo 1986 *The Difficult Dialogue: Marxism and Nationalism*. London, UK: Zed Books.

Munslow, Alun 1997 *Deconstructing History*. London, UK: Routledge.

Murray, Robin 1971 The Internationalization of Capital and the Nation State. *New Left Review*, no. 67, pp. 84–109. London.

Nash, Philleo 1937 The Place of Religious Revivalism in the Formation of the Intercultural Community on Klamath Reservation. In *The Social Anthropology of North American Tribes*, edited by Fred Eggan, pp. 377–442. Chicago, IL: The University of Chicago Press.

Nehru, Jawaharlal 1946 *The Discovery of India*. New York: The John Day Company.

Nettl, John P. 1966 *Rosa Luxemburg*, 2 vols. London, UK: Oxford University Press.

Nimni, Ephraim 1991 *Marxism and Nationalism: Theoretical Origins of a Political Crisis*. London, UK: Pluto Press.

Nisbet, Robert A. 1969 *Social Change and History: Aspects of the Western Theory of Development*. New York: Oxford University Press.

—— 1980 *History of the Idea of Progress*. New York: Basic Books.

Nonini, Donald M. and Aihwa Ong 1997 Chinese Transnationalism as an Alternative Modernity. In *Underground Empires: The Cultural Politics of Modern Chinese Transnationalism*, edited by Aihwa Ong and Donald Nonini, pp. 3–33. New York: Routledge.

Nove, Alec 1965 Introduction. In *The New Economics*, by Evgeny Preobrazhensky, pp. vii–xvii. Oxford, UK: Clarendon Press. 1969 *An Economic History of the U.S.S.R.* London, UK: Penguin Books.

O'Brien, Philip J. 1975 A Critique of Latin American Theories of Dependency. In *Beyond the Sociology of Development*, edited by Ivar Oxaal, Tony Barnett and David Booth, pp. 7–27. London, UK: Routledge and Kegan Paul.

O'Hanlon, Rosalind 1988 Recovering the Subject: *Subaltern Studies* and the Histories of Resistance in Colonial South Asia. *Modern Asian Studies*, Vol. 22, no. 1, pp. 189–224. London.

Ohmae, Kenicki 1990 *The Borderless World: Power and Strategy in the Interlinked Economy*. New York: HarperCollins Publishers.

Panitch, Leo 1997 Rethinking the Role of the State. In *Globalization: Critical Reflections*, edited by James A. Mittelman, pp. 83–113. Boulder, CO: Lynne Rienner Publishers.

Parsons, Talcott 1951 *The Social System*. New York: The Free Press.

—— 1961a Some Considerations on the Theory of Social Change. *Rural Sociology*, vol. 26, no. 3, pp. 219–39. Ithaca.

—— 1961b An Outline of the Social System. In *Theories of Society: Foundations of Modern Sociological Theory*, edited by Talcott Parsons, Edward Shils, Kaspar D. Naegele and Jesse R. Pitts, Vol. 1, pp. 30–79. Glencoe, IL: The Free Press.

—— 1961c Differentiation and Variation in Social Structures: Introduction. In *Theories of Society: Foundations of Modern Sociological Theory*, edited by Talcott Parsons, Edward Shils, Kaspar D. Naegele and Jesse R. Pitts, Vol. 1, pp. 239–64. Glencoe, IL: The Free Press.

—— 1966 *Societies: Evolutionary and Comparative Perspectives*. Englewood Cliffs, NJ: Prentice-Hall.

—— 1967 Evolutionary Universals in Society [1964]. In *Sociological Theory and Modern Society*, by Talcott Parsons, pp. 490–536. New York: The Free Press.

—— 1971 Comparative Studies and Evolutionary Change. In *Comparative Methods in Sociology*, edited by Ivan Vallier, pp. 97–139. Berkeley, CA: University of California Press.

Patnaik, Utsa 1971 Capitalist Development in Agriculture. *Economic and Political Weekly*, vol. VI, no. 39, pp. a123–a130. Bombay.

—— 1972a Development of Capitalism in Agriculture – I. *Social Scientist*, vol. 1, no. 2, pp. 15–31. New Delhi.

—— 1972b Development of Capitalism in Agriculture – II. *Social Scientist*, vol. 1, no. 3, pp. 3–19. New Delhi.

Patterson, Thomas C. 1987 Development, Ecology, and Marginal Utility in Anthropology. *Dialectical Anthropology*, vol. 12, no. 1, pp. 15–32. Dordrecht.

Patterson, Thomas C. and Frank Spencer 1994 Racial Hierarchies and Buffer Races. *Transforming Anthropology*, vol. 5, no. 1–2, pp. 20–7. Washington.

Peace, William 1993 Leslie White and Evolutionary Theory. *Dialectical Anthropology*, vol. 18, no. 2, pp. 123–52. Dordrecht.

Pelczyniski, Zbigniew A. 1984 Nation, Civil Society, State: Hegelian Sources of the Marxian Non-theory of Nationality. In *The State and Civil Society: Studies in Hegel's Political Philosophy*, edited by Z. A. Pelczynski, pp. 262–78. Cambridge, UK: Cambridge University Press.

Pickering, William S. F. 1984 *Durkheim's Sociology of Religion: Themes and Theories*. London, UK: Routledge and Kegan Paul.

Piore, Michael and Charles Sabel 1984 *The Second Industrial Divide: Possibilities for Prosperity*. New York: Basic Books.

Pirenne, Henri 1914 The Stages in the Social History of Capitalism. *American Historical Review*, vol. XIX, no. 3, pp. 494–515. Lancaster.

—— 1939 *A History of Europe from the Invasions to the XVI Century*. New York: W. W. Norton and Company.

—— 1952 *Medieval Cities: Their Origins and the Revival of Trade* [1925]. Princeton, NJ: Princeton University Press.

Pletsch, Carl E. 1981 The Three Worlds, or the Division of Social Scientific Labor, circa 1950–1975. *Comparative Studies in Society and History*, vol. 23, no. 4, pp. 565–90. New York.

Pollert, Anna 1988 Dismantling Flexibility. *Capital and Class*, no. 34, pp. 42–75. London.

Powell, John W. 1880 *Introduction to the Study of American Indian Languages, with Words, Phrases and Sentences to be Collected*, 2nd edn. Smithsonian Institution, Bureau of Ethnology. Washington, DC: Government Printing Office.

—— 1896 The Director's Report. In *Fourteenth Annual Report of the Bureau of Ethnology, 1892–93*, pt. 1, pp. xxvii–lx. Washington, DC: Government Printing Office.

Prakash, Gyan 1994 Subaltern Studies and Postcolonial Criticism. *The American Historical Review*, vol. 99, no. 5, pp. 1475–90. Washington.

Prebisch, Raúl 1950 *The Economic Development of Latin America and its Principal Problems*. New York: United Nations.

Pred, Allan and Michael J. Watts 1992 *Reworking Modernity: Capitalisms and Symbolic Discontent*. New Brunswick, NJ: Rutgers University Press.

Preobrazhensky, Evgeny 1965 *The New Economics* [1926], with an introduction by Alec Nove. Oxford, UK: Clarendon Press.

Preston, Peter W. 1982 *Theories of Development*. London, UK: Routledge and Kegan Paul.

Radkey, Oliver H. 1958 *The Agrarian Foes of Bolshevism: Promise and Default of the Russian Socialist Revolutionaries, February to October, 1917*. New York: Columbia University Press.

Redfield, Robert 1950 *A Village That Chose Progress: Chan Kom Revisited.* Chicago, IL: The University of Chicago Press.

—— 1955 *Peasant Society and Culture.* Chicago, IL: The University of Chicago Press.

—— 1962a The Regional Aspect of Culture [1930]. In *The Papers of Robert Redfield*, edited by Margaret P. Redfield, Vol. 1, *Human Nature and the Study of Society*, pp. 145–51. Chicago, IL: The University of Chicago Press.

—— 1962b Culture Changes in Yucatan [1934]. In *The Papers of Robert Redfield*, edited by Margaret P. Redfield, Vol. 1, *Human Nature and the Study of Society*, pp. 160–72. Chicago, IL: The University of Chicago Press.

—— 1962c The Folk Society [1942]. In *The Papers of Robert Redfield*, edited by Margaret P. Redfield, Vol. 1, *Human Nature and the Study of Society*, pp. 231–53. Chicago, IL: The University of Chicago Press.

—— 1962d Primitive Merchants of Guatemala. In *The Papers of Robert Redfield*, edited by Margaret P. Redfield, Vol. 1, *Human Nature and the Study of Society*, pp. 200–10. Chicago, IL: The University of Chicago Press.

—— 1962e Folkways and City Ways [1935]. In *The Papers of Robert Redfield*, edited by Margaret P. Redfield, Vol. 1, *Human Nature and the Study of Society*, pp. 172–82. Chicago, IL: The University of Chicago Press.

Redfield, Robert, Ralph Linton and Melville J. Herskovits 1936 Memorandum for the Study of Acculturation. *American Anthropologist*, vol. 38, no. 1, pp. 149–52. Menasha.

Reich, Robert 1991 *The Work of Nations.* New York: Alfred A. Knopf.

Rey, Pierre-Philippe 1982 Class Alliances [1973]. *International Journal of Sociology*, Vol. XII, no. 2, pp. 1–120. Armonk.

Riesebrodt, Martin 1989 From Patriarchalism to Capitalism: The Theoretical Context of Max Weber's Agrarian Studies (1892–3). In *Reading Weber*, edited by Keith Tribe, pp. 131–57. London, UK: Routledge.

Rivers, William H. R. 1906 *The Todas.* New York: Macmillan and Company.

—— 1917 The Government of Subject Peoples. In *Science and the Nation*, edited by A. C. Seward, pp. 302–28. Cambridge, UK: Cambridge University Press.

Robertson, Roland 1991 Globalization, Modernization, and Postmodernization: The Ambiguous Position of Religion. In *Religion and Global Order*, edited by Roland Robertson and William R. Garrett, pp. 281–91. New York: Paragon House Publishers.

Rosdolsky, Roman 1980 *Friedrich Engels y el problema de los pueblos 'sin historia': la cuestión de las nacionalidades en la revolución de 1848–1849 a la luz de la* 'Neue Rheinische Zeitung' [1964]. Mexico, DF: Ediciones de Pasado y Presente.

Roseberry, William 1993 Beyond the Agrarian Question in Latin America. In *Confronting Historical Paradigms: Peasants, Labor, and Capitalist World*

System in Africa and Latin America, edited by Frederick Cooper, Allen F. Isaacman, Florencia E. Mallon, William Roseberry and Stever J. Stern, pp. 318–68. Madison, WI: The University of Wisconsin Press.

Rostow, Walt W. 1971a *The Stages of Economic Growth: A Non-Communist Manifesto* [1960], 2nd edn. Cambridge, UK: Cambridge University Press.

—— 1971b *Politics and the Stages of Growth*. Cambridge, UK: Cambridge University Press.

Rousseau, Jean-Jacques 1973 *The Social Contract and Discourses*, edited by G. D. H. Cole. London, UK: Dent.

Rowe, John H. 1964 Ethnography and Ethnology in the Sixteenth Century. *Kroeber Anthropological Society Papers*, no. 30, pp. 1–20. Berkeley.

—— 1965 The Renaissance Foundation of Anthropology. *American Anthropologist*, vol. 67, no. 1, pp. 1–20. Menasha, WI.

Rubin, Vera, editor 1959 Plantation Systems of the New World. *Division of Social Science, Pan American Union, Social Science Monograph*, no. 7. Washington, DC.

Rydell, Robert W. 1984 *All the World's a Fair: Visions of Empire at American International Expositions, 1876–1916*. Chicago, IL: The University of Chicago Press.

Said, Edward 1978 *Orientalism*. New York: Vintage Books.

Saint-Simon, Henri 1952 The Organizer [1819–20]. In *Henri Comte de Saint-Simon (1760–1825): Selected Writings*, edited by F. M. H. Markham. Westport, CT: Hyperion Press.

—— 1976a On the Reorganization of European Society [1814]. In *The Political Thought of Saint-Simon*, edited by Ghita Ionescu, pp. 83–98. Oxford, UK: Oxford University Press.

—— 1976b Industry [1816–18]. In *The Political Thought of Saint-Simon*, edited by Ghita Ionescu, pp. 99–128. Oxford, UK: Oxford University Press.

—— 1976c On the Industrial System [1821–2]. In *The Political Thought of Saint-Simon*, edited by Ghita Ionescu, pp. 153–81. Oxford, UK: Oxford University Press.

Sapir, Edward 1949a The Unconscious Patterning of Behavior in Society [1927]. In *Selected Writings of Edward Sapir in Language, Culture, and Personality*, edited by David G. Mandelbaum, pp. 544–59. Berkeley, CA: University of California Press.

—— 1949b The Emergence of the Concept of Personality in a Study of Culture [1934]. In *Selected Writings of Edward Sapir in Language, Culture, and Personality*, edited by David G. Mandelbaum, pp. 590–7. Berkeley, CA: University of California Press.

Savage, Stephen P. 1981 *The Theories of Talcott Parsons: The Social Relations of Action*. New York: St Martin's Press.

Sayer, Derek and Philip Corrigan 1983 Late Marx: Continuity, Contradiction and Learning. In *Late Marx and the Russian Road: Marx and 'The Peripheries of Capitalism'*, edited by Teodor Shanin, pp. 77–94. New York: Monthly Review Press.

Schumpeter, Joseph A. 1951 The Sociology of Imperialisms [1919]. In *Imperialism and Social Classes*, edited by Paul M. Sweezy, pp. 3–130. New York: Augustus M. Kelley.

Scott, James C. 1976 *The Moral Economy of the Peasant: Rebellion and Subsistence in Southeast Asia*. New Haven, CT: Yale University Press.

—— 1977 Hegemony and the Peasantry. *Politics and Society*, vol. 7, no. 3, pp. 267–96. Washington.

—— 1985 *Weapons of the Weak: Everyday Forms of Peasant Resistance*. New Haven, CT: Yale University Press.

—— 1990 *Domination and the Arts of Resistance: Hidden Transcripts*. New Haven, CT: Yale University Press.

Seddon, David, editor 1978 *Relations of Production: Marxist Approaches to Economic Anthropology*. London, UK: Frank Cass.

Service, Elman R. 1975 *Origins of the State and Civilization: The Process of Cultural Evolution*. New York: W. W. Norton.

Shadle, Stanley F. 1994 *Andrés Molina Enríquez: Mexican Land Reformer of the Revolutionary Era*. Tucson, AZ: University of Arizona Press.

Shaikh, Anwar 1991a Economic Crises. In *A Dictionary of Marxist Thought*, 2nd edn., edited by Tom Bottomore, pp. 160–5. Oxford, UK: Basil Blackwell.

—— 1991b Falling Rate of Profit. In *A Dictionary of Marxist Thought*, 2nd edn., edited by Tom Bottomore, pp. 185–6. Oxford, UK: Basil Blackwell.

Shanin, Teodor 1971 Peasantry: Delineation of a Sociological Concept and a Field of Study. *Archives Européennes de Sociologie*, tome XII, no. 3, pp. 289–300. Paris.

—— 1980 Measuring Peasant Capitalism: The Operationalization of Concepts of Political Economy: Russia's 1920s – India's 1970s. In *Peasants in History: Essays in Honour of Daniel Thorner*, edited by Eric J. Hobsbawm, Witold Kula, Ashok Mitra, K. N. Raj and Ignacy Sachs, pp. 83–104. Calcutta: Oxford University Press.

Shanin, Teodor, editor 1983 *Late Marx and the Russian Road: Marx and 'The Peripheries of Capitalism'*. New York: Monthly Review Press.

Shanin, Teodor 1985 *The Roots of Otherness: Russia's Turn of the Century*, Vol. 1, *Russia as a 'Developing Society'*. New Haven, CT: Yale University Press.

—— 1986 *The Roots of Otherness: Russia's Turn of the Century*, Vol. 2, *Russia, 1905–07: Revolutions as a Moment of Truth*. New Haven, CT: Yale University Press.

Shils, Edward A. 1960a Political Development in the New States – Alternative

Courses of Political Development. *Comparative Studies in Society and History*, vol. II, no. 2, pp. 265–92. The Hague.

—— 1960b Political Development in the New States – The Will to be Modern. *Comparative Studies in Society and History*, vol. II, no. 3, pp. 379–411. The Hague.

—— 1963 On the Comparative Study of the New States. In *Old Societies and New States: The Quest for Modernity in Asia and Africa*, edited by Clifford Geertz, pp. 1–26. Glencoe, IL: The Free Press.

Shohat, Ella 1992 Notes on the Post-Colonial. *Social Text*, no. 31/32, pp. 99–133. New York.

Silverman, Sydel 1979 The Peasant Concept in Anthropology. *Journal of Peasant Studies*, vol. 7, no. 1, pp. 49–69. London.

Sivaramakrishnan, K. 1995 Situating the Subaltern: History and Anthropology in the Subaltern Studies Project. *Journal of Historical Sociology*, vol. 8, no. 4, pp. 395–429. Oxford.

Skocpol, Theda 1985 Bringing the State Back In: Strategies of Analysis in Current Research. In *Bringing the State Back In*, edited by Peter B. Evans, Dietrich Rueschemeyer and Theda Skocpol, pp. 3–37. Cambridge, UK: Cambridge University Press.

Smelser, Neil J. 1961 Mechanisms of Change and Adjustment to Change. In *Industrialization and Society*, edited by Bert F. Hoselitz and Wilbert E. Moore, pp. 32–54. Paris: UNESCO–Mouton.

Smith, Adam 1976 *An Inquiry into the Nature and Causes of the Wealth of Nations* [1776], 2 vols. Chicago, IL: The University of Chicago Press.

—— 1978 *Lectures on Jurisprudence* [1762–3], edited by Ronald L. Meek, David D. Raphael, and Peter Stein. Oxford, UK: Clarendon Press.

Smith, Anthony D. 1973 *The Concept of Social Change: A Critique of the Functionalist Theory of Social Change*. London, UK: Routledge and Kegan Paul.

Smith, Richard 1997 Creative Destruction: Capitalist Development and China's Environment. *New Left Review*, no. 222, pp. 3–42. London.

Solomon, Susan G. 1977 *The Soviet Agrarian Debate: A Controversy in Social Science, 1923–1929*. Boulder, CO: Westview Press.

Spencer, Herbert 1852 A Theory of Population Deduced from the General Law of Animal Fertility. *The Westminster Review*, vol. LVII, April, pp. 250–68. London, UK.

—— 1857 Progess: Its Law and Cause. *The Westminster Review*, vol. LXVII, pp. 244–67. London, UK.

—— 1876 *The Principles of Sociology*, Vol. 1, pt. 2. London, UK: Williams and Norgate.

—— 1896 *The Principles of Sociology*, Vol. 3, pt. 8. London, UK: Williams and Norgate.

—— 1972 *Social Statics* [1851]. In *Herbert Spencer: Selected Writings*, edited by J. D. Y. Peel, pp. 17–29. Chicago, IL: The University of Chicago Press.

Stephen, Lynn 1997 *Women and Social Movements in Latin America: Power from Below*. Austin, TX: University of Texas Press.

Stern, Steve J. 1993 Feudalism, Capitalism, and the World-System in the Perspective of Latin America and the Caribbean [1988]. In *Confronting Historical Paradigms: Peasants, Labor, and the Capitalist World System in Africa and Latin America*, by Frederick Cooper, Allen F. Isaacman, Florencia E. Mallon, Steve J. Stern and William Roseberry, pp. 23–83. Madison, WI: The University of Wisconsin Press.

Steward, Julian H. 1949 Cultural Causality and Law: A Trial Formulation of the Development of Early Civilizations. *American Anthropologist*, vol. 51, no. 1, pp. 1–27. Menasha.

—— 1950 Area Research: Theory and Practice. *Social Science Research Council Bulletin*, no. 63, pp. 1–164. New York.

—— 1955a The Concept and Method of Cultural Ecology [1950]. In *Theory of Culture Change*, by Julian H. Steward, pp. 30–42. Urbana, IL: The University of Illinois Press.

—— 1955b Levels of Sociocultural Integration: An Operational Concept [1951]. In *Theory of Culture Change*, by Julian H. Steward, pp. 43–63. Urbana, IL: The University of Illinois Press.

—— 1977a Limitations of Applied Anthropology: The Case of the Indian New Deal. In *Evolution and Ecology: Essays on Social Transformation by Julian Steward*, edited by Jane C. Steward and Robert F. Murphy, pp. 333–46. Urbana, IL: The University of Illinois Press.

—— 1977b Determinism in Primitive Society? [1941]. In *Evolution and Ecology; Essays on Social Transformation*, edited by Jane C. Steward and Robert F. Murphy, pp. 180–7. Urbana, IL: The University of Illinois Press.

Steward, Julian H. and Frank M. Seltzer 1938 Function and Configuration in Archaeology. *American Antiquity*, vol. IV, no. 1, pp. 4–10. Menasha.

Stocking, George W., Jr. 1982a From Physics to Ethnology [1965]. In *Race, Language and Evolution: Essays in the History of Anthropology* by George Stocking, pp. 133–60. Chicago, IL: The University of Chicago Press.

—— 1982b Franz Boas and the Culture Concept in Historical Perspective [1966]. In *Race, Language and Evolution: Essays in the History of Anthropology* by George Stocking, pp. 195–233. Chicago, IL: The University of Chicago Press.

—— 1995 *After Tylor: British Social Anthropology, 1888–1951*. Madison, WI: The University of Wisconsin Press.

Sullivan, Paul 1989 *Unfinished Conversations: Mayas and Foreigners between Two Wars*. Berkeley, CA: University of California Press.

Sunkel, Osvaldo 1969 National Development Policy and External Dependence in

Latin America. *The Journal of Development Studies*, vol. 6, no. 1, pp. 23–48. London.

Sweezy, Paul M. 1976 A Critique [1952]. In *The Transition from Feudalism to Capitalism* edited by Rodney H. Hilton, pp. 33–56. London, UK: New Left Books.

—— 1997 More (or Less) on Globalization. *Monthly Review*, Vol. 49, no. 4, pp. 1–4. New York.

Szelényi, Iván 1988 *Socialist Entrepreneurs: Embourgoisement in Rural Hungary*. Madison, WI: The University of Wisconsin Press.

Szelényi, Iván and Bill Martin 1988 The Three Waves of New Class Theories. *Theory and Society*, vol. 17, no. 4, pp. 645–67. New York.

Szelényi, Iván and Szonya Szelényi 1991 The Vacuum in Hungarian Politics: Classes and Parties. *New Left Review*, no. 187, pp. 121–38. London.

Sztompa, Piotr 1993 *The Sociology of Social Change*. Oxford, UK: Blackwell Publishers.

Tarbuck, Kenneth J. 1972 Introduction. In *The Accumulation of Capital – An Anti-Critique* by Rosa Luxemburg, and *Imperialism and the Accumulation of Capital*, by Nikolai Bukharin, edited by Kenneth J. Tarbuck. New York: Monthly Review Press.

Tarde, Gabriel 1895 *Les lois de l'imitation: étude sociologique*, 2nd edn. Paris: Félix Alcan, Editeur.

Taylor, John G. 1979 *From Modernization to Modes of Production: A Critique of the Sociologies of Development and Underdevelopment*. Atlantic Highlands, NJ: Humanities Press.

Thorner, Alice 1982 Semi-feudalism or Capitalism? Contemporary Debate on Classes and Modes of Production in India. *Economic and Political Weekly*, Vol. XVII, nos. 49, 50, 51, pp. 1961–8, 1993–9, 2061–6. Bombay.

Thorner, Daniel 1986 Chayanov's Concept of Peasant Economy. In *The Theory of Peasant Economy*, edited by Daniel Thorner, Basile Kerblay and R. E. F. Smith with a Foreword by Teodor Shanin, pp. xi–xxiv. Madison, WI: The University of Wisconsin Press.

Tipps, Dean C. 1973 Modernization Theory and the Comparative Study of Societies: A Critical Perspective. *Comparative Studies in Society and History*, vol. XV, no. 3, pp. 199–226. The Hague.

Touraine, Alain 1974 *The Post-industrial Society*. London, UK: Wildwood.

—— 1977 *The Self-production of Society* [1973]. Chicago, IL: The University of Chicago Press.

—— 1981 *The Voice and the Eye: An Analysis of Social Movements* [1978]. Cambridge, UK: Cambridge University Press.

Trigger, Bruce G. 1989 *A History of Archaeological Thought*. Cambridge, UK: Cambridge University Press.

Trotsky, Leon 1969a Results and Prospects [1906]. In *The Permanent Revolution and Results and Prospects*, pp. 29–122. New York: Pathfinder Press.

—— 1969b Permanent Revolution [1930]. In *The Permanent Revolution* and *Results and Prospects*, pp. 125–281. New York: Pathfinder Press.

Valcárcel, Luis 1914 *La cuestión agraria en el Cuzco*. Bachiller's thesis in Political and Administrative Sciences, Universidad de San Antonio Abad, Cuzco.

—— 1981 *Memorias*. Lima: Instituto de Estudios Peruanos.

Verdery, Katherine 1991 *Nationalist Ideology under Socialism: Identity and Cultural Politics in Ceausescu's Romania*. Berkeley, CA: University of California Press.

—— 1996 *What Was Socialism, and What Comes Next?* Princeton, NJ: Princeton University Press.

Vico, Giambattista 1970 *The New Science of Giambattista Vico* [1725], translated by Thomas G. Bergin and Max H. Fisch. Ithaca, NY: Cornell University Press.

Vincent, Joan 1990 *Anthropology and Politics: Visions, Traditions, and Trends*. Tucson, AZ: University of Arizona Press.

Voronin, Yuriy A. 1997 The Emerging Criminal State: Economic and Political Aspects of Organized Crime in Russia. In *Russian Organized Crime: The New Threat?* edited by Phil Williams, pp. 53–62. London, UK: Frank Cass.

Wada, Haruki 1983 Marx and Revolutionary Russia. In *Late Marx and the Russian Road: Marx and 'The Peripheries of Capitalism'*, edited by Teodor Shanin, pp. 40–76. New York: Monthly Review Press.

Wade, Robert 1996 Globalization and its Limits: Reports of the Death of the National Economy Are Greatly Exaggerated. In *National Diversity and Global Capitalism*, edited by Suzanne Berger and Ronald Dore, pp. 60–88. Ithaca, NY: Cornell University Press.

Walicki, Andrzej 1982 *Philosophy and Romantic Nationalism: The Case of Poland*. Oxford, UK: Clarendon Press.

Walker, Kathy Le Mons 1999 *Chinese Modernity and the Peasant Path: Semi-Colonialism in the Northern Yangzi Delta*. Stanford, CA: Stanford University Press.

Walker, Martin 1993 *The Cold War and the Making of the Modern World*. London, UK: Fourth Estate.

Wallerstein, Immanuel 1966 Introduction. In *Social Change: The Colonial Situation*, edited by Immanuel Wallerstein, pp. 1–8. New York: John Wiley and Sons.

—— 1974 *The Modern World-System*, Vol. 1, *Capitalist Agriculture and the Origins of the European World-Economy of the Sixteenth Century*. New York: Academic Press.

—— 1979 *The Capitalist World-Economy: Essays be Immanuel Wallerstein*. Cambridge, UK: Cambridge University Press.

—— 1980 *The Modern World-System*, Vol. 2, *Mercantilism and the Consolidation of the European World-Economy, 1600–1750*. New York: Academic Press.

—— 1989 *The Modern World-System*, Vol. 3, *The Second Era of Great Expansion of the Capitalist World-Economy, 1730–1840s*. San Diego, CA: Academic Press.

Wallwork, Ernest 1972 *Durkheim: Morality and Milieu*. Cambridge, MA: Harvard University Press.

—— 1984 Religion and Social Structure in *The Division of Labor*. *American Anthropologist*, vol. 86, no. 1, pp. 43–66. Menasha.

—— 1985 Durkheim's Early Sociology of Religion. *Sociological Analysis*, vol. 46, no. 3, pp. 201–18. Toronto.

Weber, Max 1946a Science as a Vocation [1918]. In *From Max Weber: Essays in Sociology*, edited by Hans H. Gerth and C. Wright Mills, pp. 129–56. New York: Oxford University Press.

—— 1946b The Social Psychology of the World Religions [1915]. In *From Max Weber: Essays in Sociology*, edited by Hans H. Gerth and C. Wright Mills, pp. 267–301. New York: Oxford University Press.

—— 1958a Author's Introduction [1920]. In *The Protestant Ethic and the Spirit of Capitalism* [1904–5]. New York: Charles Scribner's Sons.

—— 1958b *The Protestant Ethic and the Spirit of Capitalism* [1904–5]. New York: Charles Scribner's Sons.

—— 1958c *The City* [1921]. New York: The Free Press.

—— 1976a *The Agrarian Sociology of Ancient Civilizations* [1909]. London, UK: New Left Books.

—— 1976b The Social Causes of the Decline of Ancient Civilization [1896]. In *The Agrarian Sociology of Ancient Civilizations*, by Max Weber, pp. 387–411. London, UK: New Left Books.

—— 1978 *Economy and Society* [1922], 2 vols, edited by Guenther Roth and Claus Wittich. Berkeley, CA: University of California Press.

—— 1981 *General Economic History* [1923], with an introduction by Ira J. Cohen. New Brunswick, NJ: Transaction Books.

—— 1989a Developmental Tendencies in the Situation of East Elbian Rural Labourers [1894]. In *Reading Weber*, edited by Keith Tribe, pp. 158–87. London, UK: Routledge.

—— 1989b The Nation State and Economic Policy [1895]. In *Reading Weber*, edited by Keith Tribe, pp. 188–209. London, UK: Routledge.

Weiss, Linda 1997 The Myth of the Powerless State. *New Left Review*, no. 225, pp. 3–27. London.

—— 1998 *The Myth of the Powerless State*. Ithaca, NY: Cornell University Press.

Weiss, Roberto 1988 *The Renaissance Discovery of Classical Antiquity*. Oxford, UK: Basil Blackwell.

White, Leslie A. 1943 Energy and the Evolution of Culture. *American Anthropologist*, vol. 45, no. 4, pp. 335–56. Menasha.

Wignaraja, Poona, editor 1993 *New Social Movements in the South: Empowering the People*. London, UK: Zed Books.

Willey, Thomas E. 1978 *Back to Kant: The Revival of Kantianism in German Social and Historical Thought, 1860–1914*. Detroit, MI: Wayne State University Press.

Wilson, Godfrey B. and Monica H. Wilson 1954 *The Analysis of Social Change* [1945]. Cambridge, UK: Cambridge University Press.

Wolf, Eric R. 1955 Types of Latin American Peasantry: A Preliminary Discussion. *American Anthropologist*, vol. 57, no. 3, pp. 452–71. Menasha.

—— 1956 Aspects of Group Relations in a Complex Society: Mexico. *American Anthropologist*, vol. 58, no. 6, pp. 1065–78. Menasha.

—— 1957 Closed Corporate Peasant Communities in Mesoamerica and Central Java. *Southwestern Journal of Anthropology*, vol. 13, no. 1, pp. 1–18. Albuquerque.

—— 1966 *Peasants*. Englewood Cliffs, NJ: Prentice-Hall.

—— 1969 *Peasant Wars of the Twentieth Century*. New York: Harper and Row.

Wolf, Eric R. and Sidney W. Mintz 1957 Haciendas and Plantations in Middle America and the Antilles. *Social and Economic Studies*, vol. 6, no. 3, pp. 382–412. Kingston.

Wolfe, Patrick 1997 History and Imperialism: A Century of Theory, from Marx to Postcolonialism. *The American Historical Review*, vol. 102, no. 2, pp. 388–420. Washington.

Wolpe, Harold 1980 Introduction. In *The Articulation of Modes of Production: Essays from Economy and Society*, edited by Harold Wolpe, pp. 1–43. London, UK: Routledge and Kegan Paul.

—— 1985 The Articulation of Modes and Forms of Production. In *Marxian Theory and the Third World*, edited by Diptendra Banerjee, pp. 89–103. New Delhi: Sage Publications.

Wood, Ellen M. 1986 *The Retreat from Class: A New 'True' Socialism*. London, UK: Verso.

—— 1990 The Use and Abuses of 'Civil Society'. *Socialist Register 1990*, edited by Ralph Miliband, Leo Panitch and John Saville, pp. 60–84. London, UK: Merlin Press.

Worsley, Peter M. 1961 The Analysis of Rebellion and Revolution in Modern British Social Anthropology. *Science and Society*, vol. XXI, no. 1, pp. 26–37. New York.

—— 1990 Models of the Modern World System. In *Global Culture: Nationalism, Globalization and Modernity*, edited by Mike Featherstone, pp. 83–96. London, UK: Sage Publications.

Young, Robert M. 1985 *Darwin's Metaphor: Nature's Place in Victorian Culture*. Cambridge, UK: Cambridge University Press.

Index